P9-BIM-017

Gina –
Enjoy the "pearls!"

Girl with the
Crooked Smile

STUCK IN A MOMENT
... and the Pearls of Wisdom
that pulled her through it

DARAH ZELEDÓN

❧ STERLING PUBLISHING GROUP ☙

Girl with the Crooked Smile - Stuck in a Moment
... and the Pearls of Wisdom that pulled her through it

Copyright © 2013 Darah Zeledón. All rights reserved.
Second Edition

Limits of Liability and Disclaimer of Warranty: The author and/or publisher shall have neither liability nor responsibility to anyone with respect to any loss or damage caused, or alleged to be caused, directly or indirectly by the information contained in this book. The purpose of this book is to entertain and inform. While all accounts of the places and incidences cited are factually correct, many of the names and descriptions of the people mentioned throughout the text have been changed or slightly altered to protect their identity. The opinions expressed throughout the story are those of the author and the author alone. Any person who assisted in the providing of resources to complete this body of work is in no way directly or indirectly endorsing the author's outlook or beliefs.

No portion of this book may be reproduced mechanically, electronically, or by any other means, including photocopying, without written permission of the publisher. It is illegal to copy this book, post it to a website, or distribute it by any other means without permission from the publisher.

Published by The Sterling Publishing Group, USA 1.888.689.1130
www.SterlingPublishingGroup.com

Printed in the United States of America

Edited & Designed by Jodi Nicholson www.JodiNicholson.com
Photography by Celia Shapiro

This book may be ordered directly through the publisher or by contacting the author by visiting http://www.DarahZeledon.com or www.girlwiththecrookedsmile.com

ISBN: 978-0-9884656-2-6
Self Help: Inspirational | Memoir

Dedication

For Mom, you are my mainstay and number one editor. You have my undisputed respect, admiration and love. Thank you for bringing me into this wonderful world and for always supporting my bigger-than-life dreams. I love you.

For Dad, you gave me the most important gift a parent can give a child: unconditional love. And because of your faith in me, I grew up with the self-confidence always to keep my vision beyond the horizon. I miss you each day and love you always.

For "Grandpa" Warren, you are a beacon of light that illuminates the souls of all those around you. Our lives are forever enriched because of the endless love Grandpa Warren bestows upon all of us. May you be blessed with good health now and always!

For Yordana, Leah, Natan, Yair and Dalia, my five precious treasures. You fill my heart with joy and infuse my life with depth and purpose. I am in awe of your righteousness, good nature, smarts, and feel blessed to witness your transformation into confident, free-thinking dynamos! My unbounded love for each of you keeps me on my toes and inspires me to greatness.

For you, Joaquín, the love of my life, my best friend and most honest critic. Not only do you always have my back, but also you challenge me to be better in all I do and ignite my desire to "keep pedaling." Thank you for reminding me never to lose hope, for loving me more than any woman could ever dream of and for the honor to call myself your wife. Te amo, Mi Amor.

For Adam, the "Little Man" I always adored that somehow, slipped away from me. Please forgive me for not recognizing your pain. I miss you every day little bro, and will never stop loving you.

And for parents and people everywhere. Pay attention to your own loved ones lest they find themselves trapped in a dark space. And if they get clouded, fight like a son-of-bitch to bring them back to the light before it is too late.

Five Star Reviews

You fall down with her, you get up with her, you laugh and cry with her... I loved this book! And I'm not a fan of self-help things but this book is far from that. It's a memoir, with bonuses. It's funny, draws you in, and most of all it's not anything like "poor me" but more of a "come with me and feel what I felt" kind of journey. Intimate, raw, and vulnerable. The pearls are parts that I'll go back to when I get kicked in the teeth. *—Bethany Vedder*

Excellent! I loved this book so much I couldn't put it down and finished it in two days. Darah's story is truly motivational and gives the reader a great perspective on what is truly meaningful in life and what we do not have control over and therefore should not focus on or worry about. This book was such a great reminder on the importance of maintaining one's sense of humor and an attitude of gratitude during difficult times. Darah's ongoing perseverance in the face of repeated, extreme life experiences was so inspiring. I will be using this book with clients and recommending it to friends. *—Danielle Price*

The most encouraging book... Words cannot express how timely and impacting Darah's book, Girl with the Crooked Smile, was to my life. I had just recently lost my husband due to brain cancer/tumor. Darah's trials mimicked mine in a way, and her resilience to not give in to the sadness, gave me encouragement. Most women my age have lived long enough to experience some of what she went through. By no fault of her own, to have to endure such hardships at a relatively young age, is quite astounding! I was lured in by her clear and descriptive writing. She painted a wonderful picture in such beautiful detail. Her positive outlook is refreshing, and her strength to keep going to see what is just over the horizon has inspired me to keep going as well. Thank you, Darah!!! *—Lynne B.*

A warrior mom's victory over adversity... Girl with the Crooked Smile is a remarkable story of physical, emotional and spiritual survival through an amazing series of misfortunes. Overcoming one adversity after another, Darah Zeledon tells her story of becoming Warrior Mom as she struggles against health problems, grief, evil people and destitution. Also a story of hope, miracles, gratitude and wisdom, Zeledon's autobiographical masterpiece is both admirable and inspirational, giving every reader a new perspective on his or her own life. *— Robert McGreevey*

Loved it! I thoroughly enjoyed reading Darah Zeledon's book, Girl with the Crooked Smile. Darah has such an incredible gift, of making me laugh in between tears, while reading about the events of her life. Darah is beyond inspirational! She has found the strength to push through so many difficult times and shares with readers her "pearls of wisdom" on how we can all do the same. I can't wait for the next book, Darah! *—Dana T.*

This book will make you a stronger person! Reading Darah's book, I was inspired by her strength and ability to handle devastating circumstances. As it turns out, toward the end of reading her book, my dad was tragically killed in an accident. I found the strength to cope with such a huge loss thanks to this inspiring book. I highly recommend anyone to read her amazing life story. Thank you for sharing your most intimate moments. *Forever Grateful, Taimir Terrell*

Adversity, adventure, love—wonderfully imperfect... Powerful, riveting, and soulful, Darah's memoir teaches us the values of love and imperfection combined with themes of marriage, motherhood, and family, interlacing them with elements of her Jewish faith and adopted Latin American home to tell her story. A feisty, adventurous soul, Darah faces pain and adversity with optimism. But she also has a breaking point. This book teaches us how she made it through the most difficult of circumstances, persevering through shock, depression, frustration, and immense hardship, and coming out the other side as stronger, loving, and a more wonderfully imperfect woman. Darah is authentic, charismatic, and one-of-a-kind. Her true voice, clever explanations, and self-deprecating humor become even more infectious and entertaining; good luck putting this book down, and when you've finished, you too will be seeking out Darah Zeledon as the inspirational speaker for your next event. —*Lori B.*

A great summer read at the beach! I was pleasantly surprised and then completely hooked! It was so well-written, such a page turner, that I took it to the beach with me on my vacation and could not put it down! If her story were made into a movie, it would be a romantically tragic comedy! How about that for a genre?! I want the movie rights! I am so happy I decided to read this book. Darah's writing style is easy and simplistic, yet sophisticated enough to grab and hold your attention... her life story is unbelievable (except that it is true), her perseverance is an inspiration to anyone with a heart, and her pearls of wisdom are priceless. —*Keith L.*

Unforgettable! I have just finished this heart wrenching, inspirational memoir and still feel quite connected to the book. Parts had me crying real tears and shortly after, smiling and at times, even laughing out loud at the author's brilliant wit and sense of humor. The author's style of writing is gripping and each chapter presents another life lesson learned, along with her "pearls of wisdom" she shares with her readers. It's hard to believe this brave woman's struggle as she so passionately portrays it, but her courage, commitment to her husband and children, and "joie de vivre" reaches out to all of us and makes us stronger, more compassionate individuals. —*Queenie*

Exceptional read! Darah Zeledon's book was exceptional. It made me laugh, cry and gave me insight on how to get through difficult times in my own life. Darah is a very gifted writer. I finished <u>Girl with the Crooked Smile</u> in two days. Once I got started I could not put it down. Darah keep on writing and I for one will keep on buying your books. —*Jerry Riz*

Wow! What a page turner! This is one book that I couldn't put down. It's hard to believe that Darah, by the age of forty, had experienced so many tragic life changing situations. It makes one realize how important a loving family, good friends, and faith in God help to give us the strength to pull through life's adversities. Her sense of humor and words of wisdom are very effective in her writing style. While reading, you can feel Darah's high energy, optimism and passion for life. It makes you appreciate how important it is not to sweat the small stuff. Darah's life story is an inspiration to all that read it. —*Nancy Gronich*

Tour de Force!! Powerful. A roller coaster that keeps going up until you cannot catch your breath. Truth more alarming than fiction. Riveting, Funny and Insightful. This is a book you want to share. It inspires courage. Well done, Darah Zeledon. —*M. Zilant*

A true "must read!" As a lifelong avid reader of fiction as well as biographical non-fiction, I have had the extreme pleasure of being totally captivated by numerous authors during my lifetime; however, as a general rule, self help....introspective books would fall into my least favorite category. Therefore, imagine my surprise when I began reading Girl with the Crooked Smile and realizing that I couldn't put it down. Darah's writing skills are so good that they are hard for me to describe—other than saying her precise choice of words, the rhythm of her story, the manner in which you actually "feel" what she is saying... topped off by her valuable pearls of wisdom, are truly remarkable. I guess you could say that I "sort of" liked the book! —*Walter Hollander*

Perfect book club book! I read a lot of inspirational books and this one really captured my attention. The author's openness and vulnerability drew me in—she took me through her ups and downs and I found her hopefulness both refreshing and uplifting. I found myself flipping back to reread her lessons (called pearls). I have recommended this book to several friends and we just chose it for our next book club so we can all discuss how we would have tackled each twist in this riveting book. I loved it and can't wait to discuss with the rest of my group! –*T. King*

Inspirational! Fantastic, fluid read! She is not only inspiring, but you can completely relate to her human conversational writing style. I couldn't put the book down. The universal messages resonate with any woman who has ever lived through any life changing event. Truly engaging and I hope to see more from this author. —*N. Levy*

Girl power: cheesy cliché, but true! As a mother to two sons and one daughter, this book is full of validation for all women and coming from many different situations. It reminds readers of the complexity that embodies all women and the inner strength that is inside each and every one of us. —*P. Flick*

Clear your calendar - you can't put this book down. Girl with the Crooked Smile is a riveting book which was difficult to put down, and a book that I read in one day. Darah took me through a journey of many difficulties. There were tears and laughter but I was left with a feeling of inspiration and hope that all is possible with a loving family and friends by your side and the courage to endure. I look forward to Darah Zeledon's next book. —*Maddie Phillips*

Riveting! Most riveting book that you will not want to put down until you are finished! This is a story that is not "Hollywood" but so true in every detail. I cannot wait to read future books written by Darah. —*Ira Kent*

Contents

Foreword

By Darryl Appleton, M.D.

In architecture, an **egg** is often considered to have the perfect shape. If one holds **it** in their hands end-to-end, it can absorb enormous amounts of pressure without breaking; if held in any other orientation the fragile shell can break easily and cause egg to splash in your face. *Girl with the Crooked Smile... Stuck in a Moment* provides one with the tools needed to move their proverbial **eggs** to the perfect orientation to allow surprising strength to come from what was previously thought of as tenuous circumstances.

Girl with the Crooked Smile begins with Darah describing her return to Barcelona, Spain twelve years after her glorious honeymoon with the radiant sun beaming down upon her face wishing the moment would linger just a little bit longer. The chapters in her book that follow describe her life experiences from six years previous to that day in Spain, and chronicles her program of tough training and discipline that turned an untried civilian into the Warrior Mom that she is today. Each chapter ends with takeaway *Pearls of Wisdom* that we can all utilize in our daily life. She seamlessly employs all of the skills in her repertoire: her psychology degree, her graduate level degree in international relations in studies of relationships between countries and systems, and her life-coaching and personal expertise are all utilized to keep her sane in times of madness.

Kismet is a term from Arabic origin that means fate or destiny. People often say that timing is everything: I met Darah at a time that corresponded to the beginning of her loving relationship with her husband, Joaquín, the beginning of my burgeoning relationship with my wife-to-be, and the start of my career as a psychiatrist after moving to the warmth of Miami. I shortly realized that I have always gravitated to help those considered to have poor chances of recovery from chronic insomnia, fatigue, pain, depression and anxiety. As an expert in these fields, I have endeavored to help those that seemed to have lost their way, who may feel hopeless, and who need a helping hand. Amazingly, Darah has experienced all of these in spades and often at the same time, and devised her own, novel way to get through these conditions. Yet, Darah has always provided me with a shining example of one who despite a seemingly relentless string of bad luck, has always had a beaming (now crooked) smile with the unmistakable aura of positive energy, and a wicked sense of humor that belies the pain beneath her wings. People in these situations often pray for a change in their bad luck, ever searching for a transformational moment.

New pioneering treatments can provide just that, a true paradigm shift in medical technologies (such as rTMS) that has recently provided me with enormous professional pleasure as I see previously "treatment-resistant" patients come out of their deep abyss and propel towards wellness. But what is truly needed is the strength to persevere when they think they can't go on, and understand that without pain there is indeed no real pleasure; one needs sustenance of the soul that we medical physicians cannot always provide.

That is why this book is so crucial; it is truly a game-changer. This book will be prescribed reading material for all of my patients, and will continue to be used personally in my life. It will be on my list of items needed if one were stranded on a desert island, and should be utilized by all mental health practitioners in their practice.

If you ever have the occasion to hear the Warrior Mom speak, which I strongly suggest that you do, I contend that you will be forever changed in spirit, and you will come out soaring with a newfound strength with Darah's ability to pass on to all those that listen the pearls of how to harness the warrior spirit in all of us that may transiently leave our consciousness in the face of adversity.

I would be remiss not to mention that in the true spirit of Tzedakah (righteousness, charity) a percentage of the proceeds from this memoir will go to the *Florida Initiative for Suicide Prevention's Adam Silverman Memorial College SUN Program*. I am writing this foreword because I believe wholeheartedly in not only the book's message, but in the need to facilitate programs designed to teach college-aged young adults vital coping and problem solving skills to help prevent and heighten awareness about suicide which takes far too many of our bright young adults each and every year.

Girl with the Crooked Smile teaches us that we must constantly fight from our core, have continued faith and resilience. The courage of the Warrior Mom is available to all of us if we take a moment to allow ourselves to stop, take a deep breath, nourish our spirit with the yolk from within, and realign our eggs to the perfect alignment. By using Darah's *Pearls of Wisdom* from her life story, we too can prevent the cracking of our thin-shelled exteriors forevermore.

- Darryl Appleton, M.D.

Dr. Darryl Appleton is board certified by the American Board of Psychiatry & Neurology (ABPN), the American Board of Sleep Medicine (ABSM), and the American Board of Independent Medical Examiners (CIME). He completed his medical internship and residency in psychiatry at the University of Miami as well as at the University of Toronto. As founder of the Appleton Clinic in Toronto, the Sleep and Fatigue Treatment Center and co-founder of the BrainStim Health and TMS Center, both in Delray Beach, Florida, Dr. Appleton has been recognized internationally for his research, evaluation and treatment of major depression, mood and anxiety disorders, and sleep disorders.

Preface

To date, this book has been, by far, the biggest project of my life. What started out as a series of disjointed (poorly-written) blog posts over three and a half years ago, has become the product of thousands of hours of reading, writing, re-writing, and introspection.

I have poured my heart and soul into this book—oftentimes to the blatant disregard of all else—and have exposed my darkest, most discombobulated thoughts because I wholeheartedly believe the higher purpose is that important. If you take anything away from reading this book, I hope it is this: In this life there is no choice but to confront adversity head-on with courage, confident that eventually, time will march you out of it. When? How? Who knows? As counterintuitive as it seems, we must find comfort in the uncertainty, in the unknowable. And as we develop the coping skills necessary to trump through our toughest moments, we find ourselves stronger, wiser and more resilient.

I know my story may not resonate with everybody. Yet, I most fervently believe that the *Pearls of Wisdom* I share here will offer hope and inspiration to most anyone, from any walk of life, going through a rough stint. I want to make you laugh, make you cry, make you feel. And most of all, empower you to live your life—the good, the bad and the ugly—with the passion and spirit of a warrior.

If you find yourself trapped in a dark space, as most of us inevitably do at some time or another, know you are not alone. Find that proverbial life raft—that friend, that special place, that creative outlet, whatever brings you light—and take hold.

Never, ever, seek the easy way out—ending your life is no solution. There is always the promise of a better tomorrow. Keep pressing on. I am.

You don't know what you're made of until you are ripped apart.

Introduction

After a week of revelations and epiphanies that compelled me to see my past through a new optic, my initial thought was to rewrite the entire manuscript for the eighty-sixth time. Because that trip to Panamá in November 2012 was a real eye-opener, a directional game-changer in my overall evolution as a human being. Yes, the premise of the trip was to undergo surgery for yet another body part rendered injured from that near-fatal bike accident in April of 2011. The plan was simple: rest, recover and relax. Yet, most striking was the unanticipated tsunami of emotions that prevailed over me after I arrived.

Straddling two worlds, as my dear friend Bethany says, is unsettling. But more than that, stepping back into time, another culture, and another world, left me torn and unable to cope with the surrealism of it all.

You see, it had been four long years—years jam-packed with robust change and continued ups and downs since I'd last stepped foot on Panamanian soil. And despite having fled slightly embittered, disheartened and in denial of any emotional ties to the place, I found myself paralyzed, dazed and confused about what had been and what it all meant. How do I come to grips with this former life that is so foreign to the one I lead today? I muttered to myself every waking moment.

Friends indulged me and hauled me everywhere I wanted to go. And everywhere I went, I snapped photos and cried, deep guttural wails that sprung forth from the inner bowels of the soul. These intense reactions were perplexing. It wasn't that I longed for those days; life today is rich in love and meaning. It's that I physically felt the weight of the passage of time as more than a decade flashed through my mind's eye within seconds.

And whilst standing in the shadows of a life that used to belong to me, I found myself drowning in a sea of nostalgia. I yearned to recapture the excitement that hammered inside my chest when we first arrived to Panamá over a decade ago, fueled by Joaquín's promising new career, our new marriage and newborn daughter; we just were starting out. You know the feeling, when your entire life is still ahead of you.

During those first few years in Panamá before Joaquín resigned as the general manager of Credomatic, our days were full of promise. Our expectations were high. Each day I awoke full of hope and ready to conquer this new land, excel at my new marriage and embrace motherhood.

Those are the feelings that poured out of me when I gazed upon my first house, walked our street and combed through the neighborhood and surrounding landmarks. More than anything else, these roads were littered with remnants of memories of many firsts. Looking beyond, I realize that geographically, the places were irrelevant; it was the state of mind I pined for at that moment. Revisiting my own former life on fast-forward felt awkward, ill-fitting and invoked deep loneliness. And oddly, it felt morally wrong.

However, this slap in the face of reality forced me to seek closure with the quiet conflict that had festered in my heart for years—a conflict I had neglected to recognize, ardently believing the past and this place mattered no more.

So for you, my dear reader, instead of changing the voice throughout the entire manuscript—a less-evolved, yet candid voice interspersed with sarcasm and resentment—I decided to remain authentic. I decided to let you "see" the change of heart and maturity of perspective that developed and reflected my newfound enlightenments after this trip to Panamá—a trip that proved a real turning point for this story and for me as a work-in-progress.

One crucial lesson I learned is this: we cannot bury our feelings for eternity. No matter how stoic, how mechanical, or how strong we claim to be, eventually our feelings will spill out of us. And caution because as it did for me, it can happen in the most unlikeliest of places, when we least expect it.

I now accept that yes, I am tethered to Panamá, and in spite of all the grumbling done over the years about the unbearable climate, corrupt politics and immature work ethic of the people, this country is part of who I am. Undeniably, the experiences lived on this soil stained my younger heart with indelible impressions regardless how much I sought to negate it. Four of my five children are Panamanian and were brought into this world with the help of two of my favorite people, Dr. Velarde and Dr. Carbone.

But most important of all, after this defining trip, this grown-up-in-progress finally found gratitude. Not forced politeness or feigned gratitude, but real heartfelt appreciation; the kind only a handful of fortunate people sense after a near-death experience, survival of an unspeakable tragedy or at the end of a long, well-lived life. Because had it not been for the collaborative efforts of the Panamanian Jewish community and many close friends in particular, I wouldn't be the woman I am today—both inside and out. For starters, I wouldn't have my two upper front teeth and my spirit, well, that wouldn't be of the grateful warrior it is today.

So allow me publicly to say thank you, Panamá. Thank you for welcoming my new family and me into your warm Latin-Caribbean embrace and for affording us a chance to lead a plentiful life. Thank you for all you taught me about Judaism, friendship, community, and motherhood. Thank you for what you taught me about real life and for churning out a confirmed grown-up.

Forever in my heart. Forever in my soul. I accept you as you are and thank you from the bottom of my heart.

Girl with the
Crooked Smile

STUCK IN A MOMENT
... and the Pearls of Wisdom
that pulled her through it

DARAH ZELEDÓN

∞ STERLING PUBLISHING GROUP ∞

"You gain strength, courage and confidence by every experience by which you really stop to look fear in the face. You are able to say to yourself, I lived through this horror. I can take the next thing that comes along."

- Eleanor Roosevelt

A pearl's journey...

Born from adversity, pearls begin their formation as a grain of sand or piece of shell that accidentally slips into the mollusk. The mollusk protects itself from this foreign substance and unwittingly transforms it into a precious gem. During this journey, the "irritant" endures years of hardship and pressure. Hidden and isolated from the light of the world, it must have faith that one day, an unsuspecting swimmer will happen upon it. Once discovered, this timeless treasure is brought up to the surface to be shared with and appreciated by the entire world.

1. *A Moment of Bliss*

March 2012

With my eyes closed tight, I tilt my head up to the heavens and feel the radiant sun smile down upon me as it warms my soul.

This moment is perfect.

I'm comfortably seated on the back of a Harley Davidson clinging tightly onto my husband's familiar waist. Joaquín and I cruise north along the Carretera Costanera (coastal highway) in Spain, preparing to exit Barcelona proper. I open my eyes to drink in the awe-inspiring magnificence set before me—the infinite horizon of the Mediterranean Sea. With the cold, salty air whipping through my long hair, I breathe in the brackish scent of the ocean.

"Thank you, God," I cry, as my eyes well up with tears, "for bringing us back here, and for reminding me to trust in You, and that through unfaltering faith and patience and perseverance, all eventually comes around."

"Oh, and just one final request, if I may. Time doesn't stand still for anyone, I know, but please, just this once, let this moment linger on... a little longer."

Undoubtedly, I'm so very lucky to share this experience, once again, with my beloved Joaquín. But don't be mistaken; life hasn't been easy. We had to endure many years of unrelenting heartache and hardship before arriving to this magical moment.

This is my story—my journey—and what we had to trudge through to make it back to this place, to peace-of-mind.

Twelve years ago in 2000, I was on top of the world—young, healthy, and a wildly-in-love newlywed. We were on our honeymoon that year in Barcelona and our excitement was heightened by the thrilling sensation of adventure that also awaited us immediately after that trip. We were moving to Playa Jacó, an eclectic, laid-back surfer town on the west coast of Costa Rica. There, we would start life anew, and enter as new members of this curious and colorful society by opening our own business, a Currency Exchange Shop. We'd call it Zeman Casa de Cambio— taken from the first two letters of Joaquín's last name, Zeledón, and the last three from mine, Silverman—the quintessential manifestation of the merging of two lives into one.

The world was my oyster, picture-perfect.

However, years later in 2006, that illusion came to a screeching halt when I was diagnosed with an enormous life-threatening brain tumor while carrying our fourth child.

That was only the opening act of a series of tragic performances that came to define my very existence, and hang over my family and me like a dark storm cloud. Never knowing when fate would be back on our side, I took refuge in one singular truth: the indiscriminate passage of time.

Good times and bad times are subject to the same universal rules. Neither one lasts forever. And time, a mere string of moments, cannot and will not slow down or speed up for anyone or any situation—no matter how hard we try to make it so.

Embattled and struggling to survive, I knew the only direction to go was up, and hung onto that truism like a life raft.

And wouldn't you know it, twelve years later, almost to the day, our moment finally arrived. We slipped back in time, to that enchanted place where it all began, and our lives were first entwined in holy, hopeful matrimony...

Pearls of Wisdom ...

- o Time passes and waits for nobody.
- o Time heals.
- o Life's a cycle... at times you're up, at times you're down.
- o Press on against that relentless wind and unexpectedly, the winds will shift and be at your back.
- o Everything comes full circle.

2. *Kids Will Be Kids*

Allow me to take you back to June 2006, where it began to unfold in the Big Apple, New York City.

We step into traffic.

The offensive odor of burning rubber fills my nostrils.

"Grab tightly to my arm, Sis. Don't worry, I got your back," Adam gently lugs me across the busy intersection toward Lincoln Center.

"Thanks, little bodyguard," I smile warmly at my 6'1" brother.

It is late-morning, a day in early June full of sunshine and zero humidity with a light, heavenly breeze—a perfect hair day. I am on top of the world. Four months pregnant with my fourth child, my husband and I are about to begin our own business at home in Panamá, Central America. The kids are home safe and sound with "Papi," their Dad, and he's got a full domestic staff to help ready the kids, prepare Shabbat meals and tidy up the house. Here I am in the center of the world, New York City. Can life get any better than this?

Mom, her second husband Warren, "baby" brother Adam and I all flew in for the auspicious occasion, David's medical school graduation ceremony. My sister-in-law Amy is also here and we're all ecstatic to be together. We are so proud of David—who would've thought? Despite my usual pregnancy-induced clumsiness, I am ready to party.

David was the prototypical middle child. Textbook. Everything ever written about the middle child's plight unerringly describes him—sloppy, beleaguered, and sweet. Frankly, nobody ever really expected him to achieve this level of academic success.

If only Dad were alive to witness this miraculous victory. He'd be pinching himself.

Dad passed away without much warning. It happened on April 24, 2000, barely a month after my wedding celebration. He had been too ill to attend. In the Jewish religion, it's bad luck to cancel or postpone a simcha[1]. You don't do that. So waiting around for him to recover wasn't an option.

---

1 Hebrew word meaning gladness, joy, or festive celebration.

In 1994, after twenty-four years of marriage, Mom and Dad called it quits. For years, they had one of those low-conflict, low-stress melancholic marriages, and absolutely nothing in common. Dad moved out as soon as they sorted out their finances and relocated to an unofficial retirement condominium. Via aggressive marketing tactics, the development was trying to reel in younger couples. It had renounced its long-standing classification as a senior community, but all the locals knew that was a crock.

Dad grew old and depressed rapidly. The stale building reeked of yesterday and old age—not a propitious environment for a recent divorcee looking for love and a tennis partner. Nonetheless, I was sickened after each visit to that dreary place. Dad was only sixty when he moved in and this move ultimately aged him at lightning speed.

Years after my parents split, Dad went for a routine hip-replacement surgery. The following year he got himself a girlfriend who doted on him lovingly. During this time, the Parkinson's was under control; in fact, it hardly progressed at all.

Tragically, his happiness, stability and love life proved short-lived. A year after his hip replacement operation, he took a fall while alone in his apartment and ended up back in the hospital—this time though, the VA, the public one.

His Parkinson's began to advance rapidly, and his concomitant depression was in full swing. The lady friend disappeared as soon as Dad could no longer take her to dinner. Already debilitated mentally and physically, he began to spiral downhill and contracted sepsis during his hospitalization. The bacteria ravaged his system and led to septic shock. He passed away two days later.

Nana, Dad's shrewd mother, based all decisions—life and death ones included—on economics. Sadly, she chose to admit him wherever it cost the least. Because he had spent a few years in the army, she chose the Veteran's Affairs Medical Center in Miami.

Weeks after marrying, I was an emotional wreck. I recall trying to reconcile deep feelings of grief and guilt with the elation of being a passionately-in-love newlywed. My heart functioned on two parallel tracks. I was fraught, and acted psychotic.

Joaquín and I would make love and seconds later, I'd be coiled up in a fetal position wailing my eyes out.

"Are you okay, Mi Amor? Did I hurt you?" My new husband didn't know what to make of my disturbing behavior. I couldn't even come to grips with my own feelings as they swung wildly between emotional extremes. I certainly had no compunction to burden him with this inner turmoil.

He'll run for sure, I thought.

Distraught by Dad's abrupt and untimely death, I comforted myself with the notion that soon, we'd be getting out of town. My salvation was simple: run away.

I knew if I were to stay, local landmarks would inundate my memory and remind me of the happy childhood I wanted so desperately to forget for now.

Months before we became a couple, Joaquín had resigned from his well-paying executive job at Citibank, taking the bold initiative to opt out of the comfortable, self-indulgent South Florida lifestyle he had led for years.

"I'm going back to my country, to Costa Rica," he announced, when we first saw each other again at Shira's thirtieth birthday bash at a popular joint on Fort Lauderdale Beach, moments before the love spark shot between us. "I want to find a wife, settle down and start a family. Plus, I'm sick of Corporate America and want my own business."

I was game for anything, and ready to embrace the unknown. It was a really good time because I had arrived home, days earlier, after a year away in Jerusalem, where I had been hard at work on my Master's thesis studying the impact of Russian immigration on Israeli society after the collapse of the Soviet Union, and all the while scouring around for information on the local Russian mob. It was nearly impossible to extract hard data from any "official" about the mafia's whereabouts and activities. People were reluctant to admit it even existed, but it was fun trying.

So together, we decided to start a life together and pioneer new business terrain in Costa Rica. We headed to a quaint, laid-back surfer-town to open our own business, a Casa de Cambio[2]. Joaquín visited the area several times and saw a golden opportunity. Our only competition would be three national banks whose low-priority money exchange service was unbearably inefficient. Exasperated tourists often waited hours in slow-moving queues. Our plan was simple: bring good American customer service to the market with clean bathrooms, air-conditioning, and friendly, speedy service.

---

2 Currency exchange office

We both had high tolerance for risk and weren't intimidated by the unknown. Plus at that time, we had absolutely nothing to lose. We had socked away a total of $7,000 to fund the venture. We'd invest $2,000 for personnel, equipment, and office space refurbishments. We'd recycle the other $5,000 between our business and the bank until we'd begin to see a profit.

That is what we set out to do.

In early June 2000, we moved out of South Florida and set up shop in Playa Jacó, a popular beach town on the Pacific coast of Costa Rica inhabited primarily by pothead surfers, American misfits and Costa Rican renegades. This was our first adventure, the commencement of our marital journey. At that time, I wholeheartedly believed fleeing my hometown, so abruptly after Dad's death, would enable me to skip the predetermined emotional stages of grief—the whole damn process. My solution: plunge head-on into this new marriage, new country, and new business.

Follow the plan and don't look back.

Unfortunately, that never worked and months—even years— later, I found myself languishing in sorrow. My poorly-made decision to evade, rather than confront head-on, the reality of Dad's death would resurface for a haunting second go-around six years later.

Since my wedding day on March 19, 2000, my life, a suburban life that began as rather uneventful and conventional, has been punctuated by one major occurrence after another. Once we set out on our marital voyage, perpetual change buoyed and excited us. There was never a dull moment. Never.

I have no complaints, no regrets. Because the highs we experienced were that much more exhilarating because of our willingness to take chances.

But that's all neatly stowed away in the past.

It's now June 2006, and I am in New York City celebrating my brother David's scholastic achievements. For a week, I will disconnect from my charmed life back in Panamá and my frenetic social life and focus on the moment, this moment—David's moment.

I can't help but yearn for my father.

He was always so devoted to us. Months after he passed away, in a dream, my Dad came to me. The image was clear. I was sixteen, busy and like most vibrant teens, always on-the-go.

I am approaching the threshold of the den en route to the front door to meet my boyfriend. Dad appears. "Where are you off to in such a hurry?" he asks. I sigh, annoyed by his attempt to derail me, yet strangely, am compelled to stop and look up at him. When I do, I see crusty, little seeds sprout out from the corners of his eyes and a pus-like matter seeps out of his face and neck. "Dad," I scoff, "you must rinse this gook off when you first wake up."

"Oh, Tuti,"[3] he chuckles, "it's just that I love you so much, it's oozing out of me."

In the dream I hug him with all my might, bury my face into his soft, sturdy chest and breathe in his familiar scent; a hint of Irish Spring still lingered on his skin since his morning shower.

When I finally awoke, I lay in bed awe-struck and stared at the ceiling trying to recapture every detail. I'd been enlightened. Dad's well of love had no bottom. Indisputably, his love had a stronger presence and ability to connect us to each other and to him, albeit deceased, than death's power to tear us all apart.

I disclose my aching heart with nobody as we continue to traverse through the spacious courtyard toward the entrance of Lincoln Center.

Adam and I make a mad scramble as we push our way through the heavy glass doors. Suddenly, we find ourselves treading in a sea of people running in all directions, taking photos, exchanging greetings, congratulations, hugs and words of praise. The atmosphere is electric. Hundreds of students have realized the dream of a lifetime—the fulfillment of an objective that demands no less than unfaltering dedication.

Dr. David is beaming. His frozen grin reads a mixture of astonishment and pride. We snap the same photo from a hundred different angles.

Mom and I escape off to the restroom and I find myself staggering behind her like a drunk. People are coming straight at me from all directions, almost knocking me off my already unsteady feet.

"Mom, give me a hand. I'm getting run over!" I giggle nervously, colliding into the walls.

She spins around, backtracks about thirty yards and fetches

---

3 Short for Tutical, an abbreviated version of the silly nickname Dad created for me. My brothers' nicknames were all equally goofy, all rhyming and with the "tical" suffix.

me. I clutch onto her elbow as she pulls me through the multitudes to the restroom. Minutes later, we walk out drying our hands on our pants and notice the crowds have thinned.

We sprint around the entire building perimeter, lost, desperately searching for our designated entrance. Of course, neither one of us can interpret the brochure diagram of the building's layout. Finally we find the right passageway and thrust open the swinging door. Panting, we climb into our seats. The keynote speaker is perched over the podium, about to begin. Baby brother Adam is at my right, all nestled in. He looks up at us and chuckles out loud.

During the various speakers' discourses, Adam and I dare one another to shout out random cheers for David when he finally appears on stage. When together we are always silly and outright immature. I love that. Always being La Señora and La Madre Responsable[4] with real responsibilities to my family and community in Panamá, it's a welcome relief to disconnect and regress back into familiar patterns of childish conduct. After years rehearsing, my brothers and I have perfected our comedic repertoire. Our imitations and interpretations would rival those of any professional comedian.

In Panamá, I don't get to practice my silly impersonations. Despite being bilingual, language and cultural barriers do exist— even with my close, English-speaking friends. More importantly, I have this image to uphold as the señora of a large household, religious woman, and wife of a high-level executive. It'd be incongruous to act this way.

I oftentimes pine for a stage to perform such amateur dramatics and manifest my Peter Pan spirit. I think that's one thing my brothers and I have in common. We feel completely at ease acting outright stupid together.

Minutes pass and Adam taps me on the knee.

"Darah, Sis," he winces, "what's up with your eye? Are you okay?"

Glancing down, I realize unconsciously I've gone through an entire travel pack of tissues in an effort to control the stream of tears gushing from my left eye.

"I don't know, but it's shooting out like a freaking geyser," I

---

4 The Mrs. (Misses) and the responsible mother

whisper, trying to get a grip and dab lightly. I don't want to smear my painted face.

Strange paradox. My eye feels bone-dry and irritable, yet sheds tears uncontrollably. I cut off the flow of tears by creating a dam with a fistful of Kleenex and watch the rest of the ceremony straining with my right eye.

Adam and I continue conspiring for our moment of glory. Since our last name begins with S, we have ample time to strategize and prepare for the perfect execution of yelps that will consist of quick, recognizable one-liners from childhood.

Our goal is not only to embarrass David a little, but also to transport him down memory lane. We want him to lose his composure—for just a second. Like school-aged pranksters, we grow increasingly giddy with excitement as the time draws near.

I am having the time of my life.

While the R names are announced, I latch onto Adam's arm and we creep out of our row, tiptoe towards the side corridor, and crouch down in front of the cluster of amateur photographers.

We spot David approaching the stage. Once his name is pronounced, in a true tag-team fashion, we bellow out no less than eight familiar Dad-isms in twenty seconds flat. David cracks up in spite of himself.

Mission accomplished!

We parade back to our seats, victorious, and wait out the remainder of the ceremony.

Tears continue to flow from my left eye and trickle down my neck.

After all the photos are taken and congratulations proffered, we march out of the building. Adam, my bodyguard, insulates me from the fast-moving hordes, extends his arm and together we catch up to the rest of our group practically skipping ahead en route to The Boathouse, a lovely restaurant on the water in Central Park.

For the first time in a very long time, I haven't a care in the world. It's the first time I have traveled alone—no husband and no kids—since getting married in 2000. All I have to do is take care of my pregnant self, and that's easy; it's my fourth time down this road. I got this. No diaper bags to schlep, no overloaded strollers to push, or totes brimming with toys, snacks and bottles. Oy, and no worrying if I brought the extra pacifier.

I'm still in great shape and rarely get sick.

After the predictable first trimester morning sickness, my pregnancies usually are drama-free.

I'm a fucking rock. At least I still think I am.

The following day we stroll around the city aimlessly and once lured behind heavy, velvet curtains in Chinatown, shamelessly stock up on fake designer purses, belts and wallets.

Just around the bend, I notice a Help Wanted sign adhered to the grimy window of a convenience store. Playfully, we pester Adam about his recent unemployment status. David jostles him to go in and apply for a job. Adam is between jobs at the time, and despite his obvious smarts and enviable work ethic, he's confused about the future.

He likes so many things, or rather, the idea of doing so many things. Like so many college-grads his age, he still struggles to hone in on his true passions. He has yet to identify what his life purpose may be. He changed majors several times in college, and has worked in a variety of industries. He doesn't explicitly express it— Adam's quite enigmatic and reserved—but I know he's anxious to pinpoint his true calling.

I felt that way after graduating with a degree in psychology. I faltered at times, eventually embarking on a semi-desperate mission to find my higher calling. Yet only after many years of travel, study and dabbling in several fields, did I even begin to see the light. It's a lifelong process, one that I'm still figuring out.

In the end, you have to be comfortable living with the uncertainty.

To my mother's disappointment, at one point, Adam enlisted in the military. It was just before we went to war with Iraq in 2001. Thankfully, he was discharged shortly thereafter when accused of medical fraud. He'd failed to document his Lasik surgery on the intake forms. Oops.

Thank God for that, though.

His life had been spared.

Everyone was confident Adam would find validating work after our New York soiree. This hiccup would allow him time to disconnect from the grind of looking-for-a-real-job. He'd be able to re-group and return home with batteries recharged. For now, nobody was worried about him. Not really. It was a typical journey of self-discovery that'd require time and patience.

In the meantime, it's fun to tease him all the same. He seems to get a rise out of it. He makes a beeline toward the dingy door, enters and emerges seconds later with a huge, impish grin plastered across his face. He waves the application around proudly as if it were a school banner at a college football championship.

We're bowled over that he just did that; he has real chutzpah.

The sibling closeness we feel derives from the solid foundation of our shared, kooky past. It's a past grounded in the innocence of a carefree childhood, void of any real, life-altering hardships. We didn't suffer much from Mom and Dad's lackluster marriage, either. Most of the time, they managed to conceal their own marital troubles by re-directing their energies into us.

What most resonates about my childhood are the fun times hosting Sunday barbeques, poolside with family and friends. And someone was always entertaining, whether strumming a guitar or doing a stand-up act. Our family was quirky and corny and we were always laughing.

We were blessed.

My New York experience echoes of days long gone. We press pause on our real lives back home and with the button stuck on rewind, enjoy these precious, fleeting moments reminiscing about Dad and re-enacting scenes from old-time movie favorites.

Thrown back in time, our conversations consist of little to no substance and oftentimes, are just a back-and-forth banter of one-liners from a funny movie or lyrics from some eighties rock song. Adam always gives a stellar performance when impersonating his favorite comedian or the dance moves of his choice hi-hop or rap musician. His humor is insightful and his delivery, dry and subtle.

I'll never forget the time he came to visit us in Panamá, in October of 2004, to celebrate the bris[5] of our third child and first son, Natan. Adam had never traveled outside the United States before, and he was as wet behind the ears as they come. He couldn't wrap his brain around the concept of live-in help—something that took me years to get used to myself.

The morning after his arrival, we gather in the kitchen for breakfast.

It seems the kids' nanny developed an instant crush on Adam. She eagerly waits on him from the minute he sits down at the table.

---

5 Ritual Jewish circumcision performed when a healthy baby boy is eight days old.

Upon serving him his requested scrambled eggs and toast, she soon realizes she forgot to take out the butter. When she squats down to spread the butter on his now-cold toast, Adam looks at me bewildered, then back at her, and shrugs. Face pointed toward her, he opens his mouth in anticipation of a bite of toast. He assumes she'll be feeding him as well.

We were in stitches.

This trip to New York I will never forget.

Little did I know, I would never see my little brother again.

Pearls of Wisdom

- o   Be a kid.
- o   Cherish the moment.
- o   Life can turn upside without warning.

3. *"Bomiting"*

"We're told that men are strong and brave, but I think women know how to endure, accept defeat, and bear physical and mental agony much better than men."

- Lisa See, Shanghai Girls

June 2006, Panamá, one week later...

Home just one week from David's graduation ceremony, I lean my head all the way back and look directly overhead to examine the roof twenty feet up. A bit weathered and dated, yet gorgeously rustic. Perfect. Revealing signs of past celebrations, miniscule traces of tape and ribbon have sun-baked onto the wooden beams and are now part of its permanent structure. The cedar construction merges into a perfectly symmetrical A-frame. Despite being a country home in tropical Panamá, a land close to the Equator, it feels like the inside of a gigantic ski lodge. Soon we'll call it home.

The room is vacant and lonely; it yearns for furniture and wall décor. We are the aspiring tenants and will fill that void in fifteen days. Move-in date is set for June 15, 2006. I am exchanging niceties with my future landlord, discussing last-minute details about the house. She willingly discloses a few more idiosyncrasies about this old, rickety 5,000 square-foot farmhouse, and confesses what ostensibly will require maintenance.

Our voices echo throughout all 500 square-feet of what will become our living room. The Mexican-tiled floors and broad river stones blanketing the walls beckon me home. I've always fancied myself a country girl at heart, despite having never lived a country lifestyle. I admire the imposing vaulted ceiling.

God, I love this space, and can't wait to move in.

In the dead center of this vast emptiness, the two of us stand, conversing.

How am I going to arrange our stuff to fill such a large room? Going to have to either create an optical illusion or buy a truckload of new furniture.

Suddenly, the room begins to spin out of control. A giant vortex begins to suck me inside. Señora Aleman keeps chatting, but becomes increasingly incoherent.

What the hell is she saying? Why is she slurring her words?

I don't understand her. I can barely see her lips move, as her image turns hazy. Nausea and dizziness hijack my senses.

"I have to get back to the movers and children," I mumble reaching into my purse, fishing around for my car keys. Continuing to peer into my bag, I attempt to mask my panic.

She nods, seeming not to notice a thing.

Kiss-kiss. Ciao. We bid one another farewell.

I am deteriorating rapidly. Crawling into my Volvo wagon, the scorching, leather interior startles me and burns the back of my thighs. I can barely sit down.

As usual, it is over one-hundred-degrees outside. Beads of sweat trickle down the inside of my blouse, making their way to my pregnant belly. The sticky elastic waistband of my maternity shorts rubs against my abdomen, marking my skin and causes it to itch.

Let's make it home before puking, I plead with myself.

Home is just two blocks away. I can do this. Barely able to see straight from the sun's mid-day glare coupled with the steam rising up from the asphalt streets, I clutch the steering wheel firmly and weave my way through the two short side streets toward my home. I am spiraling downhill rapidly and a rising force begins to seize control.

Recklessly, the car lurches into the driveway and by inches, I miss driving right through the iron security gate. My trembling foot loses grip of the brake. I can't make it to the bathroom in time and instead, projectile vomit all over the steering wheel, entire dashboard, and of course, all over myself. My convulsing pregnant torso rams into the horn, startling the two housekeepers.

My husband is going to kill me. There is vomit everywhere— even inside the air conditioning vents.

Immediately, the two women run outside to my rescue. Upon glancing at the wreckage, one of them slips back inside and promptly returns with towels. Together, they lift me out of my wagon.

"I lost control of the car," I confess sheepishly.

Frantic looks tiptoe across both of their faces.

Humiliated, I vow never to drive again—not until this pregnancy is over and all this inexplicably bizarre discomfort subsides ...

Within days of my burgeoning sickness due to pregnancy, new family rituals, albeit dysfunctional, are established and replace the old way things are run around here.

Despite my slippery, sweaty palms, I keep a desperate yet secure grip while I pray to the porcelain god. Having already delivered three children within the last five years, I am a "morning sickness authority" and mindful that nausea and vomiting are an integral part of my first–second trimester experience. But this is utterly incapacitating. It has come to define me and has taken over my life. My social life comes to a virtual standstill.

"Mama, Mama, where are you?" little feet stomp throughout the house.

"Here I am, Mi Amor. In my bathroom."

The kids come charging at me, one by one—ready to pounce. Sprawled out on the cold, ceramic-tiled floor, moaning and contorting with gut-wrenching convulsions, my body moves as if I'd been shot at close range.

"Mama, are you almost done 'bomiting?'"

"Just about, go outside and find the nanny. It smells yucky in here," I mutter, shooing my almost two-year-old boy out of the bathroom.

How is it possible that these kids don't mind the foul odor of vomit? Are they that oblivious?

The other two have arrived now, girls ages three and five. And fire away with demands and complaints of their own.

"Mama, she took my favorite Barbie! Plus, you promised me ice cream and I want it now!"

"Mama, I ran outside and scraped my knee. Can I please have a purple Barney Band-Aid now?" little sister sidekick chimes in.

"Does it seem like a good time to you?" I groan, panting and drooling all over the floor. Chills crawl up my spine as cold sweat beads break out across my face.

Insanely, we conduct "business as usual." We have no option; the world can't stop mid-orbit because Mommy is sick. Strangely, my kids embrace this situation with the creepy indifference of a sociopath. Thank God for kids and their peculiar barometers for normal. Incidentally, they empower me to see things from this point of view as well.

Even so, I have almost reached my limits. And by eighteen weeks of pregnancy, I want out. My teeth are corroding, my eyes are swollen and bloodshot from the lack of sleep, and I can no longer run the simplest of errands alone. I retreat into a state of hopelessness and seek assistance for everything—including getting dressed in the morning. For a strong-willed, independent woman, this is definitely a problem.

A big one.

Every friend and stranger I encounter offers his or her unsolicited advice and confidently concludes that my pregnancy hormones are skyrocketing. Great. Apparently, this means the baby is thriving. So damn healthy it is making me violently sick. What a strange correlation.

"¡Éste bebe 'ta bien pegado, oye mi hijita!"[6] each person reassures me. Desperate to buy into something, even this bubbameister,[7] it comforts me until my situation takes an abrupt turn for the worse.

I begin to tailspin.

Like a worn-out recorder stuck on rewind, the same scenario plays out night after night. I tuck the kids into bed and wobble to my bedroom. Thrusting open the door with my foot, I make a beeline for the bathroom. I take a long, hard look in the mirror, looking deep into my own eyes, searching for the rudiments of my own deterioration.

My face hasn't changed much and my eyes reflect little more than exhaustion. I pry open the medicine cabinet affixed to the wall, pull out my cleansers and creams and attempt to maintain my nighttime routine. Each evening I struggle to cross the finish line of this small marathon. Once I do, I zigzag to my bed—drunk from exhaustion and overcome with dizziness.

After climbing into my pedestal bed, I rest my head on a flattened pillow and am hemmed into this position until morning. Like ocean waters calming after a volatile storm, the fluids inside my head begin to settle into a blissful calm. At this point, any subsequent shift in head position will trigger waves of internal unrest. The pregnancy compounds my problem, and like most pregnant women, I need to empty my crushed bladder several times a night.

Yet given my current state of turbulence, I have to hold out until morning. Each morning I reconsider wearing an adult diaper,

---

6 This baby is really clinging onto (the mother) and thriving, ya' hear my little girl?
7 Yiddish for everyday nonsense or old wives' tale

but by mid-day I am convinced it isn't necessary. I can get through another day. It's almost over and can't last forever. Besides, I am in denial and will prevail over this impending menace—whatever it is.

I fight this revolting sensation by pretending I am like any ordinary pregnant woman—uncomfortable and wobbly. And basically, it all boils down to two choices each night: stay in bed and disregard my urge to urinate, or, get up to relieve myself and subsequently vomit. On a good night, neither situation plays out. On most nights, it gets messy.

Nonetheless, my contribution to the household "graveyard shift" is minimal. I am responsible for alerting the hardworking oblivious snorer asleep at my side should tiny visitors care to arrive. My job consists of nudging him when I hear the teeny footsteps approaching our door. I lay awake each night and wait for them to come. Even if they do not come, I stay awake waiting anyway. My goal is to awaken him before the door is violently shoved open lest he think a pack of armed gangsters are busting in.

Joaquín is clueless about what is happening to his uncommonly fragile wife. Yet, he diligently assumes all physical work inherent in the nighttime duties. When you have a pack of toddlers and babies, there is certainly plenty of nighttime action. Sadly, not the kinky kind. I am his moral support, and cheer him on as he darts out of bed several times a night to hunt down sleepwalkers, console terrified nightmare-sufferers, and change sheets drenched in urine.

I feel distraught and deflated by my fading mothering abilities. Guilt plagues me for my husband's increasingly fatigued state. He doesn't get more than two hours of uninterrupted sleep a night, then gets up to work a ten-hour day. I have been reduced to a mere "maternal advisor"—physically useless.

Surely, pregnancy cannot be my only excuse.

During the day, I stumble about the house grasping onto the walls. Whatever I carry slips from my quivering hands. Once it hits the floor, it's out of reach. Gone. Even if it is just below my feet, I cannot bend down to retrieve it. This is the most unsettling sensation I've ever experienced—worse than the nastiest hangover imaginable.

To function, I combat this ghastly sensation by maintaining my head on one plane all day. Consequently, I attain perfect posture. My erect stance rivals that of any indigenous woman skillfully balancing a basket-full-of-sustenance on her sturdy head. I keep my eyes staring toward the horizon on a forty-five-degree angle while ambling throughout the house.

What the hell is happening to me? What kind of pregnancy is this? Am I still human?

The exhausted housekeepers—thank God for them—trail me, calling out all items, one by one, as they fall from my arms and hit the floor.

"Señora, sus llaves (keys), cellular (cell phone), botella de agua (water bottle)..."

These women become my seeing-eye dogs, my arms and my legs. I can only see directly in front of me; it's as if my vision were severely impaired. If I look down, up, or to either side, the room begins to spin out of control and I will topple over.

Who knows what they really think of me, and my antics?

Surely, they must find me to be a melodramatic and complicated "gringa."[8] Really, who ever heard of such strange symptoms associated with pregnancy? Perhaps it would be plausible if I were blind or wearing a neck brace after a major spinal injury. But pregnant? These women spit their babies out waiting in line at the bus terminal, and are back working a week later. I, too consider myself as brawny and resilient as they are, but in reality, I am falling apart and losing control of the woman I once was.

My magnificently naïve children postulate that the baby in Mommy's belly is making her sick and assume complete uselessness during pregnancy is par-for-the-course.

God love 'em for their innocence and ability to accept and explain the world with such simplicity—just the way they see it.

Peculiarly, as if part of a massive conspiracy, everybody agrees—including several of the country's renowned medical experts. In retrospect, I question, how could so many learned professionals have bought into such a preposterous theory?

Everybody that is, except for a dear friend of mine. We have some great friends and lead a very active social life. Entangled in the social web of such a small, affluent community means you're invited to most everything.

Moreover, an entire week goes by bouncing from one affair to the next. Each year our social obligations grow exponentially, as we

---

8 American girl

become more drawn into synagogue events and engulfed by business-related obligations.

Often I've considered working part-time until the kids return from school. However, this would pose a problem. It would interfere with the abundant social engagements we are committed to attend. Indeed such affairs consume most of my time and interrupt my trying-to-be-more-than-just-a-mom ambitions. The amount of hours invested before each event between trips to the gift shops, department stores, beauty salon and neighborhood seamstress to prepare for parties and luncheons and gatherings is unremitting and time-consuming.

No doubt, we are entrenched.

Being part of this small, elite circle does have its benefits. For starters, if something unusual is transpiring, everybody knows about it. Secrets and privacy do not exist in this small town. If you're having an affair, everyone already knows. On a much brighter note, the notion of dropping dead in your home and the body remaining undiscovered until days later would never happen. What a relief.

Nonetheless, we can't simply "drop out" of society for a while. Our friendships and status confer social expectations upon us. And we want to uphold our commitments and do it all. So onward we march, despite my decline. Thankfully, I enjoy four-hour stints of relief from my misery with an expensive, hard-to-come-by drug called Zofran, typically used to alleviate extreme nausea in chemotherapy patients. Each pill runs about twenty-five bucks a pop and Joaquín smuggles it in from Costa Rica. It is considerably cheaper and easier to get over there.

I must feel better. Our friends, the Eisenmans, are hosting a gathering at their penthouse on the thirty-first floor of their new, luxury condominium. Built just off the shore in a prosperous sector of town called Punta Paitilla, the building faces the Panamanian Bay that merges into the Pacific Ocean. The view is breathtaking. The international cargo ships, cruise liners, and miscellaneous ocean vessels wait in queue to cross the Panamanian Canal, and appear vividly on the horizon.

The building's veneer resembles something right out of Robin Leach's 1990's television program, Lifestyles of the Rich and Famous. After passing the two guardhouses, we muscle our way through the heavy glass doors leading into the building's foyer.

Once inside, it is utterly majestic—like the inside of a king's private quarters—opulence dripping from every square inch. Solid marble blankets the floors while masterful oil and acrylic artwork canvas the walls of this vestibule. Lavish furnishings upholstered with fine, satiny imported fabrics are positioned throughout.

We step into the spacious, high-speed elevator. When the mirrored double doors slide open onto the thirty-first floor, we exit the elevator and enter directly into the private foyer of our friends' penthouse. Each floor of this building consists of one 6,000 square-foot private residence of sprawling luxury. Indeed, many have been featured on the glossy pages of the country's most glamorous high-end home décor publication, Selecta.

We ring the bell. The imposing hand-carved mahogany double doors slowly crack open.

A well-groomed housekeeper, one of many, clad in an all-white uniform, cordially greets us. "Buenas noches, Señores[9] Zeledón."

She escorts us directly to the front living room, where several other elegantly dressed couples are gathered, cocktails in hand and conversing amicably. We greet the other guests, most of whom we know quite well.

My girlfriend suddenly emerges from the bedroom quarters, effervescent and impeccable, cloaked in the finest European threads. Always the life of the party, she loves to host events at her home. She sees me and smiles; her blue eyes sparkle like diamonds.

Dorita and I are kindred spirits, and although we've only been friends less than a year, it was instant chemistry. She's a sweet girl, introspective, yet outgoing and all-around dynamic.

She teaches etiquette both privately and in the local schools. After authoring a book on the subject, she was asked to develop a curriculum and share her knowledge with others—mainly unruly, self-centered adolescents in need of manners-training.

She has the gift of gab and talks to everyone—from the homeless woman begging for change on the street corner to the president of the country. She has met them all.

She asks me how I'm doing. No personal questions, please, I think. The last thing I want to be at a festive gathering is an aguafiestas.[10]

"Everything is fine," I lie, shifting my gaze off to the side.

---

9 Good evening, Mr. and Mrs. Zeledón
10 Party-pooper or killjoy

"You really have a knack for interior design, you know," I flick my wrist toward the new, stately-looking furnishings.

However, stupid she is not. Amused by my failed attempt to change the subject, she presses me for information.

"Seriously, how's it going, amiga? Tell me. Do you feel any better?" she insists with a gentle stroke of the back of my hair.

Now I am putty in her hands. And must come clean. Because she touched my hair.

I attempt to downplay the harsh realities of my tumbling world and in lieu of a straight answer, entertain her with a theatrical play-by-play of the nighttime chaos.

As you probably noticed in the last chapter, I come from a family that has always relied upon slapstick humor and self-deprecation to gloss over life's challenges; now I resort back to this coping method and am in my element. I perform spot-on imitations of myself crashing into the walls, and offer fictitious confessions of being a just-out-of-the-closet bulimic.

But nothing works. She doesn't appreciate my inappropriate stabs at comedy. Visibly agitated, she shrugs it off, edges forward, and looks me dead in the eyes. She furrows her brows. "Darah, I order you to get your inner ears examined by both an auditory specialist and an ENT doctor. Get two opinions."

"That makes sense," I sigh in resignation, whispering under my breath.

In Panamá, most major industries run differently than those in the United States. Private insurance is one of them. It operates more like a PPO than an HMO. One must not first consult with a primary care physician to be referred on to a specialist. Patients can simply intuit what type of specialist they need based upon identifiable symptoms or through a friend referral, and make the appointment directly with that particular physician.

As long as the specialist is part of one's network, it's fine. If you find yourself with the wrong kind of specialist, you simply continue making appointments with others until you find the one best trained to solve whatever problem you have. Generally, one pays a fifteen–to–twenty–dollar co-payment regardless of the doctor's specialty. My plan is called PALIC, or Pan-American Life Insurance Company. It is very inclusive and straightforward.

That following morning after Dorita's gathering, I phone the two recommended doctors and make the appointments. Due to last-minute cancellations, I'm able to slide in with both the ENT and auditory specialist within two days.

And just like this, my official quest to uncover the mysterious truth behind these debilitating symptoms has begun.

My husband accompanies me to both appointments. The ENT, supposedly the best in the country, performs a superficial exam and is very forthcoming when he tells me that this enigmatic culprit is none other than the hormonal surge brought on by pregnancy. He diagnoses me with rough pregnancy and a possible build-up of inner ear fluid. While escorting me to the receptionist to pay, he urges me to re-think any future pregnancies. "You're body doesn't seem to respond well anymore," he concludes.

The next day we meet with the auditory specialist. A kind, burly man, he subjects me to a battery of tests to determine the status of my equilibrium—similar maneuvers cops make inebriated drivers perform to determine their degree of intoxication. Afterward, he opines that I have some loose debris in my inner ears that ought to be shaken loose.

He props me up on an examination table, wrestles me into submission, twists my limbs this way and that, and snaps my neck from one side to the other. In the end, I sway out of his office like a clumsy, drunken sailor on the verge of puking. I clutch onto my husband's arm for stability.

I can't believe I am paying for this crap!

Not only were his martial-arts techniques ineffective, but days after this barbaric treatment, I feel worse. In the meantime, I've been consulting with my sister-in-law Amy, a physical therapist, who gives me some medical insight into what's doing inside my inner ears.

She explains the shifting of fluids that takes place upon the execution of these maneuvers. Apparently, had my problem consisted of loose debris, these tactics would've proven helpful and stabilized me, and all the symptomatic dizziness and nausea would've tapered off. But that's not my case.

I'm starting to lose faith in this strong healthy body I've worked so damn hard to condition.

Each day is markedly worse than the one before. The symptoms mount rapidly.

Another week passes and I am involuntarily winking with my left eye. At first, I think it is a nervous tick, but later I realize that

I've acquired some sort of uncontrollable twitch. One evening during dinner, my husband, who appears even more deeply embedded in denial than me, is undeterred and refuses to take me seriously.

He finds my winking endearing, if not outright seductive.

Seductive? Libido? Are you freaking kidding me?

"I can't stop it and it's annoying," I clarify, urging him to shut up and eat.

But love is blind and he has a hard time recognizing that his reliably well-built wife is no longer at the helm of her failing vessel.

The following evening, we attend a religious class. Dorita is there. I report back that both specialists were a waste of time.

"One expert diagnosed me with 'tough pregnancy' and the other with 'sand in my ear.' What a profound analysis," I guffaw.

"Get this one," I continue, "I can't stop winking with my left eye. And the funniest thing is that I was never able to wink before in my life."

Incidentally, within days of this most recent symptom, my eye gives way to sudden, unmanageable tearing as it had in New York.

In my signature quirky fashion, I try to make her laugh. "Joaquín is bursting with pride now that his uncoordinated wife finally has mastered the seductive art of winking."

But she doesn't take the bait. In fact, I've never seen her so damn serious. She stares at me sternly, seizes me by the shoulders and snaps, "Darah, YA CALLATE!" You must see my neurologist tomorrow. I will call her myself in the morning. Her name is Dr. Muñoz."

"I know her well," she goes on, "and will make the appointment for you. I had problems years ago and nobody could give me an accurate diagnosis. And on the very first visit, she knew exactly what was wrong with me. I was so relieved."

It'll be a waste of time, I silently conclude, but why not? Insurance covers it all and nobody else seems to know what is going on. Because in this small town of mine it's all about name-dropping, that following morning we find ourselves in the presence of the eminent neurologist, a woman that my friend beholds in the highest regard. She is arguably the most knowledgeable neurologist in the country. High honors and degrees from American Ivy League

---

11 Darah, shut up already!

universities blanket her office walls.

I know I am in good hands.

After five minutes of get-down-to-business conversation, she brings my husband and me into her examination room.

With her assistance, I wrangle my way on top of the examination table. Once settled in, she subjects me to more of the same basic coordination tests I had already performed for the other guy.

Is this really so necessary that I had to leave the movers?

We are in the midst of moving homes and I have movers with boxes and supplies at my house waiting for instructions. I had told everybody, including the three housekeepers, that I would return within the hour to label and classify everything.

Meanwhile, here I am performing the basic gross motor skills I mastered as a toddler.

What a waste of time! I can barely concentrate as my mind keeps wandering back to the house. I had told the movers to box it all up and not do anything more until I got back.

Get me out of here!

All of a sudden, I am brought back to the here and now upon the realization that I can't execute the simplest of movements correctly.

I try to bring my left hand toward my face and touch my left index finger to the tip of my nose. Simple enough, right? But no, instead of this happening, my left arm takes the hand on a long, windy detour and it gets lost, unable to find my nose. In fact, I enlist the help of my right hand to hold my left arm steady at the elbow and attempt to guide it toward its destination.

Why is my left hand quivering so much?

"Lay down flat on your back," she proceeds, "and with your left heel, trace your right shin, starting at the knee, and move in a straight line down to the ankle."

What a joke, really? What the hell...

But wait. I can't do it. My left heel slips off my right shinbone as if the surface of the leg were full of grease. The left leg begins to tremble uncontrollably. I look down to witness this travesty and am both shocked and embarrassed by my awkwardness.

My limbs have developed a mind of their own.

"It's nothing, Doctor," I comment coolly. "I'm just stressed out with the move and haven't been sleeping well since the pregnancy began."

She dismisses my rationale, evidently finding it superfluous if not obstructive, and clearly, is not the least bit interested in my self-diagnosis. At once, her eyes begin to dart about the room as her brain computes the data. I can almost see her neurons firing. Then with her right thumb and forefinger, she massages her chin, and for a brief moment, slips away into deep thought.

Something is up. Within seconds, she perks up and rushes back into her consultation room, and summons us to trail behind. Still silent, she yanks one of her fifty-pound medical tombs off a shelf, opens it and thumbs through the pages. She finds what she is looking for when she lands on a page with a detailed illustration of the brain.

"Sit down Mr. and Mrs. Zeledón, and look at this."

She points to the cerebellum.

"This is the part of the brain that controls coordination and movement. Pregnancy hormones have no influence whatsoever over the functioning or malfunctioning of coordination, dexterity, and equilibrium," she asserts. "Whatever you've been told until now is absolutely incorrect."

Okay, so what does that mean? Are we getting any closer to identifying what the hell is going on with me? Being in Limbo, in the Not-Yet-Knowing-Stage, is driving me nuts.

She says nothing more for what seems like an eternity.

Then, she picks up the phone and makes a call to her colleague's office, the country's most renowned neurosurgeon, Dr. Uribe. She speaks to his secretary and instructs her to squeeze me into his schedule sometime the day after tomorrow. She wants him to examine me after the MRI brain scan she insists I take tomorrow.

My husband glances down at his shoes and as if speaking to his feet, mumbles under his breath, "Claro que sí, doctora, ahora mismo llamaré para sacar la cita para mañana."[12] She frowns, nods solemnly and offers no further explanation for this sudden sense of urgency, or for her cold bedside manner.

My husband, full of concern, gently presses her for more information.

"So what do you think is the matter, doctor? Any idea if..." he trails off, not really knowing what or how to ask what he really

---

12 Of course, Doctor. Right now I will call and make the appointment for tomorrow.

wants to know.

She doesn't budge.

"I will only discuss matters with you after the MRI results are available—no sooner."

She rises and with that cue, we tear ourselves from our chairs and with rounded shoulders, head toward the door.

I must be clueless about the severity of the situation. Staring at my watch, the only emotion I'm experiencing is a rising irritation. I need to be home by now, tending to the crew of movers. Everyone is hanging around, waiting, and doing God-knows-what to kill time.

They cannot possibly make important packing decisions without first consulting with me. Because I always have to be in control, I need to supervise everything or my entire world will come crashing down. My Type-A neurosis shields me from the looming battles of my near future.

I have no idea at this moment what is yet in store for me. What I had formerly known as "chaos" was minor league stuff in comparison to what awaits me.

That evening, I call everyone I know and grill them about the ins and outs of the MRI experience. My test is the following morning and I seek advice and suggestions from anyone who has ever undergone what seems to be a terrifying procedure. I must visualize the entire disturbing experience. This is how I prepare mentally. Blissfully unaware of the seriousness of my situation, my sole concern is getting through the whole MRI ordeal without suffering a full-blown panic attack inside the coffin-like contraption.

Waves of panic temporarily overcome me as I envision being physically bound to a freezing, metal examination table. Visions of my head locked in a brace while subjected to relentless clamor have me scouring around for advice, meditation techniques, and most significantly, drugs.

Fortunately, Dr. Carbone, my wonderful Ob-Gyn and confidant, prescribes a safe, light relaxant to help me coast through the required exam more gracefully.

If I can get through this, I can then get back to the work at hand—the move—I coach myself. There is so much to do and I want it to go smoothly.

Here in Panamá, good private health insurance gives us access to the best specialists and procedures right away. I never have to wait more than two days for a consultation. And because a lot rides on "who you know," if agendas are full, I'll mention my husband's recent position with the bank or drop a name. Besides, almost every doctor I need to see somehow is related to a friend of mine. That is how we make accommodations. I love that about living here, the special treatment and privileges inherent in being part of the "it" crowd, or upper class—whatever you call it.

The exam is scheduled for that very next morning at the new Hospital Punta Pacífica, a state-of-the-art facility that's affiliated with John Hopkins Medicine International—the place I plan to deliver this fourth baby.

Joaquín starts the car. Already having swallowed half a sedative, my face slackens. I stretch out my limbs and relax, communing with the comfortable leather seat of his BMW.

Once we arrive, loose-limbed and arrogant, I swagger into the waiting room ready for action. The receptionist confirms my full name and exam-type, "La Señora Zeledón para una resonancia cerebral,"[13] she shouts at the top of her lungs, as if I'm also hard of hearing. (I am by the way, but just don't know it yet.)

Patient confidentiality doesn't seem to exist and now the entire waiting room knows why I am here.

My husband is outside in the corridor on an important business call.

I spin around and scan the room to scope out a seat. An entire waiting room of quizzical eyes is gazing directly at my bulging abdomen. Like a two-step country-dance routine, all sets of eyes immediately dart up to make eye contact with mine. It's as if they're requesting an answer to their collective question: why are you, a pregnant lady, getting a brain scan?

Within minutes, the attendant calls me in to get prepped. After removing my jewelry and handing my stuff over to Joaquín, the technician settles me into this futuristic device. I start to zone out. Initially, my husband comes into the room and caresses my legs, to let me know he's by my side.

After a while, he must get antsy because he walks outside.

If I almost close my eyelids, and glance straight down toward my feet, I can see his silhouette. Back and forth, back and forth, he is pacing like a lion. He's up and down the corridor and tugging at

---

13 Mrs. Zeledón for a MRI brain scan

his face for what seems like a long time. What I cannot determine is whether he's on the phone.

Maybe he's annoyed it's taking so long and he's missing work.

Thanks to my drug-induced serenity, I don't mind and the hour passes quickly.

The MRI finale is transcendental. The last few minutes of deafening clamor transport me to another realm of consciousness. In fact, the racket is so mind-blowing and intrusive that my skull vibrates. I find myself on the cusp where pain and pleasure melt together into one indefinable, intense emotion.

Then, silence. The ringing in my ears continues for several long minutes but I'm unperturbed. Like a balloon, I inflate with pride.

I did it! I was graceful under pressure!

They unleash me.

I pop up.

"Let's go grab a sesame bagel and cappuccino, Mi Amor. I'm starving!" I cheer, rushing toward the exit.

"Ok... one... sec," Joaquín replies, transfixed while glaring at the screen's images.

While exiting, he asks the technicians if we could take a quick sneak-peek at all the successive computer screens to see the different-angled pictures of my brain. He saw them mumble amongst themselves and point to something on the screen during the exam.

He wonders what is up.

They agree to allow us into their tight control center for a preview, yet confess that they are not equipped to provide any medical explanation or accurate diagnosis.

But we are living in Panamá, a third world country by all definitions, and right now, in this place and on this particular day with these two lab coats, the rules appear as nothing more than a mere suggestion.

So when my husband asks about a large, amorphous image jumping out on the screen, the two technicians answer him, and rather confidently—despite having previously disqualified themselves for their lack of veritable credentials.

He studies the black and white lunar images and whispers in hushed tones with the two men. I'm not concerned, or frankly, that interested right now. I am confident that worst-case scenario, it is no more than a ball of fluid that has gathered in my inner ears, something that will require drainage. This was one of the ENT's brilliant theories; I liked it, so I chose to believe it.

From a few yards away, with my right foot already out the door, I see my husband oddly erect. His head hangs low and he seems to be gasping for air. Whatever they must have said scared the living daylights out of him because a terrified expression ripples across his face. He glances toward the door to where I am waiting, rather impatiently, and as soon as our eyes meet, his distraught look subsides into one of doubt, then sorrow.

I quickly dismiss our exchange of marital telepathy. For now...

For the first time ever, I'm the one rushing him along and motion him to get moving. It is time for that prized cappuccino and then time to get home to the movers.

Oh, the movers! I'm moving houses tomorrow and have so much to do!

First, nothing is going to eclipse my MRI-survival soiree.

"It's probably just a big ball of fluid that requires drainage, Mi Amor. That's what the ENT doctor thought, remember?" I blurt out confidently in response to his earlier gloomy look.

He nods pensively without saying another word about it.

We walk out and climb into the car and jet over to the breakfast bistro. It's late-morning and the place is near empty. Our food arrives almost immediately and I am in heaven—relishing each bite of my scrumptious veggie omelet while nursing a frothy latte.

I love eating out—even if only for a cup of coffee.

Although Joaquín is distracted, I chatter away tirelessly about the move, new house and kids. There's a lot going on and I'm sticking to my blueprint of how it's all going to play out.

We pay the bill and step cautiously into the searing car. As usual, the heat and humidity is unbearable. Because of the climate, this place is arguably uninhabitable most of the year. And pregnancy only exacerbates my personal heat index. Pools of sweat drench the inside of my blouse within seconds.

We drive a few short blocks and Joaquín is oddly quiet. His silence hangs like a shroud until we get home. I notice everything, even my own neglectful naïveté, yet choose to divert my focus toward the move. Multi-tasking has never been my forte.

He drops me off at home so I can get busy before he heads to his provisional office to polish-up a business proposal that targets co-investors. George Weeden, a close childhood friend, generously let Joaquín set up "shop" in his office. What a Godsend.

As soon as I cross the threshold of the front entrance, several desperately bored and hungry men bombard me. I know this because it is almost noon, and at that precise hour daily, a cacophony of rumbling bellies all but shuts the entire country down.

"Señora," I hear different voices calling me from all directions, "donde quisiera usted que pongamos..."[14] Without skipping a beat, I disconnect from the MRI episode and spring into action.

My mission: bring order to the moving fiasco.

I bounce around between the three bedrooms, kitchen, formal dining area, den and garage. I oversee how all items are packaged and subsequently, how each box is labeled.

The sponginess of the items' insulation doesn't concern me much. We are only moving a few blocks up the road, but I do want our stuff properly packed and easy to identify upon tomorrow's unpacking. Each time we move, Joaquín and I grow manic and restless with desire to have the entire new place set up with wall hangings, furnishings and ornaments almost immediately. And each time, without failure, we slave away refusing to stop until one of us collapses from exhaustion or comes down with a cold.

I'm in the zone now but keep getting distracted as calls come in from friends and family around the globe. Everyone had been on stand-by, eagerly waiting to learn about the MRI incident. At least, that's what I think they want to know about.

In reality, I learn later that day, all they really want to know are the results—something I had no concern with during this busy time.

One by one, I assure my family and friends that the worst of it is over and insist they needn't worry. The MRI was a breeze—thankfully. Now it's time to focus on the move, the new house repairs that must be carried out right away, and impending birth of our second son, I tell them all.

This stuff really has me stressed out.

However, all are abuzz with questions and only want to discuss my health. How morose.

I, in turn, only want to gripe about the clumsy movers. And go

---

14 Ma'am, where would you like us to put...?

on and on about how these incompetent men are mishandling our fragile stuff. My local friends indulge me in mind-numbing chitchat as we collectively commiserate about the workers' lack of drive and disinterest in a job well-done.

Such mundane babble keeps the existential thoughts out of my sick head.

Feeling industrious and full of adrenaline, I busy myself with a plan: get the kids' beds assembled in the new house ASAP. I set aside three sets of fresh linens, pillows and towels and stuff them into a giant, black trash bag. I order the movers to load their bed frames, mattresses and cribs into the truck last so it'll be unloaded first.

Who knows how long it'll take to assemble everything else, but at the very least, the kids will feel settled into their new home by nightfall, I triumphantly decide.

They're all too little and have enough sleep issues as it stands. This way the night's sleep won't further be disturbed by the transition. By single-mindedly focusing on this short-term goal, I continue to disconnect from my own reality, immersed in my plan.

That evening my husband returns at nine-o'-clock with the MRI film and the radiologist's results in hand. The image is contained in a huge manila envelope and accompanying results printed and folded into a small letter-sized white envelope.

He clasps both documents firmly in his right hand.

"Stop working already, Mi Amor. Sit down. I need to talk to you."

He wants to discuss what he already knows, what he just found out, but I am beat. All day I've been directing a crew of fifteen while looking out for the kids. I don't want to feed the beast. Maybe if I ignore it, it'll disappear.

"Enough already! What else to talk about?" I rant, consumed by denial.

His face turns ashen as he breaks the news gently, yet firmly.

"Da-rah," he begins in monosyllables, "the radiologist discovered a mass the size of a tennis ball situated right inside your left inner ear canal," and he deliberately affixes his glasses with the other hand after pulling the image out of the large envelope.

He points to the diagram on the film with his Mont Blanc, resembling an old, tenured professor.

"Look here. This growth is feeding like a parasite off the

abundance of hormones produced by the pregnancy. It's putting continuous pressure on your brain stem."

"That's why," his voice softens to a whisper, "you're dizzy, nauseous, off-balanced, and losing your hearing; the tumor is obstructing the left ear canal."

My eyes glaze over and I enter into another realm of consciousness. My body feels weightless. I leave my body. Suddenly, I am floating—actually hovering—over the room looking down upon the two of us in mid-conversation. My mind fills up with static. The blood drains out of my face.

I open my mouth to speak, but cannot produce a word.

My characteristically composed and objective husband, witnesses my abrupt transformation, grabs me and hugs me with all his might.

His eyes are swollen, and swell with tears.

"Mi Amor, I'm so grateful what you have is probably benign."[15]

He plants a gentle kiss on my forehead.

And waits.

I latch desperately onto my stomach and double over.

The wind is knocked out of me. I've been kicked deep in the gut. The room spins out of control. I'm faint. Need air. Can't breathe.

"Wait a minute, back up," I charge, in need of further clarification.

This demanding new reality usurps center stage and hijacks my trusted mechanism of denial.

"What? What are you talking about?" I cringe, peering at him incredulously. Bleary-eyed, I hobble over to the desk to grab a hold of it as my knees go limp and buckle.

Please just let me lie down and go to sleep. I wanna skip this part...

"I have something? You mean it's not just that..."

Silence.

As if time has stopped, his stiff body remains motionless. He patiently watches as I swallow this bitter pill.

Benign? Tumor? Mass? Growth? Me? Miss super-healthy,

---

15 The next day he confessed that he spent the entire day researching brain tumors on the internet and the ones that most resembled mine were all malignant. Friends that ran into Joaquín at the local drycleaners and Kosher restaurant that same day, later told me he looked like he'd seen a ghost.

fitness freak have a brain t.t.t.t.t.t.tumor?

Sporadic thoughts jump about inside my head like a pinball bouncing frenetically in all directions. You mean this whole ordeal isn't over yet? C'mon, I have a move to contend with, another baby on the way, a bris[16] to plan... no time for petty distractions.

"I'm not really making it up?" I challenge defiantly. "I'm a drama queen—you know me dammit!"

"Yes, Mi Amor," he exhales pensively and clutches at his chest, "but most likely your tumor, which is called an Acoustic Neuroma, is not malignant."

My tumor? This is not MINE. I don't own this thing. Don't want it. Get it the fuck out of me, now!

It is undeniable. Time is not on my side. This monster, this intruder—my tumor—has to come out immediately.

My so-called plans are worthless.

And unbeknownst to me, pathology aside, I am in death's imminent grip.

So on this day, the groundwork was laid. The heart-mind connection severs.

From here on forward, in spite of sporadic displays of emotion, I'm comfortably numb. An impenetrable exoskeleton protects my entrails.

I've transformed into a robot.

Pearls of Wisdom...

- o   Carry on as if all were normal until the time comes to confront adversity.
- o   When you're in the mouth of mayhem, pragmatism is the key to survival.
- o   Focus on others during times of chaos.
- o   Distract yourself with the mundane while embroiled in turmoil. It's too early to process anyway.

---

16 Ritual Jewish circumcision performed when baby boy is 8 days old.

4. *Stoic, Raw & Not Ready To Die*

June 14- 26, 2006

Joaquín drops the bomb that fateful evening and I board the train of emotions just before turning into a zombie.

A million feelings swiftly sweep through me as though I were watching some old black and white Super 8 film on fast forward. Except the movie reel is rolling inside my head, and I have not the time to stop the tape to consider what just played inside my mind's eye.

My recalcitrant body also rejects the news at first. My fists tighten and the visceral flight-or-fight mode powers on. A sudden rush of emotion, a mishmash of fear, despair, grief and rage, instantly overwhelm me.

I am drowning from the heaviness in my own heart.

It's too much to accept.

The timing can't be worse.

Pregnant, and with three small children to look after, the eldest just turned five. Our living situation is in a state of flux and there are months of unpacking and sorting in my foreseeable future. Everything happens so fast.

After initially receiving the breaking news, I never again have the luxury of time to contemplate my dismal fate during this experience. No real opportunity to process it at all.

Those next few days, my moments of solitude come while camping out in the bathroom. In this small space, I begin to confront my own mortality. At once, a wave of sadness pulls me under. Down, down, down...I am being sucked into a vortex of sorrow. Widower, orphans...

Fortunately, it never lasts long. Upon exiting the restroom, if not met by ornery toddlers, one of the movers is waiting in earnest, with a question or a suggestion. Gratefully, that yanks me out of my dark, inner abyss and returns me to the present.

In retrospect, the irony and hidden blessing behind this whole predicament was that circumstances forced me to hold it together from the very start; we were in the midst of this move and with children so young, I didn't want to complicate their lives further by transferring worry onto them.

In short: I was wrapped up in an emotional straitjacket and had no way out. My break from reality, and choice to focus on the mundane, was the only reason I continued to get out of bed each morning.

I never considered myself that brave of a person. But now, there was no option. Courage was needed. It boiled down to two options: face my fate head-on and fight like a son-of-a-bitch or shrivel up with self-pity and perish. The latter would have provoked mass hysteria and ultimately, the disintegration of my family.

So I chose to fight. I am good at fighting—just ask Mom and Joaquín.

My heart turns to stone. Stoicism becomes my modus operandi. Raw adrenaline fuels my actions. My body accomplishes tasks mechanically and not once, consults with my heart. It feels as though I were swimming underwater. Detached and aloof, I watch my own life unfold much like a journalist observes a dramatic scene unravel from the back of the bus.

If I panic, like a chain reaction, my kids and husband will, too. Moreover, the hysterical housekeepers—the helping hands we need so very much—certainly will abandon us. When they smell trouble, they take the low road so I have to stay cool or risk losing them. More on this later, promise.

My logical left-brain enters into business mode. It regularly engages in strategic discussions with my husband. My enchained heart—shunned-out and held hostage—will not be heard from again until much, much later—with the exception of an occasional cry-out in the sleeping hours.

Will I come out of this alive? Will my baby make it? What will happen to my children if they grow up without their mother? Down, down, down... Help, I'm asphyxiating. Shut up, Darah! Don't even go there. Forget it.

I wake up and stop these sinister thoughts dead in their tracks.

From June 15, 2006 forward, my devoted companion and I strap on our blinders, roll up our sleeves, and dive head-first into a muddy sea of work.

We take it all on at lightning speed—no-holds-barred. In addition to my medical arrangements—where I'm advised to plan for an estimated six weeks of time away from home—the logistics that go into arranging for our kids' care, well-being and physical safety is daunting.

I am a nothing more than a soldier with a clear mission: take care of the children, make this new house a safe home, and police hubby's mental state. Oh yeah, and stay alive.

Easy enough, right?

If I never felt like a bona fide adult before, this is quite the inauguration into a grown-up world.

When I do experience a sudden flash of daytime vulnerability, I console myself with one inspiration: *Darah, you're embarking on a personal rite of passage journey. One day, this'll transform you into someone much stronger, and much better than the woman you are today.*

Deep inhalation. No time to wallow. Suck it up. Dive into the fear, Darah. Embrace the unknown, and one day you will wear that damn warrior badge.

My functional psychosis serves me well as we check major decisions off the list—one by one. We have but a few days to pull it all together. We work around the clock and barely sleep. The pressure is crushing.

From a logistical standpoint, obtaining the information we need to make educated decisions about surgeons and accommodations is a calamity at best. Our entire life is stored inside an eighteen-wheeler parked outside of our new home—one with an eight-foot deep un-fenced-in hole in the backyard. We have no phone line in either the old house or the new one. The internet installation service is scheduled in three days, which in Panamanian terms means: whenever we get around to it sometime within the next two weeks.

We don't have local television and therefore, little knowledge of the outside world. Our newspaper still hasn't been programmed to arrive. Our cell phones—our only form of communication with the rest of the world—ring off the hook from all four corners of the globe.

I remain numb, a machine—day after day. Like this, I operate most successfully, and thrust all feelings aside each time they defiantly dare to surface.

Damn heart, stay the hell out of it! I got work to do!

The word about my diagnosis spreads through the grapevine like wildfire. People in the community come in droves to our country home to visit.

And I realize now, to say their good-byes. Told to me much

later was this: public opinion was I was already dead and buried.

Some people organize masses. The Jewish community arranges for groups to recite Tehilim, or psalms, on my behalf. Our new landlord—a dignified and kind-hearted woman we hardly know—holds a mass in Mexico City to plead for my survival. She is Panamanian but temporarily resides in Mexico City due to her husband's political post. Other people acquainted with us—and some we don't know at all—beg God to spare my life for the sake of my husband and small children.

Again, people told me all of this after the fact—after I began to recognize and accept my fate.

Some "friends" never stop by and simply avoid Joaquín and me. It breaks my heart that some of the people with whom I have invested years building friendships, can't even face me in my hour of need. Other folks however, who aren't close to me, show up daily. Many offer to help care for our children, do our food shopping, and manage our expenses. Others send over homemade pastries. A few recommend doctors, hospitals, and volunteer to supervise the construction of the much-needed child safety gate around the circumference of the backyard pool.

People react so differently in times of crisis. True colors emerge when times get tough, I realize. I am disappointed by some and pleasantly surprised by others.

The pool weighs heavily on our minds. We originally planned to tie up this loose end once moved in. Now, circumstances have changed and so have our priorities. The children are so young; the eldest just turned five and she is the only one who knows how to swim. Worse yet, the housekeepers—the adults in charge of supervising the children in our absence—are themselves, petrified of the water. It's not a good situation.

Ideas, suggestions, advice and assistance are like bullets—fired at us from all directions. We absorb it all, open to anything that makes sense. This hodgepodge of information swarms around our heads as frantic bees buzz around their beloved queen. Moreover, every detail of this sticky situation merits our undivided attention.

Little by little, like a slow-burning forest fire that devours one tree at a time, it engulfs our every waking thought. In fact, there is nothing else to discuss but this.

Seeing the amount of work set before us, some friends send

over their housekeepers or male domestic workers for a day or two to help lift and unpack heavy boxes. The interior movements of my new house mirror the inner workings of a large factory; there is a constant hum of activity and collaboration between so many people—most of whom have never met one another before.

Workers come and go. Visitors stop by. Friends help me set up some of my closet drawers. Others come to inspect, bring food, world news, bestow gifts and blessings, and motivational reads. A few of the more spiritual ones set out to detoxify the bad energy that envelopes our family by offering to change mezuzahs[17] and re-Kasher[18] our kitchen.

This goes on for five consecutive days and nights. Non-stop. I am not only walking erectly like a robot, but also void of feeling toward my own destiny. So caught up in this frenetic pace, I don't even realize my days are numbered.

Time ticks away and sound decisions need to be made about my approaching surgery. But where to begin? What criteria do we use to choose the best surgeon for the monumental challenge of performing brain surgery on a pregnant woman? Is it possible to ensure the fetus' survival? No.

Many of the world's renowned surgeons with whom we consult say it is an impossible feat, and admit to a lack of experience in a case like mine. Frightfully, a grand majority opine that we have to sacrifice the baby's life. On more than one occasion I hear, "Mrs. Zeledón, regretfully, first we'll need to remove the fetus, and then we can...." Some of the younger, more cutting-edge physicians also assert that the baby will never survive the operation and insist on removing him first.

Fuck that. Next. I need a hero who can save us both.

At twenty-three weeks gestation, the fetus would have no chance of survival—at least as a normal healthy baby. Several acclaimed, high-risk Ob-Gyn doctors urge me to wait another six weeks to operate, and then force a Cesarean at thirty weeks. Yet this scenario still would not guarantee the baby's survival and subsequent thriving.

I feel woozy with expert opinions. Too much to process. Who to believe? What are my own preferences? Do I even have them?

---

17 A piece of parchment usually contained in a decorative case inscribed with specified Hebrew verses from the Torah, or Old Testament.
18 The act of making a Jewish family's kitchen Kosher.

Incredibly, with scant resources and on minimal sleep, somehow, we manage to make our selections. After forty-eight consecutive hours of reading and researching surgeons all around the world that are qualified and willing to perform a procedure comparable to the removal of a fuzzy tennis ball entangled in hundreds of sticky tentacles, we narrow it down to two. Fortunately, for us, both of these renowned masters practice in the same city, Manhattan.

Even after we identify our two top choices, friends and relatives continue to protest and present their own opinions about how, why, where, and when to operate. Everyone, including our community rabbi, has something to say. It doesn't help much that each point of view is at odds with all others on the table.

Looking back, what really plagued me was that I did not want to leave the country for so long and entrust the children's care to others unrelated to me. If my days in Panamá taught me one thing, it was not to trust anyone who watches your kids—especially those you have to pay to do it. To this day, I still don't.

Thoughts of abandoning my three babies quickly drove me into a state of despondency, and a few times, I felt my repressed heart wriggle in protest. More than once, I was tempted to turn my back on myself—on the whole damn medical ordeal—and seek refuge in my precious children.

Being with them at that time was more important to me than fighting the battle of my life. At least if I was going to die, I considered in a moment of clarity, I'd know that in the end we had spent quality time together.

What if I simply avoided it all, I thought, and stepped into a parallel reality—one where nothing ever happened? Can I "will it" to disappear?

These absurd thoughts crossed my mind more often than I care to admit...

However, all the neurologists and neurosurgeons that had reviewed my MRI images unanimously agreed that baby aside, I couldn't wait more than two weeks, at best. This invasive mass had to be extracted immediately. Freeloading off the profusion of pregnancy hormones, this characteristically slow-growing tumor was swelling unpredictably—at lightning speed—and shoving itself up against my brainstem. Spontaneously, without a moment's notice, I could fall to the ground and suffer massive seizures resulting from hydrocephalus, or water on the brain.

One starlit night, after hours meditating alone on the back patio and listening to the familiar chants of the grillos[19] and howls of neighborhood street dogs, or tinakeros, I threw my hands up in the air, resigned to my fate. I knew what I had to do—leave the kids. Undergoing surgery in Panamá, just to stay close to them, was not an option; there were no neurosurgeons qualified to take on the job.

And so the faith-I-never-knew-existed kicked into high gear.

Close your eyes, Darah. Take a deep breath. And jump. What else can you do? Just ride it till the end.

Here are just a few things we had to do. We arranged for a dear friend to come and stay at the house to supervise the children and oversee the nannies. Tía Bonnie was the most unselfish person I ever met and she loved our kids. Single, her two children were older so she was flexible with her time. She would move into our home for the duration of our time away.

She would function as the "supervisor of everything in our life" and we trusted her implicitly. Thank God for her. With no family in the country to love on our children, we were damn lucky to have someone willing to put her own life on hold to bail us out. If it weren't for her, we wouldn't have known what to do with the children.

Tía Bonnie is coming.

Check.

With that under control, we updated all the insurance policies and paid all deductibles. My husband met with our insurance agent, Lorena, to discuss strategies for coping with the impending labyrinth of paperwork. He had an international plan specifically designed to cover catastrophes and emergencies. This policy secured treatment for urgent care anywhere in the world—only once the insured paid the $10,000 deductible in full.

Money wasn't a real issue back then. We had the liquid cash available at the time. Months before we'd earmarked it to invest in our own business. Bit once again by the entrepreneurial bug, Joaquín had resigned as the general manager of Credomatic—a Nicaraguan-founded bank and credit card issuing institution— leaving it as the country's second most successful credit card issuer

---

19 Crickets

since he started the business five years earlier. "I want my own cab," he told everyone.

It was a risk, but a calculated one. So, why not? We were used to taking chances and trusted our instincts. Most importantly, it would make him happy. My industrious hubby had toiled away for a solid year perfecting his business plan—a plan that could have served as a model for any MBA program.

Joaquín was in his groove pitching investors, and felt optimistic. Unfortunately, his momentum was disrupted when priorities suddenly shifted. And all the previously allocated funds were to be invested in my head. His dream put on hold for now.

After confirming everything with Tía Bonnie, I tackled what was next on my list.

I called the pool company and in light of the new finding, that being my brain tumor, emphasized the job's urgency. They were receptive and claimed they'd arrive the next day to install a gate around the backyard death trap. That was a major hurdle to overcome before we left town. We trusted no one to rescue one of our children from accidentally falling in—none of the supervising adults knew how to swim!

We phoned the children's pediatrician, Dr. Carlos Velarde, and explained my condition and subsequent absence should a visit to his private consultation be necessary. He was very reassuring and wouldn't hesitate to make a house call if need be.

We solicited the phone, cable, water and internet companies to connect services immediately. I knew that if we didn't get these jobs done ourselves before leaving, we wouldn't have reliable communication with our children once gone. Magically, most every company arrived at its scheduled appointment to install, connect and repair. It seems that once you say the words "brain tumor," people really jolt into action.

I had one last visit with my trusted Ob-Gyn, Dr. Juan Antonio Carbone, and made copies of all my pregnancy records—past and present. I personally spoke with each of the children's teachers and in no uncertain terms, begged them to extend extra emotional support during the upcoming six weeks. We left monies for food, monthly bills, school activities, and car keys with Tía Bonnie—the one who would be running the asylum.

By the time we left our new house, just six short days after officially moving in, most of the boxes still remained sealed shut. It was impossible to find anything and as a textbook Type-A, it irked me to no end. But I had to just sever myself from it all, let it go and leave it as is—disorganized and filthy.

"The house looks like a tornado just blew through," I'd comment apologetically to each person as they stepped foot inside to pay me a visit. It was a form of saving face; I didn't want them to think—God forbid—that I didn't keep a tidy home. Truth be told, mostly it was directed inward, to myself. It was implausible considering my nature, but I repeated this catchphrase repetitively, in an attempt to re-program my cerebral hardware and emancipate myself from the grips of perfectionism.

To detach from my respective responsibilities, and delegate them to other people—many of whom I did not know—was the antithesis of all I'd ever known or done.

But I did it.

Perhaps I will come out the other end a classic Type-B, I fantasized. Wouldn't *that* be wonderful?

Nevertheless, this cyclone of chaotic energy spun around and around, enclosed me, and wove a virtual cocoon. In fact, the entire period was surreal; it was as if I were residing inside a gigantic bubble. Inside this dome I floated, shielded from reality, in a never-ending out-of-body experience.

I use the bubble metaphor because of its transparency. Essentially, I peered out onto this other reality—the actual truth—and watched it unfurl before my eyes. Moreover, because this thin veil protected me, I never had to touch it.

That's *how* I did it. Insulated inside this other sphere of reality—this other dimension—I survived for weeks. I knew what was happening intellectually, but emotionally, my system already had shut down. I was no longer human.

I spoke about my own mortality with the indifference of an aloof newscaster, reporting on tragedies in distant lands. "Yeah, the doctors say that the baby will have to be taken out now, and obviously not live, and I may emerge brain-damaged."

On many levels of consciousness, I had no clue it was happening to me.

What is all the fuss and tears about? What is it with these people and their Mexican novelas?[20]

---

20 Soap operas.

Brain surgery felt almost like an afterthought, like one of the many tasks penciled into my To-Do list together with "make appointment for bikini wax" and "schedule flu shots for the kids."

Looking back, I realize that the detachment that naturally evolved, or rather, this self-delusion, is the only thing that saved me from falling apart. It kept me isolated from my own heart, and never allowed it to take me into the dangerous realm of emotional vulnerability.

Operating under the auspices of this parallel universe, I was able to preserve a few remaining strands of sanity.

It's amazing how the brain functions. Defense mechanisms and psychological breaks-from-reality serve an invaluable purpose: they enable us to persevere in times of unbearable stress.

"It is not what we accomplish in life,
but what we overcome that earns us the respect of others."
—Unknown

Pearls of Wisdom...

- o Stay busy to keep emotions from clouding judgment.
- o If need be, hold on for somebody you love.
- o Be loyal and forever grateful to those that stayed true while you were down.
- o If overwhelmed, throw hands up and surrender. Have faith.
- o Be bold and go against your nature.

5. *Life In The Big City,*
Surgeons & A Leap of Faith

The last week of June 2006...

Prior to our arrival in Manhattan, we had scheduled interviews with the two neurosurgeons selected. We would have to decide between them and schedule the surgery within a week, by the last days of June.

It was a tough call because one was a revered guru—the chief neurosurgeon for over twenty-five years at the internationally acclaimed Memorial Sloan-Kettering Cancer Center on York Avenue between Sixty–seventh and Sixty–eighth Street—and operated with a Dream Team of surgeons. His operating colleagues, the ENT surgeon, high-risk Ob-Gyn and anesthesiologist came from New York- Presbyterian/Columbia University Medical Center located directly across the street from Sloan. These physicians were worldwide sensations and had worked together on many famous people.

This crew, in fact, recently operated on the former Israeli Prime Minister, Ariel Sharon. That impressed us. Although didn't he remain in a coma after surgery? So who really knows what good they did for him?

The dynamic between the entire surgical team was fundamental because the neurosurgeon would need to operate alongside an ENT surgeon and a high risk Ob-Gyn, who would carefully monitor the fetus. The group also would consist of the anesthesiologist and a slew of surgical nurses and technicians. Each one, in their own right, had excellent credentials and was critical to the team's success.

The second neurosurgeon we had researched was at NYU Medical Center located on First Avenue and East Thirty-fourth Street, adjacent to the East River. His waiting room was jam-packed, standing room only.

I never knew how popular brain surgeons were.

After a two-hour wait, the doctor emerged and extended his right hand and with a twinkle in his eye, introduced himself. "Good afternoon. I'm John Golfinos. Sorry you had to wait so long. Come follow me please."

He immediately led us into his private consultation room equipped with tables and chairs, a white board, sink, counter and vanity. I noticed boxes of tissues strategically positioned throughout.

Dr. Golfinos mentioned having studied the MRI film we express-mailed him days earlier from Panamá. I found him spunky, optimistic and affable, and estimated his age to be about fifteen years the guru's junior.

He gave us a brief overview of his experience, credentials and glimpse into his weekly routine. Effectively, Dr. Golfinos was in his prime operating years. An energetic Greek with an infectious smile, he seemed to melt my worries away. Stats-wise, he was performing an average of six to eight brain surgeries a week. He was on fire.

He specialized in benign tumors like mine; namely, Schwannomas also termed Acoustic Neuromas, Meningiomas and Atrocytomas—to name just a few. He was notorious for a procedure called Gamma Knife. My tumor was too large to annihilate with laser so it had to be removed surgically. However, his Gamma Knife fame was relevant because chances were that after extraction, whatever post-surgery residue remained would be aggressively attacked via this precise laser treatment.

We all felt instant chemistry with Dr. Golfinos and intuitively trusted him. He clipped my sizeable MRI images up on the board and with a long pointer, explained to us exactly what we were looking at. He informed us that this audacious and unpredictable mass was swelling rapidly and seizing valuable real estate inside my small head.

He asked me to stand up and walk in a straight line—about fifteen yards to the wall, and back.

C'mon, Darah, I thought, try to walk real straight and maybe they'll re-diagnose you.

He studied my movements carefully and once we had sat back down, said in the most charming and un-alarming way, "If it were my wife, I wouldn't even let her walk out that door right now."

Yes. He wanted me admitted that very day—that very second. "The problem is," he articulated, "the pregnancy hormones are exacerbating the tumor's growth at speeds exceptional for a tumor of this nature. And its movements are shifting erratically. I can't predict what will happen next. At any moment you could suffer convulsions."

The mass was enormous. It was roughly the size of a tennis ball and it was displacing the brainstem. This constant pressure on the brainstem made it dangerously close to causing a blockage of cerebrospinal fluid which would create a condition called hydrocephalus, as mentioned previously, known commonly as "water on the brain."

This was a really big deal. For the first time, I realized just how deadly my situation had become.

His sense of urgency was the ultimate litmus test, what undeniably tipped the scales in his favor. He sniffed out the severity of the situation and leaned on the side of caution. Between the two surgeons, he was the one already most careful with my life.

However, the deal-breaker was when we returned to consult with the chief neurosurgeon at Sloan-Kettering the following day. Unfazed by Dr. Golfinos' assessment, the guru encouraged me to pop steroids and hang out in the city for a few weeks awaiting his return from a family ski trip to the Himalayas.

No contest. We'd book the operation with Dr. Golfinos and his talented team at NYU Medical Center.

It was—pardon the pun—a no-brainer.

Hence, three hours later, while Mom, Joaquín and I mulled it over at a nearby Starbucks, we made the two-minute phone call to the NYU Medical Center Admissions Department, and I was good-to-go.

Surgery was set for June 30th, just a few days later.

One more thing to cross off my To-Do list.

Is the worst part over yet?

Mom had flown up from South Florida to join us. Having taken a month hiatus from work to be by my side, she also helped us make these tough decisions.

Upon our initial interview with Dr. Golfinos, I remember him asking me straight out if I'd prefer to sacrifice my hearing on the left side in order to most likely save my facial nerves.

With a steady grin, he poignantly inquired, "Would you rather risk losing both the facial nerve-functioning responsible for the left side of your face, and the hearing in your left ear, with a small probability that we end up preserving both." "Or," he continued, still unflinching, "we just puncture straight through the left ear canal, with a retroauricular incision, and sacrifice the entire hearing but not touch the facial nerves—which may yield a higher probability of success?"

This scattershot line of questioning was critical because there were two strategies vis-à-vis the head-drilling point of entry. He clearly had his drilling preferences as a seasoned specialist, but it was indeed protocol, as awkward as it seemed, to inquire about the patient's post-surgical expectations.

What followed next, after being asked the strangest question I ever heard, was a synopsis, in layman's terms, of all other things— known and unknown—that still could go wrong during the procedure. No matter what tactic was selected.

Struggling to appear poised considering the absurdity of his inquiry, I glanced over at Joaquín and Mom, both nodding mindlessly, staring blankly at and almost through Dr. Golfinos. I shrugged my shoulders.

Hmm. What were my choices again? 1) High likelihood of facial paralysis and probable deafness on the left side, or 2) guaranteed left-sided deafness with a high probability of no droopy face, or 3) a degree of unconfirmed damage to either of the above-mentioned plus God knows what else. Wait a minute. What the hell am I doing—choosing toppings on a pizza?

Nevertheless, I opted for one-sided deafness over a hanging, twisted face. Seemed like a better deal at the time.

Despite all the debating about piercing through my cerebellum or puncturing through my inner ear canal, and the apparent moment of levity of it all, deep, deep down, I remained indifferent. It still hadn't penetrated. Not yet.

In a twist of fate the next day, the worn-out proverb: "Be careful what you wish for," achieved perfect manifestation.

My husband was days away from turning forty and on numerous occasions had stated his desire to eat "Kosher Chinese food in New York City." To him, that'd be the quintessential celebration. Party animal.

He did not want an ostentatious party. He wanted only those closest to him at his side. So two days prior to my hospital admittance, his dream became reality. And at Mr. Broadway, a popular Kosher Chinese restaurant on Thirty-eighth Street and Broadway, there sat the three of us—Mom, Joaquín and I—fraught with anxiety, while Mom and I struggled to feign happiness and bestow birthday wishes upon my now-chain-smoking-and-on-the-verge-of-pneumonia hubby.

Unfortunately, the experience was far from the pleasant one he had envisioned months before. The coveted Chinese cuisine turned bitter as it traversed the lumps in our bone-dry throats. We couldn't even swallow. We paid the bill and fled the restaurant, heartsick. Three full orders of food remained untouched atop the celebratory table.

This episode taught me an important life lesson. From that day forward, I was convinced that you always get what you ask for in some form and from some direction; you just cannot predict nor control under which circumstances it will materialize in your life. Needless to say, I'm very careful about verbalizing my desires out loud to the universe. Because I know I will get them, yet have no control over the conditions that'll precipitate their delivery.

I've always been a spiritual person, and one that knows how to surrender—okay, only after exhausting all available resources, including everyone's patience. However, this lone aspect of my controlling nature has saved me from many dangerous situations— at the very last minute.

Several times over the years I'd found myself in precarious situations. Yet only after careful deliberations to ensure my own safety, eventually I surrendered my destiny to a Higher Power. Thankfully, each time I came out unscathed.

My husband and I, both Jewish—me by birth, and he by choice—became baal teshuvim, or more observant, upon marriage. The literal translation of these words from Hebrew to English means "those that return (to the religion) or repent." However, it is more than this. A baal teshuva is not born-again in the sense of the Christian that suddenly repents, accepts Jesus Christ as the Savior, or the Messiah, and reflectively becomes more pious.

Many Jews gradually discover their longing to get closer to God either through a stricter observance of Halakcha, or Jewish law, or via disciplined Tefillah, or prayer.

Others have a grand epiphany after a life-altering experience that almost overnight, quenches an unfulfilled longing and as a result, embrace the religion wholly and without reservation.

Regardless of the reasons why or how many people come upon their personal spiritual awakenings, as a couple, we made a conscientious decision to step up our level of observance when we got married. And over the years, little by little, grew more religious. It was a world foreign to that within which I grew up, yet we had chosen that path for our future children—to give them a solid sense of Jewish identity and sense of belonging to an ancient community that has thrived against all odds.

When the news of my catastrophe first spread amongst Jews in Panamá, many organized prayer services to recite specific psalms, or Tehilim, on my behalf. The fact that they included me in their pleas to God was not only comforting, it was flattering. I believe that prayer in numbers is very powerful. Many believe that psalms have the power to break through all barriers and reach Hashem, or God, directly, and furthermore alter God's decree.

Frankly, I hadn't the wherewithal to plead for my own life—heck, I was swathed in a blanket denial—so I was grateful that others were taking care of this for me.

My husband took a liking to Chabad, a group and philosophy of Orthodox Judaism and part of the Chassidic movement. All Chassidic Jews are originally from Eastern Europe and there was a Chabad-Lubavitch dynasty of seven leaders that all originated with the first Chassidic leader, the Bal Shem Tov. This faction spun off the ghetto-life of Eastern European Jews and sought to infuse their Jewish customs and practices with more singing, dancing and celebrated joy.

At the time, this was quite distinct from other sects of existing Orthodox Jews that were very dogmatic, consequence and fear-driven. Over the course of several years, my husband developed an affinity for Chabad and introduced me to it conceptually. The spiritual principles and sense of justice upon which pure, untainted, Orthodox Judaism is rooted are beautiful and awe-inspiring.

I would never define myself as a "Chabad-nik" or as a very religious person; I've always maintained a natural aversion toward indoctrination of any kind—heck, I never even wanted to join a sorority for that very reason. I was loath to surrendering control over my own mind. Even every attempt made over the years to hypnotize me failed.

I tried to live the lifestyle of an Orthodox Jew for many years, when we lived in Panamá. It was highly encouraged and fashionable, and there existed immense societal pressure to do so, but deep down I felt like a fraudster. The prevalent beliefs never genuinely penetrated my heart as it had with many friends of mine.

Within this orthodox community, I mingled and participated in most all activities.

After each shiur,[21] I strove to adapt the recent teachings toward the modification of my life, like changing a behavior or incorporating yet another ritual into our household routine—another prayer, blessing, or a more stringent level of Kashrut or Tzniut.[22]

Yet I always found myself unable to follow through. Half in, half out. I guess I wanted to believe more than I actually did.

But nobody, with the exception of a few close friends, knew just how much I struggled, and how I always felt like an outsider. Nose pressed up against the glass.

And frankly, as far as Orthodox Judaism goes, the time-consuming, labor-intensive tasks, and endless stream of work required to maintain this holy lifestyle completely overwhelmed me. Maybe I was lazy, but pious-living recipes never sat well with me.

What I did like, though, was that it was embracing and promoted service to God with a happy heart. The "Lubavitchers" described God as loving, forgiving and understanding. That, I could deal with.

I needed to believe in a God that'd give me a lot of chances.

The story continues that this philosophy arrived in the United States just a few years after World War II when the sixth leader of this dynasty, Rebbe Yosef Yitzchak Schneersohn, left Eastern Europe and immigrated to Crown Heights, a neighborhood in the central portion of the New York City borough of Brooklyn.

He focused on educating the less religious American Jews about all the beauty and wonders of their own religion. A great many of these disenfranchised youths were disenchanted with (their erroneous concept of) Judaism and what it actually had to offer in terms of mystics and other worldliness. They were lacking guidance and actively exploring similar principles in other religions such as Buddhism. I've met many of these soul-searching backpackers while traveling over the years.

Nonetheless, his son-in-law, Rebbe Menachem Mendel Schneerson, the seventh leader in the Chabad-Lubavitch dynasty who just passed away in 1994, is arguably the most phenomenal

---

21 Hebrew for lesson.
22 Hebrew for modesty or privacy, specifically in one's speech, behavior and clothing.

Jewish personality of modern times. He met with many heads of government from all over the world and both Jews and non-Jews alike respected him as a wise leader and spiritual guide.

He had acquired hundreds of thousands of followers, admirers and millions of sympathizers from around the globe. He was and still is, undoubtedly, the one individual more than any other responsible for rousing the conscience and spiritual awakening of Jews around the world.

He began a system of schulchim, or emissaries. These rabbinical scholars were assigned to the most remote corners of the world. This innovative approach broke the traditional model that Orthodox Jews could only live in popular designated cities that were within walking distance of synagogues.

Now the Jewish educators and spiritual advisors were on a mission to proactively seek out the unaffiliated Jewish people in an effort to bring Jewish life to them—be it India, Ecuador or China. It's true. I remember when we lived in Playa Jacó, Costa Rica, several of these young recent-rabbi-grads drove hours through tropical storms from San José to reach us along with the handful of other wayward Jews living in our small, beachside town. You may know these emissaries for their trademark black Fedora wide-brimmed, cowboy-style hats, long black coats and ZZ Top-length beards.

One belief that resonates throughout the Jewish world-at-large is that of the infinite power of davening, or praying, at the gravesite of a tzaddik, or righteous person. The Divine Presence is said to hover over the burial site of all matriarchs, patriarchs and tzaddikim at all times.

If a person prays to God in the merit of one of these prophets at their respective place of burial, the righteous person's soul, which never dies, intervenes on one's behalf. Therefore, the person's supplication is taken straight to God. In other words, the tzaddik acts as an intermediary by delivering the message directly into God's Hands.

This is not to say that the Jew doesn't have a direct relationship with his Maker and needs the help of this third party to be heard. Simply stated, the request will arrive faster—think of it as Federal Express Overnight Delivery versus the United States Postal Service's Parcel Post service—and with a special endorsement from someone who can get God's immediate attention.

Jewish sages claim that the righteous are even greater after their passing than during their lifetime and the Ohel, (lit: "tent,") refers to the structure built over the resting place of a tzaddik. It has become a center in and of itself—a place where thousands come from all corners of the world to receive inspiration and blessings from the Rebbe, albeit deceased.

Prior to entering the cemetery, one must obey strict customs such as the removal of his or her shoes, if leather. Typically, devotees recite a slew of blessings in an effort to remove any spiritual blockage. Many men immerse themselves in a fresh, circulating water Mikveh, or ritual bath, to purify themselves morally before entering this holy space. Many followers come prepared with their petitions already expressed on paper, and paper and writing utensils are offered to those not as prepared.

Some people hang out for long stretches in the preparation area just outside the cemetery before walking the fenced-in path leading to the two tombs, that of the Rebbe and his father-in-law, Yosef Yitzchak. Many are so overcome with emotion, having made the pilgrimage from thousands of miles away, and having programmed the particulars of this visit for months—maybe years—beforehand. Some people just sit in silence, undeterred, absorbing the sacredness of the area.

Instructional brochures, a coffee machine, restrooms and video-clips broadcasting the Rebbe's powerful sermons stock the welcome area. When ready, one walks roughly fifty yards to the constructed area encircling both tombs. There is a mini-library housing a myriad of prayer books and books of psalms.

If you don't bring your own prayer books, these are available for use as it is standard procedure to recite specified psalms as well as one's private appeals aloud at the grave. Upon finishing with the readings, many spend additional time simply reflecting, and some get enraptured in deep concentration or overtaken by raw emotion.

The spiritual vibration is palpable and there is no denying that some godly force hovers over this site.

Before leaving, it is customary to tear one's personal notes to shreds as well as those sent or read on behalf of others not present. Subsequently, all is tossed into a large pit where everything, eventually, will be collected and destroyed.

My husband did not want to leave any stone unturned. I needed all the help I could get. The best physicians for the job were hired, so now all that was left to take care of was the intangible, the ethereal side of things.

All of the aforementioned is to provide an understanding of where and why my husband left before dawn that next morning after our foiled Chinese dinner birthday celebration.

Full of hope and unfaltering devotion, Joaquín had to catch the train to Crown Heights, and daven with the early morning minyon[23] at 770 Eastern Parkway, the address of the late Rebbe's office and synagogue. Then, he had to take the thirty-minute cab ride out to Cambria Heights, the location of the Ohel.

He went to beg God for my life and that of our unborn son—just two days before my scheduled hospital admittance.

What a dedicated husband, doing all that he could to keep me alive.

I was, and still am, so lucky to have him.

And that's not all about the Rebbe. A devout group of Chabad followers employ a mystical practice called Igrot Kodesh in order to receive continued guidance from the Rebbe, albeit deceased, for whatever's plaguing them. For decades, people wrote letters to the Rebbe asking for blessings, advice, mystical clarifications and explanations, and strength—all with the goal of tuning into his divine prophecy.

A compilation of thirty-to-forty books was published—much like an encyclopedia set—containing all the Rebbe's thoughtful and divinely-inspired replies to each and every heartfelt inquiry ever received from devotees around the world. These texts are considered, still, an invaluable resource for life's biggest and smallest problems.

According to protocol, one writes a sincere, detailed letter addressed to the Rebbe explaining one's predicament. Then the person himself, a Chassidic Rabbi, or some other trusted individual with access to this sacred anthology, opens a random volume and arbitrarily slips the written petition between the pages. Whichever written reply emerges on that particular page is considered the answer to that person's quandary.

Although it's arbitrary, it's believed that despite an initially

---

23 Group of ten Jewish men, of Bar Mitzvah age, that are needed to recite specific prayers such as Kaddish, which is said daily for the first twelve months after the loss of an immediate family member.

perceived irrelevance, on a more profound level, the corresponding letter is fitting. Many times, the reply sounds totally "off," alluding to a change in scholastic environment or place of employment when one seeks guidance for a troubled marriage. I'd been told of an older gentleman who'd received a reply that referred to a young girl's despair over her dead cat. But the letter that, once randomly selected, responded to my health problems was eerily on target.

On the cab ride over to New York University Medical Center, a call came in on Joaquín's cell phone. It was from Israel. A couple, very close friends of ours and devout followers of the Rebbe and the Chassidic ways, were brimming with excitement.

"Oh thank God, thank God, you answered," breathless, my best friend from high school, a convert herself who now resides in Israel continued, "we have such good news. It's amazing. Unreal. Never happened before." Apparently, her husband crafted a letter to the Rebbe on our behalf and wedged it between the Igrot Kodesh pages.

We were told that Efy petitioned the Rebbe to intervene on my behalf, and ask God to alter my fate so that my life and that of our baby's would be saved. He also implored the Rebbe to ask God to ensure the well-being of my husband and three children so that they'd be blessed with the strength and faith they'd need to toil through the tough times. I'm not certain what else was written, but the precision of the reply was compelling. It was undeniable that intangible, celestial forces were at work.

The likelihood of receiving a spot-on response, undeniably relevant to your unique life situation, is slim to none. That night they faxed the reply to the apartment.

The title of the reply letter was: To the lady undergoing surgery. The end of the letter read: Not to worry; you will receive a lifetime of nachas[24] from your child.

Here is what it said in-between:

Regarding your operation, I asked for a pidyon (redemption of the soul) for you and a speedy recovery. Surely, you are following the instructions of the doctors. Healing comes from G-d but the Torah tells us that it should be done through a messenger, namely a doctor, and the medicine he subscribes. However, we must remember that

---

24 Yiddish for good fortune, happiness.

the main cure is the good deeds which Hashem has commanded each one of us to do, and they provide us with health and strength.

With blessings for a quick recovery and regards to your son, may he be well.

Although I wasn't a firm believer, this mystic coincidence made my skin crawl.

I knew someone was looking out for me.

And that wasn't the first time I felt such gratitude—a feeling that someone was watching over me.

Let me take you back eighteen years, to 1994, to one incident in particular. Thinking about it now, I don't know how I ever could've taken such a blind leap of faith.

At the time, I remember staunchly believing it was a calculated risk, a well thought-out alternative to the original plan now stymied for reasons of stupidity and pettiness. And come to think of it, as a mother, I can tell you with all certainty that I would die if any of my kids, even the boys, ever did something so irresponsible, and consciously put themselves in harm's way.

It was October of 1994, and I was visiting a friend, an American girl named Diane, in Quito, Ecuador. She was logging a few classes at a local university as part of an exchange program. I flew down from Costa Rica to pay her a visit and explore another country.

Don't quite remember what triggered it, probably something related to her new elitist, Ecuadorian boyfriend and jealousy, but after a hurtful exchange of accusations on day two, we decided to part ways. She left me in the center of town, a lone gringa with a loaded backpack hanging lopsidedly from my weary shoulder and a heavy duffle in hand.

There I stood stunned, on the street corner of the busy Calle Orellana, with ten days left on my ticket. I was alone, didn't know a soul, and had nowhere to go.

Where was I to go? How would I spend the remaining time before my flight back to San José, Costa Rica? Back in San José, I had been renting a room at the home of a sweet and pious elderly widow, Amelia, who lived in Tibás. It was a small town located near my English teaching job at El Instituto Costariccense Interamericano. I was using my vacation days to travel to South America and having a friend all set up in Ecuador facilitated that experience. We had planned to journey throughout the entire country as she was also on break from classes.

She had been there four months. She knew people. Got herself a local boyfriend and had made plans for us to travel with him and his fancy friends. We were headed to the beaches of Guayaquil, quaint town of Cuenca—where the cobblestone roads transport you back in time—and the famous Otavalo market.

This giant outdoor mercado[25] is set deep within a breathtaking mountainous backdrop. It's the place where indigenous men, women and children weave their vibrant-colored fabrics into intricate patterns that reflect their spiritual beliefs and semi-nomadic way of life. They also exhibit exquisite, hand-painted artisans and soft leather wares. I planned on making a lot of purchases. I had promised to bring gifts for friends and loved ones back in Costa Rica and South Florida.

But that plan fell through...

I walk up and down both sides of the broken sidewalk that run parallel with this highly-transited city artery. Twilight is fast approaching and I need to make some decisions; I must arrange a place to sleep for the next several days.

I was supposed to stay with her at her host family's mansion in the upscale neighborhood of Guapulo for the first five days. And I had been looking forward to it. The house was a stately home decked out with a private tennis court, over-sized pool overlooking the valley, and a full staff of domestic help. The lush sprawling estate grounds were home to many plant and animal species.

The patio in particular, with its wraparound porch, made my heart aflutter from the moment I saw it. I quietly promised myself to spend my early-mornings there, wrapped up in a hammock meditating and writing in my journal while sipping coffee. A perfect retreat.

The interior of this colonial residence resembled the charismatically tasteful décor found in one of those quaint bed and breakfast hotels. But judging from the size of this one, I imagine it'd been a converted government office building. It boasted of long corridors and each room was unique—outfitted with one-of-a-kind tapestries and furnishings. Thick, heavy floor-to-ceiling curtains stretched wide open to reveal the magnificent and seductive landscape just beyond the other side of the glass windowpane.

---

25 market

I shake off my looming funk and come across a hopping, American-style rock bar. I stand outside for a good ten minutes to observe the element before entering. Its patrons are mostly American backpackers, local wannabes, university students, and Europeans. It is a mishmash of folks, and the joint seems safe in a familiar kind of way. The music blaring out of the enormous street-side speakers is none other than John Cougar's Hurts So Good. I have nothing to lose and nowhere else to go. So I step foot inside to find a friend.

Strolling in, I notice them immediately. They are of athletic stature, well-groomed, and cloaked in designer attire. It is the Haitian national soccer team. Pitchers of beer and chunky glass mugs cover their giant, round table set back deep inside the bar. They seem to be celebrating. Maybe they just won a championship title.

I make a beeline for the bar and climb onto a stool, still glancing in their direction, examining the interactions between the teammates and the parade of people approaching the table. Perhaps everyone is inquiring about the team's recent victories.

I summon the bartender over and ask him what's up. He tells me they are here to compete in an international tournament and had arrived a few days ago. The games have yet to begin and for now, they're checking out the local scene. He comments that they aren't drinking too much because they have to report in with their coaches early each morning.

I scan the room again, searching for a friendly face, an American student, or someone with a comforting sparkle in his or her eye. I need someone to trust. But who? How do I determine who is trustworthy and who is not in a matter of seconds? This skill requires specialized training and I am not an FBI agent, serial killer profiler, or a private detective. I am just an openhearted, wide-eyed college grad, full of wanderlust and a sense of adventure.

My appearance makes no mistake of it, either. My knapsack is stuffed and overflowing with travel brochures, English-Spanish dictionaries and several spiral notebooks I use as personal journals. A tattered Let's Go Ecuador book is jammed into the front mesh pocket of my old, reliable JanSport. Around my neck and comfortably hidden from view hangs a cloth pouch. It contains my life—my passport, airline return ticket, student identification card, insurance card, a couple of credit cards, pocket-sized address book, and $200 for emergencies. My weathered duffle looks like it has been through decades of abuse.

My face reads: if we become friends, can I trust you?

Yet behind my apparent gaze of apprehension and innocence, I have learned to travel alone. And thanks to years of studying psychology and personal encounters and work-related experiences that put me in contact with all walks of life, already, by age twenty-two, I have developed into a keen observer of human nature. Additionally, my Spanish proficiency bolsters my self-confidence. However, time is running out. I have to get myself set up by nightfall.

I glance back at that giant, round table again and notice several smart-looking, young women seated with the Haitian athletes. They are munching on bocas[26] and laughing light-heartedly. That is a good sign. I scan the bar one last time before making my move.

The other patrons are all too stoned or shady-looking to befriend. In fact, as the night drags on, this place seems to serve as a refuge for lost souls and outcasts livings on the fringes of an adopted, Ecuadorian society. Perhaps, some of these gringos have a history of confrontations with US authorities or fled from a dark past.

Regardless, my gut tells me to choose the soccer team.

Therefore, I do.

I amble over to the table. Somehow, they already spotted me because as soon as I come within earshot, several are ready to engage in conversation.

"Who are you?" asks a tall, slender mulatto in broken English. "Are you here alone?" he smiles.

I tell him and the crew, including their lady companions—who by now are all glaring in my direction—an abridged version of my recent drama. I choose to struggle in Spanish after perceiving their discomfort with English.

"But I'm not going to let this ruin my trip," I affirm with a confident grin. "There's so much here to explore and I want to make the most of my time remaining. Who knows when I'll make it back again?"

The quiet one in the corner who has been studying some sort of pamphlet suddenly looks up, winks at me and cheers, "You can

---

26 Small-sized appetizers usually served with alcoholic beverages.

come with us. We've chartered a bus and have another five days until our official training begins. We're leaving in the morning for Guayaquil and will be staying at youth hostels throughout the country."

The girls smile encouragingly. Appears they already assessed these young men. I know by their guttural accents and lighter skin tone that they are not from Haiti. I don't know anything about their level of intimacy with these guys, but based on their body language and lack of physical interactions, it seems like they met recently. And the athletes behave respectfully.

"Ok, I'll go. Where are you staying in Quito?" I question bravely, looking at no one in particular.

"We've got a block of hotel rooms at the Hilton; there are extra beds. You can stay in one," the now-not-so-quiet-one responds nonchalantly.

"Cool."

In short, I traipse around with this large group for five days. We travel to Mitad del Mundo in the province of Pichincha and snap photos standing right on the equator line. We suntan at the beaches of Guayaquil, spend an entire day at the famed Otovalo market, and visit a beach town in Las Esmeraldas. We see a lot.

Thankfully, besides the now-not-so-quiet-one professing his eternal love and devotion to me ad nauseam, I manage to escape unscathed. I become buddies with the jovial, chubby girl—the one none of the guys try to sleep with—and stick to her like glue. This works like a charm to buffer me from unwelcome advances.

My poor parents feel impotent. The entire time they are worried sick, waiting each day for that spontaneous collect-call. They insist I pay the airline fine to change my return date, and get myself back to San José immediately. They offer to send me loads of cash via Western Union to bail me out. My uncle, an international lawyer, has a wealthy client in Quito with whom I meet at his lavish offices (at Mom and Dad's insistence.) As a favor to my uncle, he offers to put me up for the remainder of my days at his private compound.

However, I refuse. Taking pleasure in defying their parental warnings, I also turn down my uncle's connections. "Not unless absolutely necessary," I clarify to my folks. I don't want to waste my trip holed up in some stranger's mansion. Who knows when I will be back here? There are so many places in the world to visit and I must live out this adventure now set before me.

My attempts to reassure my parents of my safety and good judgment fall upon deaf ears. In each phone call, they remind me of other college-aged, American girls who had traveled alone or with friends. Many became unsuspecting victims of sadistic tragedies or other unhappy endings.

Yet I believed I would be okay. I considered myself street-smart and most importantly, stayed sober. That week was a life-changing milestone; it transformed me into someone who would forever trust her gut.

Things could've turned sour, I know. But they didn't.

I was a lucky girl.

I reminisce about this precarious episode in Ecuador for one reason: Assurance.

By staying calm and sober while stepping into the unknown with faith and trust, things ultimately worked out.

I had a similar inner calm that contained me now, days before brain surgery, despite occasional eruptions of emotion. One way or another, I'd come out of this okay. I believed it with all my might.

Nonetheless, my alleged freedom was coming to an end and one long exhausting day before relinquishing my bodily rights, last-minute prayers flooded in from friends and family around the world. I talked to very few people over the phone. My hearing was fading fast and my body was stiff and uncomfortable; it already felt like a damn corpse.

Mom and Joaquín spoke for me, relayed messages and filtered calls. Both of them sent out frequent global emails, informing everyone of my status.

And it actually dawned on me that very night, the night before turning myself in to "their custody," that I may lose my life—widowing one devoted husband and leaving three cherub angels without their mother to raise them. Obviously, thoughts my husband, family and friends had been considering for weeks.

Finally, I was starting to get it.

"If I live," I reasoned out loud to make certain my husband could hear as we lay in bed, "at the very least, I'll end up partially deaf, with some degree of facial paralysis and who knows what else."

Unconsciously, I wanted to forewarn him, and myself, that I'd emerge disfigured and less attractive.

Will my husband still find me physically attractive? Or, will he feign attraction and make love to me out of pity?

All night long, I tortured myself with these destructive thoughts. Much like a washing machine stuck on the spin cycle, these ideas whirled wildly inside my head now that reality insidiously seeped into my consciousness.

And yet, in spite of all of the gloomy prenatal forecasts, I didn't fear for my unborn baby's life. I was confident he'd make it; his major organs were developed and my trusted Dr. Carbone didn't seem too concerned about the anesthesia if I were well-monitored.

I knew the baby was strong because his mother was strong. At least that is how I understood it. Despite my instincts that assured me it really wasn't my time to go, later that night in bed, this robot transformed back into a human. And in my husband's arms, I broke down and sobbed uncontrollably—for the very first time since this entire calamity began.

I missed my babies.

I loved my life.

I wanted to live.

Pearls of Wisdom...

- o   Be careful what you wish for.
- o   Be true to yourself and resist peer pressure.
- o   Come clean about what you believe.
- o   Recognize blessings.
- o   Trust your instincts.

6. *Hope & Surrender – It's Showtime!*

The next day I awoke with a heavy heart, yet full of fight. I stumbled out of bed, took one final look at my pre-surgery self in a full-length mirror, and made my way to the tiny kitchen to brew a pot of coffee.

I wanted this mass extracted from my brain already. It was not part of me. It was an unwelcome intruder. Like a belligerent squatter, it had illegally usurped the limited space inside my head, aggressively pushing all rightful occupants out of its way. I wanted to recover my waning senses. It was high time for me to move again like the agile sporty woman I always deemed myself to be.

I had evolved into this monstrously erect zombie made of flesh and bone. My metamorphosis into this alien-like creature had been so gradual over a period of many months, that I hardly noticed my strengthening deficits. My attentive body did, though. And in all its innate wisdom, continuously fought to regroup and compensate, to cope with the accumulation of debilities, as my physical senses and neurological system slowly failed.

Fortunately, we had good luck with our accommodations, if that were an omen of other good fortune yet to come. Weeks before arriving, we had come upon a realtor named Louise, a woman we found on the internet. She rented furnished apartments for periods of a week or more. She rented out people's private homes and seasonal second residences to people like us who were visiting New York and required lodging for extended periods of time.

Knowing how unaffordable New York City is, staying in a hotel for six weeks was out of the question. And although financially it made no sense, space-wise I'd need the apartment anyway to heal and rest.

It worked out well. The flat she found us was in a building conveniently located on the west side of Central Park, a few blocks from the Hudson River. The building was on West Sixty-third Street and Broadway, a long thirty-blocks from the hospital, but just two short blocks from a Whole Foods supermarket, Starbucks, movie theatre and several small Mom and Pop convenience stores.

Additionally, a Duane Reade pharmacy was just around the corner so that would come in handy, as I'd receive all prescriptions there. Our spacious, one-bedroom apartment was equipped with a full kitchen, television, cable, and fax machine. We even received personal mail delivered to our door. The set-up was cozy and perfect for the moment.

We leave the apartment unusually early that morning to avoid traffic. We hail a cab and lug my bulky suitcase into the back seat with us. The night before, I packed a few pictures of the kids, my new robe Warren's daughter-in-law gifted me, a pair of fluffy, pink slippers from Collins in Panamá that I splurged on for the grand event, and miscellaneous creams, lotions and body scrubs.

Am I going to a spa?

I am determined to continue with my humble, yet consistent night routine despite it all. At the very least, I'll be able to retain a modicum of personal dignity by doing whatever I can to feel clean and attractive.

The cab ride over is hell. The crazy cabby floors it the whole damn ride over. By the time we make it to the hospital, my face is pasty white and I am on the verge of losing my marbles. Not even upon announcing the pregnancy-brain tumor dilemma did he slow a little. Tough guy. I guess some people become jaded when their life events have hardened them to a point that nothing evokes compassion.

We are ushered into New York University Medical Center through one of the many automatic doors by a friendly guard. He instructs us to make a beeline for Admissions, a.k.a. Financial Ruin, before anything else, to talk business.

First things first, of course.

Emerging from the elevator at just seven-o'-clock in the morning, already the department is abuzz with activity. The frenetic energy and noisy chatter mirrors that of a crowded, telemarketing workplace. There are rows and rows of cubicles and machinery. The noise is unbearable; all people talk at once—to each other and on the phones. At the same time, these multitasking masters are making copies, printing documents, checking identifications, stapling, cutting, tearing hospital wristbands, running credit reports, and shamelessly emptying patients' bank accounts.

After signing what seems like a billion documents that later would set off our personal descent into financial devastation, an aide arrives with a fancy wheelchair and settles me in. Mom and

Joaquín race behind us with the bags and knick-knacks while he wheels me up to the Neurological Intensive Care Unit, or NICU, on the twelfth floor.

There he delivers me directly into the hands of the floor's intake nurse. And within just minutes, I am confined and bound by IVs, heart rate monitors, fetal monitors, and other state-of-the-art electrical devices. I am their captive. Nurses, aides and volunteers come rushing out to greet me as if I were a celebrity. What do they know about me? And just like that, all my freedom of mobility, albeit uncoordinated and unstable, is gone.

The unit head nurse explains that Dr. Golfinos insisted I be placed under unblinking surveillance four days prior to the operation. Immediately, it becomes apparent I am the Guinea-Pig/Poster-Child/Pity-Party of the ward. Actually, if there had been a popularity contest, this "pregnant lady with the brain tumor" would have won hands-down. Everyone coddles and pampers me more than ever in my life—far more than during infancy and early childhood. Admittedly, I like the attention.

This illusion comforts me. It is as if all these people truly care about me, Darah Zeledón, my unborn child, and quiet, little existence back home in Panamá. I lead myself to believe it to be so.

Maybe they know this hapless person before them isn't the real me, I think.

Teams of medical personnel are so thorough and cautious that it compels me to question silently whether my condition really merits such a fuss.

Am I really so ill that all this hoopla is necessary? Yes?

Okay then, why don't I give a shit?

I detached from this sickly body months ago, and now feel nothing.

They got the wrong woman, I secretly conclude, right up to knife-time. It is near impossible for me to reconcile this ailing woman with the spirited person I am—someone who has been blessed with optimum health her entire life. For heaven's sake, I never even get sick from kissing my snot-nosed, germ-infested kids right on the mouth in defiance of conventional germaphobe thinking.

However, my superbly-functioning immune system can't help get me out of this one. Nothing less than a highly skilled team of doctors and prayers that reach way up into the heavens is going to get me out of this alive. Nothing less than a miracle.

And so, regardless of my good health and the role it played for over thirty years, within four days of pre-surgical preparation, I am submitted to the following tests:

1. Two ultrasounds of my abdomen
2. Ultrasound of my legs
3. MRI brain scan
4. Various blood work and urine tests
5. Several allergy exams
6. Hearing loss analysis
7. Vision tests
8. Throat swabs
9. Metal cables stuck up my nose and down my throat to test weakened vocal cords
10. Tear duct testing *(Did I mention that tears were shooting out of my left eye like a geyser again?)*

I must confess that by far, the most unpleasant sensation came from number nine on the list.

I remember when the technician ambushed me with that one. Right out of left field...

There are no visitors present, and I am indulging in a rare moment of quiet relaxation, caressing my bulging belly, assuring my unborn baby that we are going to be okay. Suddenly, this stone-faced-recent-graduate who at best is pushing twenty-five, storms into my room. After mumbling out a perfunctory greeting without even looking in my direction, he pulls out some odd-looking equipment from his small, black leather satchel. "Hi there," he blurts out awkwardly. Still distracted, he continues to riffle through his bag.

"Sit still and remain calm," he commands.

Wait. Wasn't I doing just that before you walked in? How about you first introduce yourself and tell me what the hell you plan to do to me? I whisper under my breath.

He proceeds to unravel this four-foot-long, snake-like metal probe. It resembles a tool plumbers utilize to unclog extreme cases of waste blockage. Next, he orders me again to "be still" while inserting this tube up both my nostrils and down my throat.

Oh my God! Wait! I'm being raped through my nose.

My hands nervously wander about searching for something to

grab a hold of and finally settle upon my quivering knees. My fingers clutch at the frayed hem of my hospital gown. Achieving a Zen-like state of inner tranquility is impossible. Yet somehow, through fixating my gaze upon a shiny metal knob welded to the wall, I manage not to go berserk and strangle this insensitive neophyte. Lucky for him.

Minutes later, additional teams enter to take measurements of my pre-surgery facial paralysis.

Guess it is supposed to get worse, I quietly gripe. Everyone neglected to inform me well about that major detail.

Oh yeah, in my previous list I failed to mention the kidney and gastro crew—a team that subjects me to an entire cocktail of their own creation. Thankfully, a feces sample was not on their list. All sense of personal dignity certainly would have vanished with that one.

The assessments performed are more exhaustive than with your average patient because two people are evaluated—the baby and me. Therefore, an entire battery of tests also is performed on my abdomen to determine the baby's pre-surgery health.

Anyone who has gone through major surgery or has spent several nights in a hospital knows that it is indeed, the worst place to rest, sleep or recover. In my case, scores of doctors and hordes of enthusiastic residents marched in by the half dozen every half hour and instructed me perform the same dexterity, coordination and vision tests over and over again like some trained circus monkey. I just wanted to tell them to bother some other hospital prisoner and leave me the hell alone.

Why can't they share notes with their colleagues from the other units? Wouldn't that be more efficient? Or is that considered cheating? Go bother my neighbor; she has been sleeping for hours. Listen to her snoring!

So much for personal space. I yearn for a shred of privacy to have a hushed conversation with a visitor, or ponder my unknown fate, or simply urinate without the permission and witnessing of the entire staff unit, for crying out loud!

Despite the sheer humiliation of listening to a team of medical personnel—I swear I overheard this conversation—debate about whether or not I was "able" to move my bowels, a few extraordinary experiences occurred during those unforgettable four days prior to surgery. One of these incidences really stood out and to this day, cracks me up just thinking about it. At the time, it was not funny at all, but two weeks post-surgery when my sense of humor returned, I almost pissed myself talking about it with Mom...

It is June 29, 2006—one day before my scheduled brain operation. Already, I have been a NICU resident for three days. Our unit is a lofty bunch, mostly women and mostly normal—healthy, active and young-ish. Curiously, despite the fact that many of us never even caught a cold, to our dismay, we suddenly and inexplicably came down with these random, unprecedented brain tumors. Not one of the other women had a family history of tumors—no genetic link at all. At the time, there was some loose-talk about a possible correlation with cell phone use, but nothing concrete.

One post-op patient, Karen, was especially gregarious. She earned her bragging rights. She emerged from her surgery like a champion and the following day, was out and about, visiting with the other patients on the ward. Karen was the storyteller, and chatted us up about her personal tumor-related drama. Seeking to inspire all of us frightened lambs as we, too waited our turn under the knife, she became our unofficial Ward Heroine.

With her heavy New York accent, I hear her yapping away with my neighbor in the room to my left. She sounds amicable and encouraging and I am anxious to talk with someone who knows exactly what it feels like to go through it.

I am in my eight-by-eight foot cubicle. The front of the room that faces the nurses' quarters is a glass wall. Only once the pale blue curtains are drawn, is privacy attained. There's also a partial glass wall at my left, and when the wraparound curtains stretch wide open, I can peak into my neighbor's room.

I am hoisted up on a space-mobile inside this giant aquarium. Onlookers pass by and peer in with the same pitiful curiosity extended to an endangered species housed at the city zoo. From my geographical position, it seems that all individual NICU rooms orbit around the nurses' station in the dead center of the floor.

I twist my neck to the left and wait to see the shadows on the floor broaden and move in my direction. I've been listening to Karen greet all fellow patients for the better part of an hour and I'm up next. I hear blather and laughter erupt all around me. She's like some sort of celebrity.

Minutes later, they wrap it up and now it's my turn for the

sanctioned visit. In totters this petite silhouette of a woman with an entourage of family members trailing behind. When my eyes converge and settle upon her face for the first time, severe cognitive dissonance takes hold of my rational brain. Because listening to her is one thing.

Her face is another story.

It is terribly bruised and puffy. The image of Sylvester Stallone's battered countenance in Rocky IV zips through my mind. Her eyes are so heavily blackened and swollen that attempting eye contact feels intrusive.

This lovely brunette turns to greet my mother and I wince, studying her profile. Her nose is rammed completely over to one side of her face. Dried blood blankets the right side of her shaved scalp, right ear, and the blood has drip-dried mid-flight on the way down her cheek. Her hair is plastered securely underneath this cocktail of dried-up fluid as if weighted down by viscous, industrial-strength hair gel. Her head is bandaged with so many layers of thick white gauze she stands at almost six feet tall.

Meanwhile there she is, prattling on about how amazing she feels—understandably still under the effects of Morphine. Her husband Barry, a sweet-faced man donning a warm smile, observes our squeamish reactions and clears his throat, "We haven't allowed her to look into a mirror... yet."

No shit? Could have cleaned her up a little, don't ya think?

In a flash of insight, I begin to scan the room for a hidden camera, convinced this interaction is being recorded for America's Funniest Videos. Where is Tom Bergeron?

The poor thing is passing out business cards—literally—as she proudly tells us about the company she founded and runs.

But I can't focus on a word she says. Remember "The Mole" in The Spy Who Shagged Me? I know she's eager to comfort us all, but she looks like a train wreck. And she's scaring the living daylights out of me with her post-surgical mask.

When this kind soul, this ad hoc motivational speaker—and still a dear friend to this day—finally exits my teeny quarters, I exhale a sigh of relief.

Time to compute all the new data she just relayed.

But not yet.

All at once, in parades a troop of Jewish do-gooders, men and women whose mission is to pop in unannounced and pay all Jewish patients a brief visit. For Jews, one of the most important Mitzvot, or moral and spiritual obligations, is to visit the sick, isolated, homebound or distressed. The name for this action in Hebrew is Bikur Cholim.

The premise is based on the fact that God visited Abraham while he was recuperating after his circumcision.[27] The Bible tells us that human beings are created in the image of God. It instructs us to aspire to be like God by emulating His ways.

These kind people come in daily and bring me kosher food, ask about my children, recite blessings and psalms and pray for my recovery. All within forty-five seconds.

My surgery was scheduled for June 30, 2006 at nine-o'-clock in the morning on the following day. However, it was delayed because Dr. Golfinos, the neurosurgeon, Dr. Roland, the ENT surgeon, and their corresponding teams had two surgeries to perform prior to mine. They were running late, and by the time it was my turn at bat, it was rounding one in the afternoon. The waiting, the not knowing when, or if, was exasperating. I was hyped up, chomping at the bit and as ready as I would ever be. Let's do this already!

All my friends and family had phoned to confer their last-minute blessings and expressions of love. All that could be done on our end to make this operation a success was done. I wasn't nervous or frightened at this point. As delusional as it sounds, I was still buffered by an impermeable bubble of denial. Plus, I took comfort in knowing that I'd be skyrocketed to another galaxy on the anesthesia super-shuttle soon enough and oblivious to all right away.

I was concerned about my husband and mother. Waiting indefinitely is difficult for most anyone, and even more so for these folks—two of the most impatient people I know. In spite of their impetuous natures, they'd have no choice but to putter away approximately ten hours before receiving word on my status.

We were all seated in the ward waiting area pretending to watch the news. Whenever I tried to inquire how they had planned to spend the time, they changed the subject.

Maybe they didn't want me to know they were going shopping or had planned to catch the Off-Broadway matinee.

---

27 (Genesis 17:26-18:1)

Yet before I had the chance to press further, the head nurse came in to get me.

Under the knife I go.

Pearls of Wisdom...

- o Fight like hell until you can't fight anymore.
- o Be a kid and take comfort in illusions if it preserves sanity.
- o Maintain dignity.
- o Stay actively engaged.

7. *Gurney–Ride Ramblings, Pain & Morphine... Could've Been Worse*

"You're never ready for what you have to do.
You just do it and that makes you ready."

- Movie Sybil, 1976

It's a long stretch, at least twenty yards. I study the ceiling. The long, white tubular bulbs secured into the rows of overhead fixtures radiate a bright fluorescent glow. The walls however, are desperately barren, and as we cruise between them, create the illusion of being trapped inside an infinite tunnel. There is no end and no beginning.

I feel as if I'm being swallowed up, lost inside a maze, a cornfield, or at sea, perhaps. Everything goes on endlessly—the walls, the ceiling, and the floor—and sucks me into this painfully white vacuum.

How about a splash of color on the walls or inspirational quote, maybe? I could really use one right now.

Deep inhalation. A sterile, pleasant-smelling aroma fills my nostrils as this tea trolley rolls on.

My discombobulated mind wanders.

Did I lock the big freezer back home in Panamá? I left tons of expensive cuts of meat in there. I hope they finished fencing in that giant pool. Damn. Nobody knows how to swim. Who unpacked my bras and panties?

Oh shit. I forgot to tell Joaquín to clip the kids' nails when he goes back tomorrow. The nanny cannot do it and they'll scratch each others' eyes out. New York? Wasn't I just partying in this town a month ago for David's graduation? What the hell happened? It's got to be some kind of a joke.

Everybody is talking, but not to me. These scrubs are teasing one another about their golf games and waging war over who is a more devoted Yankee fan. Un-freaking-believable. Operating on a patient whose very life is on the line is just another day at the office for these folks.

Still wheeling....

How about a joke to lighten things up? What's bigger: a twenty-five-week fetus or the tennis ball-sized tumor inside my head? Who the fuck cares.

I crane my neck to gaze behind me. Joaquín is shrinking and I no longer hear Mom's loud, nasal voice—that familiar inflection that contains nothing more than a mere hint of her Brooklyn past. It's the one that always drove me crazy as a teenager and ironically, the one I now find as soothing as a lullaby.

I start to talk to my husband...or maybe I just think I am.

Sorry your business plans fell through, Mi Amor. Sorry all your money had to go to this. How much time do we have until the well runs dry? Doesn't matter. I love you. I know we'll figure something out. I always believed in you and always will.

I look up at my right, and stare at a face, the owner of the forearm that's been grasping this gurney for what seems like miles. I smile awkwardly. But he doesn't see me. I'm already invisible.

Please don't let me die. I have three small kids waiting for me at home. They don't know Mommy may never come back. I never really did say good-bye. Whose feeble body is this? It's all a mistake. I'm a fucking rock. Let me off!

"Me" is only the thought I am having right now.

The double doors entering the operating room swing wide open as the gurney careens into them. Within seconds, the crew transfers me onto a cold, sleek slab of metal. This operating table is the size of a crib mattress, completely flat and totally uncomfortable.

Guess I expected to be cradled by an orthopedic mattress since I am pregnant and going to be here a while.

This odd-looking place resembles my high school science laboratory, the place where we'd dissect animal carcasses. It's definitely not a place to set down a pregnant woman for ten hours of intricate brain surgery. The surgical table is located in the dead center of the room. The ceiling must be over twenty feet high. I find myself in the middle of a vast space stocked with tools, gadgets and boxes of supplies. Everything is arranged and labeled neatly on floor-to-ceiling shelving. It sort of resembles a warehouse or auto repair garage. No. It looks like the backdrop of a horror scene from some B-rated movie on late-night cable.

Before panic sets in, a couple of pale green scrubs approach me. With their latex-gloved hands, they pull an auxiliary contraption out from under my back. I hear a reverberating clang that momentarily deafens me. Suddenly, my arms are stretched wide open, strapped and restrained with thick white bands. I can hear the Velcro as it wraps around this jutting crucifix. I notice a pair of dark eyes hovering directly above, staring wistfully into mine.

Are you a woman or a man? No matter. Just be nice to me, please.

"Is everyone well-rested and pumped up? Let's kick ass!" I cheer out, forever the motivator.

Nobody responds. Maybe I whispered. Maybe I mumbled.

I glance at the large-faced wall clock: 1:23 pm.

The dark eyes slant and smile reassuringly. A plastic mask is brought toward my face. The soft whistle of the air jet soothes me.

"Just relax, Darah, and take in a few deep breaths. Enjoy your wine."

The inhaler blows a rush of cold, delicious air through my nostrils. It feels good. Too good.

This is a piece of cake.

Tell me again, how did I...?

Lights out.

The time is now 11:20 pm and I'm still on this gurney. Is it over? Or was the whole performance cancelled?

I run my hands up and down my still-pregnant belly. I strain to whisper to an unknown pair of hands mummifying my head, "Is my baby alive?"

Instantly, I drift back into sedation, unable to wait for the reply. One way or another, I become aware that they moved me again, but don't know to where. My eyes are welded shut, puffed-up and sore. And my hearing is turned off. Neither ear works. I only remember feeling the sensation of motion, so I assume it to be true.

How did I get back to my room in the NICU? Did Mom or Joaquín come to see me yet? It's all a blur. I'm trapped inside this malfunctioning body and don't remember much. But I do recall the pain.

It is so searing, so piercing, that I envision myself starring in one of the Godfather flicks. One of the enraged mafia bosses lifts me up by the ears. Ruthlessly, he bangs my head into the concrete sidewalk, and screams in my face like a deranged lunatic. I play this tape—this imaginary gory scene—over and over in my head, in an effort to pair images with my agony. This image represents how I feel. And how I explain to myself what happened.

Words are of no use to me; I can't speak, hear, or write. Can't communicate with anyone. All I am able to do takes place inside my mind so I create metaphorical imagery to depict the crippling pain that ripples through me.

So crushing, I can hardly breathe. I succumb to the throbbing and lay as still as a cadaver. I signal with the tip of my forefinger to communicate with nurse personnel. I keep reminding myself to breathe.

Good painkillers are unavailable to me; I'm pregnant and the strong stuff I really need could harm the baby. So I seek to transcend it by retracting my self-awareness into a tiny distant voice buried deep inside the crevices of my conscious mind. This faraway voice is the only "Me" that now exists; I detach from the body and all the rest.

Inside this thought, I hide for days. I'm merely a distant observer watching someone else's life unravel on the big screen. My heart goes out to this afflicted woman; it's not happening to me though.

The surgical team had extracted the nerve inside my left ear canal, leaving me with single-sided deafness. As mentioned previously, strategically, they needed to drill through it to remove this fleshy tennis ball successfully. Consequently, the now-unfocused hearing ear captures all sounds with a visceral force, in an effort to compensate for its partner's loss.

And all normal noise and chatter reverberates directly back into this hypersensitive ear with an amplification that instinctively causes me to clutch at my ears. It stings. Everything, even whispers and low-pitched voices, sound like the claws of a cat screeching across a slate chalkboard. It chills me to the bone and there's no way to turn it off.

To make matters worse, every visitor that steps foot into the room receives a series of cell phone calls. "Oh, yeah, she made it. Not sure about the baby. He has yet to stir. But she seems to be doing well." Yada, yada, yada. "Okay, I'll let her know..."

Shut the hell up! I want to holler, but can't speak. I swear this glass-shattering ring will be the end of me.

Overcome with queasiness and dehydration, I cannot pry my mouth open to receive water. It is an impossible feat so I choose to let my welded mouth blister from extreme dryness. The entire left side of my face is paralyzed in response to all the facial nerve fiddling during surgery.

Supposedly, this is expected to recover in God knows how long, but for now, it looks like a severe case of Bells Palsy. I'll just have to learn to live with this asymmetry for a long time. My left eyelid, after it opened for the first time, never closed again and remains bone-dry. To rest or sleep, I have to pull the lid shut like a manual window shade.

I've had better days.

My options of pain relief post-brain surgery are Tylenol and Morphine. Yep. That's right. These are the only two medications I'm told don't cross the placenta.

Are you freaking kidding me? I need to battle these mafiosos with simple headache medication or a hallucinogenic?

I choose the Morphine and to my satisfaction, find myself hallucinating profoundly, convinced I am a new-age prophet.

At one point, I transform into the lens of a satellite and peer in on my beautiful children playing in the backyard back home in hot Panamá. But when it wears off, misery consumes me and my body writhes in pain.

It is fun for a while, but doesn't do much good to mitigate the thumping. It just helps me temporarily disconnect from it by transporting me to other realities.

Inhale. Exhale. Close your eyes Darah, and go to that little place concealed deep inside your mind's eye. Repeat this mantra: *This frail and wounded body doesn't belong to me. "Me" is only the thought I am having right now.*

Whose body is this?

Relearning The Basics:
The Brain Reclaims Its Territorial Rights

I survive the fragile forty-eight hour post-op period without dying from an infection so that is a good start. However, hoards of pestering residents are at it again—tirelessly striding in and out of my closet-sized room day and night. They come from every imaginable hospital unit and instruct me to perform the same Godforsaken coordination, dexterity, vision, hearing and vocal exams over and over again.

It is like being harassed by pesky flies at a picnic.

How can I shoo them away? Am I the only patient of interest in this entire hospital?

I can barely open my right eye. It is heavy, engorged and dry as a bone. I begin to patch my left to keep it protected from the cold hospital air and bright, artificial light. When I try to open the two together, the light floods directly into them. It feels as if I were up close staring into high-powered stadium lights.

In addition, the two eyes are unfocused and like a bad marriage, cannot agree on how to merge images. I see double for eight days post-surgery and cannot achieve clarity, look straight ahead or up. It is a brutal eight-day hangover; the room constantly spins out of control. All lights and sounds torture my senses and nausea becomes my new homeostasis. What I really need are drugs, but that is denied because of the pregnancy. Therefore, in protest of the lack of relief, each one of my senses goes on strike.

For days, my traumatized mouth remains twisted and locked. As thirsty as I am, not even a vice grip can pry it open at this juncture. My mother and her first cousin Maris have to shove tiny fragments of ice chips between my lips with their fingertips. But that hurts, too. My lips crack and bleed and the skin encircling the mouth flakes off from dehydration.

By now, the little guy inside my womb starts to come out of his induced slumber and begins to stretch his limbs and churn about. Certainly, he expects to be fed something. It has been four days since he last moved.

Thankfully, by day six post-op, things begin to turn around. I morph back into a human being, albeit a much distorted version of my former self. I learn to drink and eat with a mouth that partially operates, and half of everything I attempt to ingest goes in through the right side and immediately slips out the listless left side.

Not a pretty sight.

There will be no guests for dinner or dining out in public for a long, long time. Not to have control over the opening and closing of my own mouth is humiliating and humbling all at once. Because it is impossible to completely close the mouth to chew, not only are my manners atrocious, I wind up wearing all my food and beverages like my toddler-aged children.

I struggle to embrace this new reality—this new me—for however long it lasts.

My eyes attempt to converge but the left one can't blink or close on its own. It remains exceedingly open and when I dare look in the mirror, a harrowing Cyclops stares back at me. To worsen matters, the left eye's respective tear duct no longer functions. I grow obsessed with lubricating it with artificial teardrops. If I unwittingly skip one of the five-minute intervals, the ordinary circulating air whips my eye with the gust of a desert sand storm. Everything I took for granted requires a great deal of effort and innovation in order to function normally.

But I'm not about to back down now. I am engaged in battle and in it to win it. I will be damned if I'm not getting my old self back. I made it out alive!

Up until now, I haven't dared to walk because I don't trust my vision to keep me upright. Late in the afternoon on day six post-op, Dr. Roland stops by my hospital bed for a visit. He coaxes me to get up and take a few steps. He promises he will assist me by acting like a cross between a cane and a seeing-eye dog should I need help. I am going to need it because I can't see in front of me. At his insistence, I stand up and my eyes remain averted down, staring at my slippered feet. I feel like I'm going to topple over and plan to abort the mission.

However, the lacerating truth is that I have no option if I ever want to exit this place. He isn't going to sign my hospital release until I can shuffle about on my own. Frightened and distrusting of my broken body, I reconsider and begrudgingly oblige.

For the first twenty minutes up, I feel like I'm trying to balance inside some sort of funny house. The corridors are blanketed with slanted mirrors and optical illusions. All images are fuzzy and moving.

All five senses—vision, hearing, touch, smell, and taste—are completely impaired with "services interrupted" that persist for another six weeks, and some even beyond.

Reflectively, I had to re-learn how to use them all again after the displacement provoked by the removal of this gigantic growth from the brain. They all seemed to be making a mad scramble back to their physical points of origin inside the cranium, and in the interim, were operating under new employment contracts that stipulated they would only work part-time and on their own nebulous terms.

Additionally, for a protracted period, my coordination, dexterity and gross motor skills stayed at the level of an eighteen-month toddler, or less. And like a clumsy toddler, I needed assistance for e-v-e-r-y-t-h-i-n-g. I wasn't safe by myself. In fact, I was as dependent as a nursing infant on my caretaker, Mom. Initially, she was the one responsible to help me re-gain a degree of independence once released from the hospital seven days after surgery.

Through monotonous strolls up and down the apartment building corridor, Mom helps me retrieve my gait. My legs, still suspicious of my eyes' ability to lead, hesitate, and most of the time, force me to grasp a cane, grope the wall or latch onto Mom's arm for support. Fortunately, two weeks later, I turn a corner, and my semi-restored coordination breaks through the threshold of competence. I can bathe alone and wipe myself after evacuating.

A tad of dignity restored.

Mom is uncharacteristically patient as we discover creative ways for me to drink and eat without systematically sabotaging my clothes. My left eye is the most reluctant to return to normal functioning, and to this day—almost seven years post-surgery—is still bereft of natural tears, or normal lubrication. And because of this fluid deficiency, the assiduous right eye becomes disgruntled with its hectic schedule and punishes me with migraines when it's ready to quit. My single-sided deafness is another work-in-progress that proves a bigger and bigger pain in the ass.

But in the grand scheme of things, it's all small stuff. My baby seems fine and I escaped death relatively intact. I'm awash with gratitude for the cards I was dealt.

Thank you, Mom. I don't think I ever adequately expressed my most heartfelt gratitude to you for giving my husband a break from the pressure of my misfortune. You granted him the peace of mind to return home to our three tender children in Panamá—confident that you were there to nurse me back toward the road of independence.

In essence, Mom and I were transported back in time, reliving part of my formative years when as a new mother, she had taught me these basic life skills. Effectively, we were given a second chance to bond like a young mother does with her infant baby. Sounds sentimental and sweet, but I didn't romanticize about it. No need for me to relive it a second time. Once was enough. I bitched and moaned and wanted to be whole again, self-reliant and independent. Now, dammit!

Ten days after the date of my operation, and back at the apartment just three, I attend a follow-up appointment with the handsome and charismatic Dr. Roland to examine my sutures, the newly deaf ear, and the left-sided facial paralysis.

Seated in the waiting room, I notice a middle-aged woman gazing in my direction. It doesn't bother me, most people gawk; I am pregnant and shambling around with three feet of thick, white bandages wrapped around my entire head. My eye is patched and with a handkerchief, I put continuous pressure on my lips to contain the drooling.

Granted, I am a conversation piece.

Nonetheless, after fifteen minutes of scrutiny, I begin to squirm in my chair and grow uncomfortable. As she audaciously stalks me with her eyes, I leave my seat to sip some water from the fountain, in the hopes that she'll shift her focus to another interesting attraction. Hunched over the water fountain, I feel her eyes burn a hole in my back. She whispers to a bespeckled, bald-headed man planted at her right. A stocky elder cloaked in plaid clown pants, he sits there disinterested, nodding mechanically.

We are all patients waiting to be examined and are all in pretty bad shape. Yet she wins the prize. Her face is so misshapen that her dribbling mouth has pushed its way over to the middle of her right cheek. Her bulging left eye looks as though it were dangling out of her eye socket—like her optic nerve had been severed. Like me, she presses a crumpled tissue against her mouth in an effort to control the drooling. A wide-brimmed hat with the side flaps turned down sits atop her head, obviously to veil her disfigurements.

"Hi. Can I help you?" I grin awkwardly, speaking in the same tone a store clerk would use to greet a customer.

"You look great. What kind of operation did you have?" she asks, totally unapologetic for shamelessly staring me down for the last twenty-five minutes.

"I...ahh...had a brain tumor removed here," I indicate with my forefinger, "and the doctor wants to take my stitches out and check my facial functioning."

"When were you operated?" she demands, now both eyes bulging freakishly.

"About ten days ago."

"Oh my God! Look at her, Louie!" she snorts and jostles her dozy companion. "Her face looks much, much better than mine."

"I had my operation eight weeks ago."

I shrug my shoulders, toss her a feeble grin and nod. I turn toward my mom and nudge her with my elbow, catching her off-guard and almost knocking her out of her chair.

Hours later, I left that office a very grateful lady. Things could have been a lot worse; my eyes bore witness to just how bad it could have been.

I was okay.

My baby made it through unscathed.

The doctors were able to remove the tumor in its entirety and had left nothing behind. Yes, I lost part of my hearing and my face was still a mess.

But still... it could've been worse. Much worse.

Discipline and diligence is all I really need to return to the pre-surgery, pre-sick woman I was before. I am confident I can do it and will be okay. And I repeat this to myself and to everyone else, over and over again, to stay inspired.

The first two weeks out of the hospital, together, Mom and I walked and walked around the Upper West Side until I regained some strength. I removed the thick gauze and surgical tape that blanketed my left eye and replaced it with a neutral-colored, self-adhesive patch.

I implemented and practiced a new manual technique for sipping through a straw—something that is near-impossible if your facial muscles are flaccid and your lips don't pucker. Motivated by the fierce desire to suck down a cold, frothy ice cream shake during those sweltering summer days in Manhattan, I squeezed my lips together with both hands to seal them around the straw. I was careful not to release my grip or the liquid would come shooting out and trickle down my chin and neck.

Like this, with a little innovation and creativity, little by little things started to come together nicely.

That is, until we moved to a quiet neighborhood outside the city limits for the remainder of the mandatory recovery period.

And that's when the panic attacks began.

Pearls of Wisdom...

- o Disconnect from pain by retreating into your own thoughts.
- o Talk yourself through it all, even if you appear crazy.
- o When you feel self-pity, look at others that have it worse.

8. *Panic Attacks, Marriage & A Deeper Kind of Intimacy*

Staying in the city to recover was outrageously costly. We were clobbered over the head with a per diem of $230 between lodging, food, taxis, meds, and any extraneous expenses incurred. And we were frugal.

As our pockets lightened, our hearts grew heavy. We decided to accept an offer from family friends, my newly-married first cousin's in-laws, so we ventured out of the Big Apple and headed toward their home in the Bronx. There we'd wait out the rest of the obligatory recuperation period. At this time, a budding anxiety began to breed in the pit of my stomach. But I squashed it.

My cousin's new father-in-law picked us up from the lobby of our apartment building, and off Mom and I went, to Riverdale, a woodsy city in the Bronx, bounded on three sides by the Hudson River, Broadway and the Yonkers line. We'd dwell in their beautiful stone country home for two of the remaining three weeks before I was allowed to fly back home to the Tropics.

As soon as we stepped out of the car, we filled our lungs with the fresh rural air. Dogs were romping in the neighborhood front yards, and their home was one amidst many other stone-hedged mansions. It was invigorating, and the entire neighborhood with its country lanes seemed to come from another time zone, another era. The slower pace of life was palpable.

The house itself was a quiet, cozy country home set back on a large lot, equipped with the quintessential elements required for any kind of physical healing or spiritual renewal. A forest replete with flora and faunae encircled the property. We'd recline in the chaise lounges on the backyard porch and observe all species of birds, reptiles, small deer and other wildlife. It was the epitome of soothing and in stark contrast to the loud and hectic vibe of city life.

The hosts generously went out of their way to ensure we were comfortable and had what we needed. When I had to travel back to the city for follow-up appointments, despite our protests, Artie, my cousin's new father-in-law wouldn't take no for an answer and drove us in. He'd mill away hours until we'd finished with the appointments and drive us back to Riverdale. In the evenings, we dined at home with the lovely couple.

Our hosts were spectacular, kind and pleasant.

However, after a few days, the peace and quiet grew into an eerie silence, an absolute silence that afforded me too much time to think. I needed to prepare myself for the caretaking marathons that awaited me back home. And these thoughts lurked about like monsters, and kept me awake at night. There were three toddler-aged children who desperately needed their mommy. They were too young to understand what was transpiring and couldn't yet grasp the concept of time. To them, it was as though I'd already been gone a year.

Inherent in the routine care of little kids are a myriad of labor-intensive tasks that require tremendous physical strength and stamina—a bundle of work I'd be expected to embrace despite my fragility. Although I always had live-in help, I relied on these ladies more when we went out. If home, I insisted on doing most everything kid-related myself.

By now, I was almost a month and a half more pregnant than when we had left, and getting larger and clumsier by the second. This, of course, grew by leaps and bounds after brain surgery. Because when they removed my left inner ear, it completely threw off my equilibrium. In sum, I was the consummate klutz.

My new, old country house back in Panamá—the one we moved into six days before leaving for six weeks—was a disaster. We had fled like refugees and I was anxious to get back and make it home. All of our family belongings had been haphazardly stashed away by countless pairs of hands. I needed to put some order to the mayhem, and clearly, rearrange it all.

Many jobs were left unfinished. The friends that helped tend to our children, supervise the help and ensure the overall security of the home were antsy. They yearned to return to their normal lives as well. I was fraught and thought of everything BUT my recovery.

Impatient and peeved for not being able to execute simple movements or perform household tasks successfully, as I unrealistically had anticipated, the self-induced pressure mounted to return to normal. For some reason related to my own arrogance, I thought this one-month hiatus would be unnecessary and had guffawed when this was told to me before surgery.

There was a fundamental discrepancy between what I aspired to become in a few short weeks, and the nonnegotiable physical limitations that hindered my quick advancement. In my mind, I was still the same person, or at the very least, could retrieve my former strong-woman status in record time. But in reality, I was no longer that self-professed indomitable person; perhaps in spirit still yes, but my flesh-and-bone was fragile and handicapped.

My self-esteem started to suffer. When I looked in the mirror, which I tried to avoid at all costs, I was disheartened to see this lopsided face staring back at me. I didn't recognize the reflected image and I felt trapped inside a foreign and warped body. I became intolerant and cruel, and outright unforgiving with myself for having been reduced to a shadow of the woman I used to be.

A compulsion to abandon ship and flat line gnawed at my consciousness. Therefore, I guess it's not unusual that with all these destructive thoughts fluttering about my unstable mind like dark spirits for ninety-six hours straight, I started to awake with a jolting horror, at all hours of the night. My debilitated body, reacting to this self-inflicted mental abuse, was beset with all the symptoms of a full-blown panic attack: rapid heartbeat, profuse sweating, panting, jittery limbs—the whole shebang. I'd awaken drenched in a puddle of sweat, gasping for air.

My left nostril was almost completely closed as a result of the facial distortion and all intake of air was blocked. Not having a steady, reliable airflow for breathing was a big deal. A *really* big deal. Shooting Afrin into my nose with the urgency of a strung-out junkie in frantic attempts to open my nostril was not a pretty sight.

I was suffocating.

My poor mother—morose and incapable of imparting even the slightest degree of consolation—lay at my side watching this pathetic scene unfurl night after night. At first, she tried to talk me out of them.

An unsettling ritual of behaviors took hold each night it happened. I'd leap out of bed and pace back and forth while staring longingly out of the window. Immediately, I'd begin to rub my cheeks up and down the cool glass pane.

The impulse to break free from my mind-body circumstance was overwhelming. I fantasized about climbing out the second story window or sprinting down the stairwell to exit the house through the back door. I wanted to run out to the backyard forest and wrap my arms around a tree. I grew intoxicated with the urge to be outside in a vast, open space without confinements. No more mirrors. The walls inside this tiny, cluttered bedroom were closing in on me.

Thus, in these wee hours of the night I came face-to-face with these merciless demons, creations of my own distorted mind.

Each morning, I awoke increasingly convinced how distraught I had become. Detained in another part of the world, far away from home, and not permitted to fly home to my children, my restless mind took me to the brink of insanity. Additionally, because I was pregnant and cared more about my unborn baby boy than my own diluted existence, I ingested no medication to alleviate my pounding head or calm my embattled nerves.

Nothing stronger than Tylenol, that is.

Bound by limitations, I couldn't push myself too hard in any direction. Working up a sweat through walking would have been dangerous at that point. Even a glass of wine was unadvisable because it remained unconfirmed what effect it'd have on the baby at this pivotal point of pregnancy. The soft tissue inside my head just was beginning to heal. I was prohibited from straining myself in any form so chewed stool softeners like candy.

The grievances continued to pile up. The rules were duly noted: no screaming, no lifting, no pushing while evacuating, no sexual relations, no grimacing, no exaggerated expressive facial movements and no intense outburst of emotion. My restless soul was captive inside this ailing outer shell that no longer resembled the body I once had trusted so well.

How will I release this tornado of emotion? When?

With no outlets available to discharge this rising anxiety, thoughts of imprisonment seized hold of my mind. A break from reality of sorts impelled me to visualize the "real me" temporarily handcuffed and chained to this broken, useless body. This survival technique kicked in just in time. I considered each day endured as another one closer to freedom. Breathing was the only thing left to focus on.

On a lighter note, I did score a wonderful new hat collection. I suppose most friends and family thought I'd have my head shaven bald pre-surgery, so in lieu of chocolates and flowers, I got hats. And man do I love hats. They sent me baseball caps, berets, bonnets, boater's hats, wide-brimmed, straw beach hats and artsy head coverings. I even got an assortment of colorful scarves.

Curiously and to everyone's surprise, only an insignificant amount of hair was removed just behind and above my left ear. It was barely noticeable. Of all the resulting physical defects, this was the least offensive. But I did enjoy the hats and scarves at any rate and used them often to deflect attention away from my twisted face.

Our time in Riverdale began to wind down, and it was bittersweet. I mustered all the energy I could to feign happiness and bestow gratitude to my wonderful hosts who had no clue what really was happening inside their daughter's old bedroom quarters in the middle of the night. I felt slightly more independent and Mom was ready to be "honorably discharged." Her rotation was coming to an end and Joaquín would be arriving to fill in.

Mom had to get back to work; her boss had generously given her paid time off that she hadn't yet accrued to nurture me. My husband needed to help me travel back home. Joaquín, who hadn't seen me since two days after my surgery, had no idea what to expect.

He had been home in Panamá taking care of the children and again, was browsing around for investors. We had decided that we'd spend the last mandated week together in Manhattan. We'd play tourists and enjoy one another's company and a few of the city's internationally renowned attractions outside of its excellent medical resources.

However, before we could set out on our weeklong New York City excursion, a pressing matter beckoned our attention. Joaquín, who had transformed into a chain-smoker ever since my diagnosis, had been coughing and wheezing for over a month. He barely could breathe or walk. He'd been treating his symptoms with some over-the-counter cough suppressant and refused to see a doctor. (Men!)

And of course, he dismissed his new smoking habit as having "nothing to do with it." Nonetheless, the day after he arrived, I insisted we walk right back into the same hospital, New York University Medical Center, to get him checked out. We had this comprehensive international medical coverage, and we might as well put it to good use rather than wait another week once home. Besides, I told him that our touring was contingent upon his willingness to get his own medical problems straightened out.

Walking into the Emergency Room, we were thankful that there was hardly a wait. Joaquín was admitted right away, assigned a bed, cloaked in an awful hospital gown, and his wrist wrapped with an ID bracelet.

And so the tables had turned.

There I was, gazing upon my horizontal, sickly husband and relieved to be in the caregiving role again finally. Undoubtedly, still looking like I just emerged from Armageddon myself, I floated around talking to nurses and doctors and tried to get him diagnosed and treated as quickly as possible.

After four hours of tests and chest x-rays, the diagnosis was made: Walking Pneumonia.

"I knew it," I scolded him, as we entered Duane Reade to purchase the antibiotics and inhalers.

Nothing less than that would've gotten him off those damn cigarettes, I thought.

The rest of that day we relaxed at the new apartment Louise had found us in Mid-town. I wanted Joaquín to recharge batteries and ingest a few doses of antibiotics to kick-start his recovery.

We both slept like rocks that night and the following morning, we set off to sightsee.

Like a pair of foreigners that had never visited New York, we went to the Museum of Jewish Heritage in Battery Park, the Statue of Liberty and walked all of Ellis Island. Using the sophisticated computer program, we spent a few hours trying to identify the boat on which my family had immigrated over to America from Russia in the late 1800's.

But it was nearly impossible because many of the Polish-Russian Jews had changed their surnames upon entering the United States and/or the person in charge of the registry would often misspell a difficult-to-pronounce name. We narrowed it down to a handful of family names, any of which very well could have been my distant ancestors.

We dined out at some delicious pizza and ice cream joints around the city, and returned to Mr. Broadway for a much-improved rerun of the thwarted Kosher-Chinese birthday dinner. We even saw a Broadway matinee starring Rita Wilson, and strolled throughout Central Park almost daily. Consequently, my desire to get home to the children began to wane. Spending so much time alone with my husband was a real treat and a cherished novelty.

And yet more than discovering all these wonders in the greatest city in the world, we explored an entire new dimension of our marriage. My loyal, still-wheezing husband had pushed me around town in a wheelchair, specifically the crowded venues that required an excessive amount of walking.

Joaquín also devised his own methods to assist me with my newfound hearing impairment. Admittedly, I found it most endearing to observe this dynamic evolve as heartbreaking as it was for me to come to grips with my disabilities. He was very protective of his "delicate" wife, a unique concept for both of us.

Constantly, he'd advise people to speak to me in my right ear because "her left doesn't work." This was his canned reply. He appeared confident and comfortable in his new role as caretaker, and took it quite seriously. I guess he just was happy to have me alive no matter what condition I was in. It was as though we'd been married for fifty years and he knew just how to manage my deteriorating senses.

Our love skyrocketed into a new dimension of intimacy after this experience. A much more committed, deeper one. Having learned this, I now insist... *The secret to a long and happy marriage is to grow increasingly blind and deaf with each passing year.*

Pearls of Wisdom...

- o Allow emotions to run their course then shift gears and move on.
- o Change your optic and "see" your relationships through fresh, new eyes.

9. *Sweet Homecoming, Panamá*

July 28, 2006

After a week of subdued enjoyment, our week in Manhattan had come to an end. Finally, it was time to go home. Wrought with nerves, I didn't know what to expect. So many questions lingered.

How will the children respond to me? Will my disfigured face and bulging eye scare them? Will I have the strength to care for them? How will I hear them call out to me? How will I deal with the heat? Where the hell did "they" put my panties?

I had been away too long, exactly forty-one days.

We pull into the driveway. My heart is aquiver with anticipation. I look at my watch. In exactly eight minutes, the children's school buses begin to arrive. The first is a small yellow van that transports the youngest, my eighteen-month little boy. Minutes later, the larger one is due to arrive, bringing home two girls, ages two and a half and five-years-old.

I step out of the car and take a look around, careful to move ever so slowly and deliberately. Everything looks the same as when I left six weeks ago in a haze of confusion. The palm trees, the weathered exterior of this old house, the neighborhood landmarks; nothing's changed.

Nevertheless, it feels surreal; my body, at long last, has returned, as it had unequivocally yearned to do for many long weeks. But my mind lags behind; it's still on that plane ride home, preparing for this very moment.

I wished time away, willing this day to come faster. Now that it's here, I don't feel ready.

I inhale the intoxicating and familiar whiff of the Tropics, a combination of humidity and burning asphalt. The rains are coming. This distinctive scent brings me back to the here and now. And for some reason, only through my augmented sense of smell, can I achieve fusion—my mind and body come together to the same time and place.

My two dogs bark wildly with anticipation. I spot them through the garage fence. When I call out to them, they respond by pouncing on top of one another in unbridled excitement. They become equally ecstatic when the Jehovah Witnesses stop by.

Hobbling toward the front door, I pause before entering. Another corner turned. A new life chapter begins. Sigh.

Let's do this, D.

Walking through the front door, I'm slapped in the face with a cloud of condensed heat. This singular reality reminds me that indeed, I'm back because there's no distinction between indoors and outdoors; the heat index is the same. Central air doesn't exist.

Tiny droplets of perspiration instantly form at my hairline. Panting, I shuffle over to the armchair adjacent to the wall in the foyer. Not more than a minute transpires when my lone hearing ear captures the recognizable drone of the engine. My boy's bus pulls into the driveway. I gasp for air as my heart races.

The nanny opens the door and greets him. Lunchbox in hand, still unsteady on his feet, he wobbles into the house. He's completely unaware that I am seated just a few feet away watching him, overcome with emotion. Speechless.

For a moment, he hesitates and stares at me in disbelief, as if I were a ghost. I say nothing. I detect from his body language that he's uncertain if this new version of Mommy encapsulates the one that had gone missing for so long. I can almost see the static in his tender mind begin to dissipate, as he comes to the realization that I must be a good enough replacement. Suddenly, he bolts toward me to sit on my beckoning lap.

Despite his inability to express himself well verbally, I answer his inquisitive eyes as they peer directly into mine. I run my fingers through his curly locks.

"Mommy is okay. Mommy loves you and missed you terribly. And now, Mommy is home to take care of you." He smiles coyly and wraps his meaty little arms around my neck. I can't stop kissing him.

As I sit with my baby boy wiggling on top of my knees, my delicate body feels a hundred years old.

Within a couple of minutes, just as this initial wave of emotion subsides and my pulse slows a bit, my two daughters' school bus arrives. When I hear the engine idling in the driveway, my heart hammers inside my chest.

The door swings opens. They have me locked on their radar from the second they enter the house and make a beeline for the armchair. I catch my breath while studying their approaching silhouettes.

I panic. My mind flip-flops between emotional extremes, and is on a destructive path.

When did they become so beautiful? I have been away too long; they are growing up so fast. Oh my God, I've missed everything.

The internal dialogue threatens to raze this happy moment, and blow it to smithereens.

Shut the hell up, Darah. It's gonna be okay. You haven't missed EVERYTHING. Smile, because here they come.

Both girls sprint right over to me, their braided ponytails wagging behind them. "Mommy, Mommy, you're back," they cheer, studying my new face. As they affectionately ruffle the hair around my puffed-out scar and stroke my half-frozen face with their compassionate little fingers, they softly inquire, "Mommy, how come your mouth, nose and eye are all broken and crooked if the boo-boo was only in your head?"

"Logical question," I mutter under my breath, tears of joy running down my cheeks. "I'll explain that to you later, hijitas."[28]

Leave it to children to expose our imperfections and insecurities in the most innocent and inoffensive way.

One by one, I examined the children. They didn't look like they'd been suffering without their parents' love. They seemed happy. Yes, parts of their bodies bespoke mild neglect. Their fingernails were long and dirty, their teeth yellowed, and hair disheveled; but really, who's going to care about their routine hygiene and upkeep like their own mother?

Effectively, it took no more than three hours to re-integrate back into the recognizable, domestic routine. This past six-week hiatus was merely a blip on the map, and because my self-diagnosed Obsessive-Compulsive Disorder, or OCD, kicked-in straight away, in under a week's time, I managed to sort through most every knick-knack in my new residence.

I methodically rearranged the entire kitchen cabinetry, which housed a menagerie of extraneous items and yanked everything out of my closet, my dresser drawers, re-classified it, and put it back.

And of course, rifled through stashes of miscellaneous toys and garments in the kids' rooms, all jumbled together in no logical

---

28 little daughters

sequence. Days later, I had this entire heap of stuff categorized.

So much for that Type-B transformation.

Phone calls were made to all doctors, teachers, and friends. I brought myself up to date with this life—our life—the one that had been running parallel to my other reality back in New York City. The children's schedules, our pending and missed social affairs, each family member's medical checkup, I was back in the saddle again.

I consciously followed up with hordes of helpful people to express my gratitude. It took the collaboration of the equivalent of a small army—a commingling of efforts, diverse talents and wits—to keep this household running smoothly in our extended absence, specifically during those defining move-in days.

I visited my treasured Ob-Gyn, Dr. Carbone, and local neurosurgeon and provided them both with medical reports and a synopsis of the resulting disabilities.

I advised my lovable neonatal pediatrician, Dr. Velarde, of the unborn baby's trials and tribulations and all he'd been exposed to in utero during the operation and subsequent four days before the belly jumping returned.

Yes, giftedly self-unaware, I was determined to step back into life as though nothing had happened. Indisputably, I believed I could do it, and would let nothing disabuse me of this notion. It was heavenly to be home and back in charge of my time and free to decide what I was or wasn't yet capable of accomplishing.

In record time, I organized most of the house and made some initial preparations for the new baby's impending arrival. The idea of becoming a mother again for the fourth time emboldened me to dive head first into this undulating sea of nesting activity.

Still weak yet fighting for normalcy, I was determined to recover my balance and enervated facial mobility.

Thankfully, all appeared to run smoothly those first few days home.

That is, until one early evening when I received an alarming, gut-wrenching phone call that would forever change my life and once again, test my courage, take me to the cusp of insanity, and challenge my undefined faith.

Pearls of Wisdom...

- ○ After a setback, jump (back) into a routine right away.
- ○ Stay grounded and positive by expressing gratitude often.

10. *Fight's Not Over Yet Girl, Here Comes the Knockout!*

We'd been back from New York just a few days and my husband was at the provisional office and not due home for another hour. I was home with the children and starting to wind them down for bed. The routine in order: dinner, bath-time, pajamas, books, tickles and cuddles. I was elated to be alive and well enough to forge ahead with this familiar routine. God gave me a second chance. Home again with my children, I felt indifferent toward the workload that caring for them and this old, rickety home entailed.

Of course, I had help. But even so, I insisted on doing most of the childcare-related work myself and it hadn't been a burden at all since back. Because my focus was on being together as a family, no workload, regardless of its size, could intimidate me or dampen my spirits.

Ready to tap into the nascent positive vibration surrounding our family once again, I truly believed the tough times were behind us.

But I was mistaken...

The house phone rings. My sentimental thoughts are interrupted.

Strange. Everyone knows to call me on my cell.

No way in hell I'm getting it. I'm combing my five-year-old Yordana's long, flowing hair. Through the corner of my eye I see Martha, the housekeeper, appear in the doorway. "Es para usted, señora. Están llamando de los EEUU."[29] She hands me the phone and walks out.

It is my cousin Russell calling from Miami. "Hey, Russ. How are ya? I'm just here with the kids..." I greet him gregariously.

He mutters an unintelligible "hello." The lilt in his voice is strange, one I don't recognize.

"Now, I'm going to pass you to Maris," he says.

Maris is my mother's first cousin and the two of them have been extremely close throughout their entire lives. In fact, Maris

---

29 It's for you, Misses. They're calling from the United States.

came to visit me a day before brain surgery and stayed with my mom a few days to lend emotional support. Days after surgery, between belly laughs, Mom and Joaquín told me how Maris had rotated between the two queen-sized beds in the apartment, alternatively sleeping with Mom, Joaquín and Warren. Nobody could fall asleep to her freight train snoring so the four of them played musical beds each night for almost a week.

Besides sharing the same first name—their mothers, my grandma Francis and her younger sister, Mabel mutually agreed to name their daughters after their deceased father, Morris—the story goes that both sisters went into the hospital together with labor pains. My mom was born first, and eleven hours later, her younger cousin came into the world.

Maris gets on the phone.

"Hi Dar. Listen to me. Are you sitting down?"

"No, but I will," I reply nonchalantly, continuing to comb through Yordana's hair.

At this point, I start to figure it out. She's about to unload the bad news I've been waiting for. The inevitable. She'll tell me that my frail grandma Francis—who is well into her eighties and declining rapidly—has just passed away. We've been expecting it for years—ever since her son, my uncle Shep's abrupt and tragic death back in January of 2003.

But that's not what she says. In one run-on sentence, without pausing, she bellows out the unimaginable and I am too astonished and caught off-guard to comprehend spoken English.

"Your little brother Adam shot and killed himself today at a gun range...(no pause)...the detectives found him there and we don't know anything else." She delivers this blow in one extended stream—with the cool, but concerned demeanor of a newscaster reading off a teleprompter.

What?

There's static everywhere. That familiar static returns to fill my head and cloud my thoughts.

Like a computer that suddenly crashes after a power surge, my mind shuts down and goes blank. All I hear is a slew of incoherent muddled noise on the other end of the line. The inner voice inside my still-fragile head rejects this absurd news.

I close my eyes, hold my breath, and lunge head-first into a Sea of Denial.

This is a gigantic mistake. Never would he have done such a heinous thing; he wasn't depressed or suicidal... We were just hanging out together last month at David's graduation.

She waits patiently on the phone as I slowly regurgitate it all—word by word—as if in a hypnotic trance. I ask her to repeat herself several times. I must hear her confirm and re-confirm it again and again. She does, and won't hang up until she's confident that I got it.

By the fourth or fifth time, the static in my head dissipates and my English comprehension returns. Her deliberately spoken words successfully penetrate my thick skull. The left frontal lobe, the part of the brain that controls language, processes the information.

Oh shit. I think I just understood what she said.

Without warning, overtaken by despair, I tumble off the couch and somersault onto the area rug. I clutch at my heaving chest. Oh God, I can't breathe, I c-a-n-n-o-t breathe... I cannot FUCKING BREATHE!! Like lava, the repressed emotions trapped inside my heart begin to bubble up to the surface. This volcano is active and poised to erupt.

Yet from my ground-level position, I shift my gaze upward and stare directly into my children's horror-struck eyes. At that moment, I realize it is still not time to release the mounting pressure of these pent-up emotions. I must stifle them at once and tighten the lid, to keep them from boiling over.

The children are whimpering softly as they observe their mommy come undone. My eldest Yordana, my five-year-old girl, hurtles herself into me, blanketing my body with her tiny self. I feel her nails dig deep into the nape of my neck as she holds on for dear life. She's quivering uncontrollably and in her own way, tries to console me despite not comprehending fully the reason for my sorrow.

The two female housekeepers, who have been observing this scene unfurl, have learned through my guttural sobs what happened. Unsettled themselves, one of the women reaches for the phone to alert my husband.

"Señor Joaquín, favor de regresar a casa enseguida. Ha pasado algo grave."[30]

My shell-shocked husband arrives within minutes. At the door,

---

30 Mr. Joaquín, please come home immediately. Something terrible has happened.

the housekeepers debrief him about this recent tragic episode. Later that evening, he confessed that on the drive over he had imagined a pool-related catastrophe, a drowning in fact, had befallen one of the children.

He walks into the den and I thrust myself upon him. "Please, Mi Amor. Don't. Don't get frantic. Try to breathe. Remember you just underwent a very delicate operation," he advises.

But his efforts to soothe me with logic are fruitless.

He tries repeatedly, reminding me that I have a fresh, open wound in my head and an unborn baby who already has experienced enough trauma. He instructs me to take notice of the vulnerable audience set before us. The small children are huddled together and panic as they witness their strong, stoic mother lose control. The reality of the situation is lost on them.

Shit, I still can't let go.

Again, my repressed emotions are trapped inside this inconveniently feeble body with no emergency exit.

Nevertheless, I pull myself together just enough to get the kids off to bed.

After a hellacious night of disturbing apparitions, the first call I make that very next morning is to Dr. Carbone. At my unremitting insistence, he reluctantly gives me the green light to take occasional, tiny doses of Xanax. "Darah, take only as needed and to help carry you through the funeral proceedings and seven subsequent days of Shivah.[31] That's it," he clarifies.

My neurosurgeon in New York City, Dr. Golfinos, who I immediately contacted as well, warns me to stay calm and as composed as possible considering the depth of this calamity. "The brain must stay well-oxygenated," he explains. "The soft brain tissue still is healing and any abrupt outburst of emotion could result in intra-cranial pressure that could cause an aneurism."

Something that would only further complicate our already chaotic lives, I think to myself.

How the hell can my intellectual brain convince my emotional side to adhere to the doctor's orders? Who in the world can keep

---

31 In Judaism, a seven-day period of formal mourning observed after the funeral of a close relative.

cool upon receiving such devastating news? I need a damn outlet.

How much more can I take?

Rattled to the core, the tank was on empty.

I was out of fight.

Yet, in hindsight, I realize that this particular event solidified my unyielding ability to compartmentalize my feelings and suppress my emotions.

My mind created deep fissures where I buried my vulnerabilities—only to be dug up later, while writing this book.

The rage deep inside my core stirred and gathered force, and unbeknownst to me at the time, would carry me through six more years of unremitting darkness.

The very next afternoon, after going through the household drill with the housekeepers, the pediatrician and our savior, Tía Bonnie—who had rushed right over—we found ourselves back on the plane. This time, our destination was Miami as we left our puzzled children crying in our wake...

From the instant we arrive to Mom's town house, just forty-five minutes after landing at the Miami International Airport, the grieving family and friends appear at my side—one by one. The funeral is set for the very next morning—in the Jewish tradition, it is critical to bury the deceased as soon as possible after death—but the house is packed. Everyone just walks around zombielike, mumbling under his or her breath, heads shaking in disbelief.

I work hard to disconnect emotionally and invoke my inner Buddha by transcending my physical body and practice some meditational techniques I read about fifteen years ago when my overriding problem was with a controlling, college boyfriend.

I regulate my breathing and shift my gaze from one inanimate object to another, avoiding eye contact with most people. I hold my face devoid of expression.

Remember what Dr. Golfinos said, I tell myself and stroke my pregnant belly with one hand while running the other hand's fingers gingerly over the bulging scar on my head.

Over and over again, I swallow the same rising lump in my bone-dry throat, as if it singularly contained all repressed emotions.

Be the strong one for Mom, David and Ricky, my inner voice commands. Stay calm, Darah. You must do this. They need YOU to keep it together so you can help THEM get through it.

All day long, I argue with myself, which further underscores my budding psychosis. Why must I be the stoic one? I'm entitled to have feelings, too. Somewhere deep inside I'm still human. Aren't I?

If I do not find a way to release this emotional turmoil soon enough, one day it will surface unpredictably and with a visceral force. At the very least, it will manifest as a peculiar tick. Alternatively, I may become an obsessive chalk-eater like those attention-seeking misfits on reality television. At worst, I will end up mutilating myself or addicted to some other form of pain-inflicting behavior.

And although I jest a little—as inappropriate as you may deem it to be—remember this is how I cope with the unthinkable. In all seriousness, the bottom line is this: I knew I wouldn't emerge from this unscathed. This was a frightening unknown as the primary caretaker of three—soon-to-be four—young children.

Mingling with so many friends and family for the first time post-surgery brings many perplexing, mixed emotions to the fore. Simultaneously, people express their condolences for my loss while congratulating me for my survival—as if I had anything to do with it. It is surreal. I don't know what to feel or how to respond. I arrived anesthetized.

I bicker with my husband incessantly to demand his unwavering support when I decide to eulogize my brother at the funeral service. It is the very least I can do as the big sister, I believe. Somehow, I end up standing in front of a rapt audience and deliver a touching speech that encapsulates all the special moments I remember most with Adam, my baby brother.

Ostensibly, I was unable to assuage his quiet desolation. I had no idea what was going on inside his tortured mind. He was always so elusive, so reserved and self-effacing.

I had been residing in another country for the last remaining six years of his short life and felt somewhat responsible for not having intervened sooner. I beat myself up for years, for being unable to protect him from himself.

If only I had known he was suffering.[32]

If only I would've pursued him more aggressively and persuaded him to come stay with us in Panamá to learn Spanish

---

32 In the following chapter, I'll get into a deeper analysis of why I believe he became derailed, and further explore my own perceived culpability.

and work at Joaquín's company.

If only...

No sense in entertaining such self-destructive thoughts now.

Too late. He's gone.

Miraculously, I don't become unhinged during the dreadful week of mourning. The maternal imperative to protect my unborn son keeps me together. Nevertheless, I do feel saddened to leave my mother and two brothers—David and my half-brother from Dad's previous, short-lived marriage, Ricky—stuck here, living surrounded by constant reminders of the heinous ending to my Adam's life. And yes, history does repeat itself. Because the definition of insanity is to make the same mistakes and expect different results.

 Nevertheless, like I did after Dad's death back in April of 2000, I feel that same sense of relief to be able to up and leave it all behind, and escape back to my other reality. My guilt about abandoning my mom is replaced by a fervent appreciation for what awaits me back home in my faraway, third world Panamá—my three babies.

Our seven-day Miami whirlwind comes and goes in the blink of an eye. I head back to my home in the Tropics. There I am safe, immersed in another country's culture, language, music, politics, and insulated from this grief.

I lead a double life.

Strangely, people (still) ask me all the time how I got through it all. I don't know. Maybe I really haven't. Perhaps the joke is on me and all these pent-up emotions are devouring my insides like some sort of cancer. Maybe I just don't realize it yet.

The simple truth is that I did all I know how to do: inhale, exhale and trust in the natural healing power of the passage of time.

Pearls of Wisdom...

- o When you feel you can't go on, tap into that reserve tank and push harder.
- o Focus on the basics such as the regulation of breathing.
- o Trust in time's power to heal.

11. *Near Drowning, Remembering Adam & The Miracle Birth*

We're back in Panamá now and are welcomed by our small battalion of children and staff. The mood is lighter and while still mourning, I'm busy making plans for the upcoming birth of the baby. Half-heartedly, I begin to decorate the baby's room, replacing the drab décor with a boyish motif. I reassemble the same hand-made pinewood crib we've been recycling for years. It was the same one originally bought from a local woodworker in Costa Rica for Yordana in 2001—just weeks before Joaquín accepted the big position to open Credomatic in Panamá and we decided to relocate.

Dr. Carbone examines me again and confirms that the baby is doing well and all looks fine with the pregnancy. I feel myself doing everything mechanically. Adam's death delivers a blow that affects me more than I realize at the time. He seems to figure more prominently in my life now in death, than he had in years. I replay his suicide continuously, and go as far back as to when he was sixteen and my parents first split.

I'm unable to access my feelings, though. By now, the breach between my emotions and intellect has become almost irreversible. My world just shattered ten days ago and it's inconceivable to go from disaster to imminent-celebration or normalcy so abruptly.

However, there is no alternative; this is how my life is unraveling. I am a passenger on this train, guided by forces much greater than I, and can't get off.

Living in another country certainly provides a built-in escape route that enables me to detach from my brother's loss. I put on blinders and for a short while, am able to focus on my immediate family and small community.

I was convinced that I'd succeeded in putting it all behind me; that is, unless Mom, David or Ricky called. Conversations with them really dragged me down.

At night, though, repressed emotions buried underneath neglected levels of consciousness emerge and startle me awake. Each night horrifying images of my brother killing himself come to torment me.

How did he do it, exactly? Did he pre meditatively sneak off around the bend and point the gun to his head? Did he suffer a long time, or did he die instantly?

My mind plays devious tricks on me as it tries to re-enact something of which I have only a dim awareness. I was never told the specifics about how he ended his life; I didn't want to know. None of us really did.

We knew he was at a gun range, where unbeknownst to us, he had a membership. The detectives told us that he slipped around the corner into a more private booth and put it to his head. Period.

We didn't know if this was on impulse, premeditated, or if he just acted plain stupid. We did know, however, that he'd been scheduled to work at his local hotel job that very afternoon and had plans with friends to drive up to the University of Florida, his alma mater in Gainesville, for the weekend. He had his work uniform and other related items in his car that seemed to substantiate this claim.

Regardless of my lack of understanding of how or why it happened, in the dead silence of the night, with my husband asleep at my side, I get yanked into that familiar whirlpool of panic, and contrive hundreds of suicidal scenarios—all of which are uncorroborated, and mere creations of my own inconsolable mind.

Eventually I'm afraid to go to sleep at night.

I'm afraid be alone with my mind.

Luckily, all phantoms disappear by morning.

The only lingering evidence of this nighttime unrest are the dark shadows under my eyes. During the day, I fuel up on caffeine. On autopilot, I deliberately run myself ragged with projects.

My daily goal is to collapse onto my bed each night wasted, and thwart off the evil spirits.

A gigantic, delightful pool plays a starring role in our backyard landscape, and the water is always crystal clear, cool and refreshing. Because we haven't been home much and the kids aren't allowed to bathe in our absence, swimming has yet to become a routine family activity.

The circumference of the entire deck is lined with lush tropical foliage, punctuated by towering palm trees and thriving mango trees which despite routine daily pickings, litter the garden grounds and perfume the air with their syrupy scent. Many species of wildlife venture out day and night to take part in this private oasis, and feast on the abundance of ripened mangoes.

I sit outside at night after the kids are asleep, mesmerized by the shimmering moon and its reflection off the still pool water. Each night, the pool hauntingly calls out to me, "Come in for a swim. The waters will purify you and your baby. And wash your mind clean."

Yet despite the lure of the tepid waters, I am too intimidated by the silence and solitude swimming represents to take a dip.

One morning, a week after returning from Adam's funeral, and under the pretense of regaining my balance and equilibrium, I succumb to the pressure and go in. This pool is a treasure that merits appreciation; heck, it was a major selling point when we first decided to rent this rickety, old house.

After that first morning swim, I am hooked. After the kids leave for school and Joaquín for work, I embark on a routine of lap swimming. The mild temperatures and calm silence of the water soothes me. I love listening to the remote sounds of birds singing, jackhammers drilling, and horns honking. It blends to form the perfect cacophony of distraction, an acoustic companion that keeps my mind from drifting.

An exercise buff my entire life, it has been far too long since I've been able to exert myself physically, and with each long-armed stroke, I find solace and gain strength. Exercise is my therapy, and always has been. Because, I reason, a pooped-out body will send blissful endorphins to the brain and begrudge the mind of stressful or depressing thoughts.

Adam is gone, but I am alive still, and have a lot on my plate. My husband needs me to be strong; he has his own professional pressure that keeps him up at night.

My three young children crave their mom's undivided attention.

I can't let any of them down.

I swim regularly, a minimum of four times a week for fifty-minute non-stop sessions. I wear myself out, until every muscle in my body begs for mercy.

Gradually, I begin morphing back into the old me again, although a very pregnant and still lop-sided version. However, after three weeks of this newly-established practice, my mind starts to roam mid-swim, and invariably, I slip into that night-demon space as fear ripples through my pregnant-body-in-motion.

Without warning, I envisage ghastly images of my little brother in death—disturbing imagery of his lifeless, tattooed body, heavy and sinking into the darkest depths of the ocean. When this happens, I swallow water, and knead my way poolside to regroup. Many times, I cannot control these terrorizing thoughts and am forced to stop swimming entirely. The stillness and tranquility of the water—of this enormous green haven—both excites and terrifies me.

I remember Adam in childhood. I was nine when he was born and already poised as my mother's little helper. Mom let me change his diapers, feed him bottles of milk, and help bathe him. I loved to play with him and take care of him—oftentimes, fantasying he was my very own baby boy.

He was my first real practice, which a few short years later, helped define my next two decades as a career babysitter. Through discipline and diligence, my regular babysitting gigs later enabled me to amass enough of a savings to finance my first car.

When I first got my license at the age of sixteen, in my own pre-owned, red Pontiac Sunbird, I offered to run each and every family errand. I only wanted an excuse to get behind the wheel, blast the radio and let my hair billow out the open window.

Adam was my travel companion, my little buddy. I'd buckle him into the backseat to come along for the ride. I remember taking him all the way to the beach, without Mom's consent of course, where I'd show him off to my tanning teenage friends. He was such a good sport, and would charm them all with his unimposing demeanor and shy sense of humor.

We nicknamed him "Little Man" because he consistently conducted himself like a gentleman and at most family gatherings, was the youngest child buzzing around amidst a swarm of older kids and adults.

Adam was a high-achiever and had been doing very well in school. Already a disciplined athlete by the age of eleven, oftentimes he'd arise before the crack of dawn and set out on long runs through the neighborhood. He was destined for greatness.

However, a lot changed after my parents delivered the news of their split. I had just arrived from a ten-month, post-graduation trip abroad to Costa Rica, where I studied, worked and backpacked around the country. David was away at college in Gainesville. Adam was sixteen and in tenth grade, living contentedly in the big house alone with Mom and Dad.

We were all worried how he'd fare—being the youngest and most vulnerable of us all—absorbing a daily dose of marital breakdown. Many times, he was caught in the crossfire of accusations exchanged between our parents and unwittingly used as a pawn. "Come stay at my house tonight," Dad would insist. "You can study here. I've set up a great room for you."

I don't think Mom and Dad ever devised a legal custody arrangement. It wasn't an area of contention and therefore, a mute point. Adam's home was the same house he'd grown up in since birth and Dad understood that. But I think out of remorse for Dad's slow-emerging depression and lack of social life, Adam agreed to stay half the time with Dad at that Godforsaken unofficial retirement community.

Dad needed Adam desperately and in the end, became an emotional burden for Adam. Adam, forever loyal, was always a pushover when it came to the father he had adored and admired very much as a young child.

Instead of providing the paternal guidance Adam craved as he prepared for college beset with questions about puberty and school and overall life direction, he found himself in the role of caretaker and companion for my rapidly deteriorating father. Never overtly expressing it, I know Adam felt lost and robbed of a father who'd be able to mentor him as he matured into a young adult. Maybe that is when his zest for life started to vanish and he lost his way.

After he left for college, he began to flounder, and changed his major several times, not quite certain how to reconcile his desire to study a particular subject matter with the potential career opportunities and monetary compensation that corresponding field could bring. Each time he wavered, he consulted with no one—not me, not David or either of my parents.

We were always on "stand-by" eager to help him out, in whatever he needed. We expressed our commitment to him constantly so he must've known he wasn't alone.

He knew we were all there for him, didn't he? Did I tell him often enough?

But stubbornly, he'd maintain he was fine and knew what he was doing. He always alleged to have consulted with a guidance counselor. But because of FERPA, or the Family Educational Rights and Privacy Act—a federal law that protects the privacy of student education records once they turn eighteen—my mother, the only one really paying attention after Dad passed away in April 2000, wasn't privy to the reports of the failing grades he'd been receiving semester after semester.

Sadly, I was disconnected and busy with my own life in Panamá to notice.

Because of his passive unwillingness to disclose his private world with even those closest to him, none of us ever suspected just how much Dad's death crushed Adam. Not until we discovered upon his death, the forever-concealed, upper-arm markings that permanently stained his skin. His disturbing tattoos included an undecipherable array of cryptic Aramaic-looking letters, the platitude about money being the root of all evil, and the most devastatingly telling, yet hidden one of all was painted over his heart:

Dad, c u soon.

Suddenly, at the very end, when it was too late to rescue him from his own damaged thoughts, it became painfully obvious that my little brother suffered intolerably after Dad's sudden death. Forever drifting, he got stuck in the sorrowful aftermath, and never moved on.

Unmistakably, he was further conflicted by the bleak financial future he perceived for himself. Having graduated from college already drowned in debt, he questioned his own ability (and desire) to make the big-ticket career choices needed to get his head above water. A loyal and disciplined employee who was well-regarded by peers and superiors alike, Adam displayed an uncertain contentment with "just getting by."

Yet paradoxically, Adam had developed an outright dysfunctional relationship with money and all the symbolic power and glory he associated with having lots of it, as evidenced by his unseemly tattoo.

Oh my God! The writing was on the wall!

Why didn't we see this coming?

Where the hell were we?

WHERE THE HELL WAS I?

WHAT KIND OF BIG SISTER...?

Dammit, Adam, why were you always so tight-lipped when it came to talking about yourself? Not even your best buddies knew any of this stuff!

How did you manage to hide those disturbing tattoos for so long?

Unequivocally, in some way or many ways known and unknown, Adam wasn't who he thought he should be. That operative word 'should' negatively affected his already-diminished self-worth. He lived his young adult life undercover, and aside from his smart sense of humor and pleasant, easygoing manner, never opened himself up to anyone about anything personal. He must've been petrified of humiliation or worse yet, out-and-out rejection.

I hardly remember seeing Adam much after our parents divorced. I moved out right before they sold the house and divvied up the spoils. Together with a roommate, we put a deposit down on a lovely rental apartment forty miles away from Mom and Dad, and just a ten-minute drive to my new place of employment. Recently hired for my first after-college professional job, I'd become absorbed with work and simultaneously, swept up in a lustful, new relationship with the athletic conquistador who wooed me with his heavy Bostonian accent. Seemed I'd found another life altogether and subconsciously, disconnected from our now-broken family.

I ran away when the illusion of our once-happy household shattered to pieces, and could no longer bear to stick around and witness Dad's decline juxtaposed with my now-dating mother's ascent. Their separate residences and new identities were too awkward, too real.

At this time, a young and impressionable Adam inadvertently got spun around by this centrifuge of disorder and lost in the shuffle. When I left home, along with my parents' failed marriage, he too began to fade into a mere ghost of the past...

Adam, I am so, so sorry!

What a senseless loss of life!

Lucky for me, after several weeks, my near drowning episodes began to taper off after I unloaded and confided in a close friend. After ingesting a daily dosage of it-wasn't-your-fault-and-there-was-nothing-more-you-could've-done friend therapy, this self-destructive narrative eventually stopped rolling inside my warped and beleaguered mind.

When the anticipated random spastic tingling returned to the left side of my face, I set out to work with a physical therapist to stimulate my awakening facial nerves. Dr. Roland explicitly had told me that until I felt this sensation, I couldn't begin to exercise the facial muscles.

The goal was to bring some symmetry back to my face. I tried to limit my gesturing and control my facial expressions out of insecurity, although it began to smother my vivacious spirit so eventually I stopped trying.

The therapist, a bubbly, young woman named Jenny, would initiate each session with a light facial massage, using only her fingertips. Next, gently she'd press a portable electronic device, a battery-operated electrical stimulation machine, to my face to shock the muscles and get them to respond. Once the muscles were electrified and twitching involuntarily, she'd lead me in front of a mirror where we'd begin the hard work, and practice twenty different facial expressions.

Each gesture—be it a grimace, frown, surprised expression, eyebrow furrow, smile or inflating balloons—would demand tremendous effort. She encouraged me to hold each position for twenty seconds, and by the end of each of the one-hour appointments, I was wiped. My facial muscles would tremble uncontrollably all night long following these bi-weekly therapeutic sessions, only to stop upon my awakening the following morning.

I never imagined exercising the face would be such hard work. It was disheartening because the improvements reaped after weeks and weeks of painstaking work were minimal and hardly noticeable. Many times I considered quitting. However, when I did skip an appointment or two, my face would freeze out of protest.

Furthermore, my left eye, in condemnation, would dry out and remain exaggeratedly open. My mouth would lose elasticity and its ability to stay closed while chewing food or drinking. Being the consummate masochist, I'd play this childish game with myself and try to fool each new person I met—to see how long I could engage them in conversation before they acknowledged my imperfect, asymmetrical face.

Getting used to the single-sided deafness was, and still is, the biggest challenge of all. In sum, it has proven to be much greater than a computed fifty-percent hearing loss.

Indirectly, this impairment has affected my vision, my reaction time, and my sense of location and dimension. My street-side self-confidence has shrunken in correlation to the perceived inability to defend myself if caught by surprise. I've become less independent as a result—a reality I still struggle to embrace.

Thus, with unrestrained resolve I pressed on with my swimming, walking and working-with-Jenny routine. I strove to restore a sense of banal normalcy to our domestic lives—however that could be defined during this time.

Thankfully, the days passed by rather uneventfully as I kept busy with the kids' activities and my own religious classes. We all gathered momentum to prepare for the incoming new member of the family. The very anticipation over the new baby's arrival uprooted the sadness that had planted itself in the pit of my stomach since I first heard the tragic news about Adam.

Before I knew it, two months flew by and the baby's scheduled birth date, October 4, 2006, came barreling around the corner. Showtime.

Forced to have a mandatory C-section because of my inability to exert the intra-cranial pressure that naturally occurs during a vaginal delivery, I couldn't help but to see it as a cop-out. Understandably, C-sections are a necessity under a litany of circumstances, but for me, a woman who had had three relatively easy, run-of-the-mill vaginal births, I deemed it inessential.

I remember that just days before the having-a-baby appointment, I phoned Dr. Golfinos in New York, and insisted that being my fourth child, a C-section needn't be obligatory in my case.

"Doc, this one's going to drop out of me while standing in line at the supermarket," I half-joked. "My second and third came out in two easy pushes; in fact, with the third, the doctor hadn't even time to pull on his scrubs." I was certain I'd be able to coax him into it. "Besides, I've been swimming and walking, and am in great shape again."

My rationale did nothing to convince him otherwise and he denied my request. When I called the next day, I got his surgical nurse practitioner Jessica, his right hand, on the phone and she emphatically reiterated Dr. Golfinos' unchanging stance on the matter. "Darah, Dr. Golfinos says that under no condition will he allow a vaginal birth."

I followed up with a few pestering emails concocting all kinds of scenarios that wouldn't require the exertion of intra-cranial pressure, all to no avail.

Finally, two days before my programmed delivery, I gave up.

Lucky for me my neurosurgeon was so adamant because when

they opened me in the OR, the team of doctors and nurses discovered a double-knot in the umbilical cord. No, it wasn't wrapped around the baby's neck—which traditionally happens on occasion—but like a long garden hose, the cord had two independent knots that were causing major obstruction.

This unusual situation was undetectable via ultrasound. Similar to a slackened hose all coiled up on the ground, it was nearly impossible to identify until they saw it up close, in the flesh.

So the big, earth-shattering news was that had a vaginal delivery been attempted, the cord would've stretched completely, and the knots would have tightened and closed. The result would have been a restriction in the baby's airflow, which "...would have ended tragically," in the exact words of my neonatologist, Dr. Velarde.

As the incurable optimist—who is far from Polyannish and can bitch and moan with the best of them—I took note of the miracles emerging from this calamity.

My brain tumor saved my life and ultimately, my baby's life, stunned, I repeated to myself day and night.

By some fluke or stroke of luck, my pregnancy exacerbated the tumor-related symptoms, which inevitably, brought me to a proper diagnosis. Just in time.

Months later, I had that mandatory C-section delivery which afforded my baby his only chance of survival. Already, a perfect symbiotic relationship existed between us—long before his miraculous arrival into the world.

For the first time in a very long time, I felt truly blessed and thankful, thankful to this new life, to my newborn son, and for my own life.

Another mysterious coincidence that came to our immediate attention was in relation to the birth weight of the baby. My son weighed in at exactly six pounds, thirteen ounces.

In Judaism, these numbers represent the 613 Mitzvot, or good deeds and obligations, the Torah ordains a Jew to respect. We were taken aback when one of our religious friends brought this mystical correlation to our awareness.

It was unquestionable that God was channeling messages through this baby.

My frozen heart started to thaw out, and I was beginning to feel. Again.

Pearls of Wisdom...

- o Allow acoustic distractions to take your mind away and off your worries.
- o Recognize blessings and miracles.
- o Know when to surrender.

12. *Naming the Baby, Comedy & Perks of One-Sided Deafness, & The Unglamorous Realities of Live-in Help*

Cuddling in the hospital bed with my miracle baby, I noticed he had a striking resemblance to my maternal great-grandfather. His long fingers were befit for a pianist and he possessed the characteristic Ashkenazi profile with big hollow eyes and a pronounced nose. "This one looks like my side!" I gloated to my husband, whose genes are so dominant that the other three children emerged from my womb like a tribe of his mini-clones.

Although I wanted to name this baby after my late brother, my religious beliefs dictate that when a soul passes due to suicide, it takes a solid year for that soul to rest peacefully and subsequently, ascend to heaven.

Additionally, I believed that if I didn't comply with this mandate—that indeed appealed to my sense of reasoning as well—and named my new son after my deceased Adam, this would attract bad fortune into the baby's life.

A few weeks after our return home to Panamá following Adam's funeral, Joaquín and I had consulted with a spiritual guru, a world-renowned Sephardic Rabbi visiting from Israel, who was said to have mystical insights. People throughout the community were flocking to his side during fifteen-minute scheduled sessions to seek advice from this hacham[33].

We figured we'd sign up and give it a shot, and ask his thoughts on the naming of our baby. Once we shared our sad story, misty-eyed, he looked up to the heavens and seemed to slip into a trance for several, long minutes. When he snapped out of it, he assured us that he had received a name befitting our baby, based upon the baby's foreseen mazal.[34]

However, his loyal translator cautioned, "...once the great

---

33 Hebrew for sage, or wise leader.
34 Hebrew for luck or fortune, and by those who practice astrology, the term has acquired the connotation of cosmic fate or fortune.

Rabbi announces the name aloud, there's no turning back. It becomes cosmically chosen for your child only."

Oh shit. What are we getting ourselves into? What if we hate the name; or worse yet, can't even pronounce it?

But hey, we were desperate for guidance and chose to go with it, whatever "it" was. Therefore, instead of using the name we originally had chosen, we obliged and called the new baby the divinely ordained name, Yair. In Hebrew this name means, "he will shine."

Fortunately, Yair was born perfect. He was alert and healthy despite the New York high-risk Ob-Gyn's hypothesis that he would be born with withdrawal symptoms due to the extensive exposure to anesthesia. Four days after giving birth, I was discharged from the hospital and we brought him home for all to marvel over. The entire Panamanian community was inspired by this tiny creature that had come into the world peaceful and intact after all he had gone through in utero. His bris[35] was a most-celebrated community affair. Many people we didn't know arrived to see this little miracle with their own eyes.

Moreover, in spite of his mother's tension and heartache, he was always an easy-going baby, never fussy, and blossomed as he reached each subsequent milestone. To this day, he hugs us with all his might and fills our hearts with joy.

We were blessed.

With the birth of our son scratched off the interminable To-Do list, my focus shifted once again. My new mission: acclimate to the hearing impairment. What was happening to me was disconcerting, as nobody had bothered to explain any of it. The ENT surgeon never fully defined or prepared me how to cope with all the secondary effects; I guess he assumed I'd figure it all out on my own.

My discomfort rose gradually, over the course of a year. The heap of inconveniences the deafness generated continued (and continues) to grow.

Hearing anything was hard work—a task requiring enormous, conscientious effort. Initially, the hearing ear had become super-sensitive as it worked frenetically to compensate for its partner's

---

35 Ashkenzai Jews' pronunciation of the Hebrew word for the ritual circumcision that typically takes places eight days after the healthy, full-term delivery of a baby boy.

abrupt loss. I found myself unable to hear someone speaking to me from two yards away because distinguishing sounds based on their proximity or filtering out the background noise from ten yards away was impossible.

At night, the hearing ear picked up high-pitched tones not meant for human, auditory consumption. Echolocation, vibrations emitted by nocturnal creatures such as those used by bats to locate their prey, was a regular nighttime phenomenon occurring in the yard, just beyond my bedroom window. These under-the-radar reverberations ricocheted inside my head like rapid-fire bullets all night long while I tried to sleep.

My husband thought I was experiencing auditory hallucinations; he never heard a thing. Not even with a thick, foamy earplug shoved deep inside my right ear canal, could I drown it out. It was as if my entire vestibular system was going haywire and playing pranks on me.

Another strange occurrence was that at times, the good ear would create phantom sounds. I'd spend the entire night, tossing between sleep and wakefulness, convinced that one of the children was somewhere trapped and sobbing. However, it became clear upon inspection that all four were in their beds fast asleep. I had the same problem with car alarms, cell phones rings, and doorbells. I heard the nagging, high-pitched ding all day long.

Through trial and error, I realized one of the many obstacles of one-sided deafness was the inability to localize sound. You hear almost every sound in the vicinity, yet have no idea from which direction it comes. For example, when I took my baby out in the stroller, whenever an approaching car would honk or biker was at my heels, I reacted with a startling jerk.

Oftentimes, people stand to my left and strike up conversations. Completely unaware of their presence until physically tapped on the shoulder, it triggers waves of panic.

I never know how long someone is at my side, watching me and waiting for a response.

I feel exposed and defenseless.

These sentiments are tough ones to reckon with considering a need always to be in control.

As a result, I've grown excessively paranoid, and while walking, glance over my shoulder every couple of minutes. Engaged in conversation at any indoor gathering, or open outdoor area is unnerving. I'm unable to focus on socializing as I crane my neck in all directions, scanning my surroundings suspiciously, in anticipation of a noisy ambush.

I'd imagine it quite comical from an outsider's point of view. Oftentimes, I'm running like a madwoman when the children call me or I hear someone crying. Effectively, I charge off in the polar opposite direction from wherever the racket originates.

At least I'm consistent; every time I get it wrong. In addition, my work always doubles as I backtrack to my point of origin to begin again. When the house is full, I'm subjected to a perpetual stream of the following:

"Mommy, come."

"Mommy, help!"

"Mommy, he's (hitting, biting, punching, bothering, annoying, hurting, killing) me!"

"But where are you?" I shriek, while spinning 360 degrees looking for a child-sized body.

Most of the time my little hypochondriacs are a few feet away and just out of eyesight. My knee-jerk reaction of taking off like a crazed maniac in lieu of asking for directions proves futile on the rare occasion that it is something important. However, I'm training the children to specify their location if out of visual range or to enunciate clearly and make eye contact when addressing me within range.

I continue to master lip-reading, which is nothing more than a survival instinct. Our home habitually models a surveillance drill in action. Everyone constantly updates me with his or her geographical position.

"Mommy, I am by the door. Come, I need help."

"Here I am, Mommy, by the kitchen entrance. Please pour me a cup of juice."

"Look to your left, Mommy; I'm standing here with my nose bleeding."

"Darah, Mi Amor, look this way, I've just stepped out of the shower and need a towel because I'm dripping wet!"

Am I oblivious?

Indisputably, the most hilarious scene unfolds once my cell phone rings. Notorious for losing it several times a day, I set it down, get absorbed in or distracted by some task and have no recollection where I originally put it. When this happens, it might as well be in another city because the chances of me finding it alone are slim to none.

Here enters the inability to localize sound. Because when I hear the phone ring, although it is within reach or nestled into my own coat pocket and I do hear it, if I cannot see it or feel it vibrate, I will never find it.

My partial deafness affects us socially as well. After we attend a group event, by the time we leave, my head gyrates as if it were an overstuffed washing machine stuck on the spin cycle. With one-sided deafness, not only am I unable to localize the sound, the sound also lacks dimension.

Curiously, I perceive words spoken by a couple conversing privately at the next table as loudly as those spoken by the person sitting adjacent to me. The competing noises actually cancel out one another and if I were to close my eyes, it'd be utterly impossible to recognize which sound is closest in proximity.

The various, simultaneous conversations merge into one giant surge of noise, and oftentimes usher in a nasty migraine.

Although my internal hardware goes mad trying to function semi-normally, some may interpret this as a gift. Unwittingly, I find myself eaves-dropping on other people's conversations by tuning into the wrong frequency. Seriously.

It's not my intention and although I'd rather focus on who I'm with, through the bombardment of numerous competing sounds that my right ear detects at the same decibel-level and closeness, I've no option.

Perhaps I have a promising future in detective work. Maybe I can aspire to be an international spy.

Picture this routine chaos: my forever-competing children all talk at once. Each kid's entranced in his or her own disparate monologue, jockeying for the spotlight, for Mom's undivided attention. Although I'm ill-equipped to do so, all expect me to carry on a slew of simultaneous, disjointed conversations with ease. Curiously, the lone, hearing ear seems to be developing a peculiar aversion to my own children's voices.

The background acoustics are comprised of barking dogs, the obnoxious ring of a misplaced cell phone, washing machine and drier hubbub, and the deafening drone of neighborhood lawnmowers. Additionally, I have three housekeepers that call out to me randomly and frequently from all over the house, to inquire about mealtime preparations and how to quick-fix whatever they recently have broken.

In other words: lots of ear-splitting, disorderly hullabaloo, a real life Tower of Babel.

Hyped up on un-tempered, un-medicated anxiety, I assume the open stance of a seasoned New York City deli butcher bracing for the Friday afternoon lunchtime blitz.

"You first," I yell, index finger pointing to a child.

"One sec. Hey, wait up," hand suspended in a pause position, holding the impatient interrupter at bay.

"No, not yet. Wait until you're called," I sneer at the loudest and most obnoxious.

Now enters the patiently waiting, slow-talking one, "Go ahead, you're up. Please talk fast because the others want to speak and the nannies are calling."

"Quiet. No, it's still not your turn," I bellow out to the sneaky one trying to foil my attempts at order.

Crying and protests proceed.

The throbbing headache further intensifies.

However, I always conceal my angst and maintain my composure so the housekeepers feel safe and sound. Unbelievably, the live-in help are witnesses to the mayhem and like children, study their employers' (our) behaviors for a living.

If we are on the fringe of losing our minds, sniffing out our vulnerabilities and desperation, they'll either demand a hefty raise, i.e. bribe us to make them stay, or up and quit. That's just the way it is.

Allow me to explain.

Here I digress from the above scene to provide an overview of what life with live-in help is really like in Panamá. Especially for those of you who consider it nothing less than "glamorous." For starters, a live-in housekeeper earns an average monthly salary of US$250 plus room and board.[36] Most every residence, albeit small, is constructed with special maids' quarters—typically adjacent to the kitchen and laundry area.

With the employer's initial investment of $150 for uniforms, work shoes, aprons and basic toiletries, the housekeeper is ready to

---

36 Salaries vary depending on how many children are in the household, the relative affluence of the neighborhood and cooks typically receive higher wages than nannies.

begin. Most of our friends and acquaintances have two live-ins, and one that "travels," or commutes daily via bus. Sometimes this third person only works several times a week.

This commuter—usually a male—is responsible for the more cumbersome, labor-intensive chores of pool/hot-tub maintenance, deep furniture cleaning, wood polishing, silver shining, hand-washing cars, gardening, and floor-to-ceiling window scrubbing.

Additionally, many families also employ an "ironer" that comes weekly or bi-weekly to press the entire family's wardrobe—including, but not limited to: children's clothes, tablecloths, fancy napkins, sheets, men's work shirts and slacks. Generally, the live-in help refuse to iron because they're afraid to "heat up their hands."

Amongst all domestic workers, tales abound of people that had spent hours ironing, got wet and developed facial paralyses as a result. Others, it was said, contracted a nervous twitch or full-blown pneumonia. Some got pregnant. Others grew a fifth extremity. It was a tough case to argue. Of course, for a handsome bonus, it was relatively easy to convince them otherwise.

This was all new to me when I first moved to Panamá from Costa Rica back in June of 2001 when Yordana was just six weeks old. When I was single, I often spent my Saturdays ironing a week's worth of wrinkled clothes, showered right after to go out dancing and never faced a medical emergency.

Aside from the ironing drama, countless times the nanny left without warning and I'd be without help for a week or two. Most certainly a cultural problem, many of my friends struggled with the same dilemma; namely, high turnover due to a lack of loyalty. In such a small town where everyone knows each other, social responsibilities are great and expectations, high.

Accommodations for childcare are unavailable at the local gyms, religious classes, parties, teas, or most any other venue where adults congregate.

As the general manager of Credomatic, Joaquín was expected to wine and dine colleagues visiting from other countries in the region, or he needed to schmooze a local client at dinner. He always brought me along. The other executives also brought their spouses. That's how it was. So for that reason, I depended heavily upon the domestic help to support our active social life.

But these women, the housekeepers, also had a thriving social life of their own. When their employers weren't home, they'd spend hours chatting, full-throttle, with each other from their personal cell phones, engaged in line-by-line comparisons of their respective jobs.

"I have a television in my room. Do you? After the baby falls asleep, I'm off-duty and can go outside and meet my boyfriend at the diner, can you? Oh, really? You get bonuses for all the holidays and on your birthday. Hmmmmm..." Wheels churning.

This is how these dialogues ensue and before you know it, your kids' favorite nanny or award-winning cook abandons you to begin working at the neighbor's house for a mere ten dollars more a month, a weekly conjugal visit or for an extra helping of meat.

It's unfortunate, and a pervasive problem. Moms socializing at children's birthday parties are hesitant to bring their nannies along—fearful she'll be "stolen" by another señora. Disloyalty on behalf of the domestic workers toward their employers is the norm. And these women are masters of deception.

As frustrating as it was to live with such ambiguity, the way many Panamanian women treated their housekeepers—like private property—disturbed me. They'd order them around like indentured servants and not permit them to converse much with outsiders. In fact, many of these ladies spoke of their domestic employees like an experienced jockey talks of his award-winning racehorse.

"Mercedes has been working hard all day polishing silver. I'm going to rest her tonight and take Juanita to help out at the party tomorrow."

"María was up all night with the colicky baby so today I'll give her a break and put her in the kitchen instead."

Oftentimes it was difficult to make, or rather keep, plans. These tenuous relationships caused me great anxiety. I was always on-edge, and worried that my helping hands would abandon me without warning. I wasn't the only one grappling with this issue; this epidemic spread throughout households with lots of children, mainly in the Jewish community.

In lieu of the caveat, "if God wants or God willing," after expressing a desire to do something or go somewhere, I'd qualify my intention with, "only if the nanny returns."

I had friends that had to cancel international trips, lost plane reservations, and missed weddings—all at the last minute—because the nanny returned late from her day off. Or worse yet, didn't come back at all after having committed to stay with the pets or kids or housesit during a programmed trip.

Lying is expected and practically culturally acceptable and therefore, causes widespread societal problems. Because when one's word carries little weight, relationships are strained at best. Herein lied—pardon the pun—the instability in which we lived.

Domestic employee-employer contractual agreements are unenforceable, a real joke. I always had to be a step ahead with a back-up plan. Many times, I had to fire someone for stealing something from my home or mistreating one of my children and it'd take a few weeks to replace her. Retreating into my comfortably familiar "alternative reality," I'd pretend to have a recruiting office across the street—inside the local cafeteria-diner, Niko's on Calle Cincuenta, or Fiftieth Street.

My desk was a weathered, brown vinyl booth adjacent to the kids' play area. There is where, over a piping hot cup of eighty-nine-cent coffee, I met and interviewed too many women to remember while my kids played joyfully in the germ-infested ball pit.

Most of the time, I had at least one person I could call on to lend a hand with the kids, help with the housework, or run errands should I find myself in a bind.

But like my vibrant social life, this interviewing, hiring, training and firing cycle devoured many hours of my time.

There you have it. Now you know why I had to keep calm in spite of the mounting pressure brought on by the discombobulated interaction, or verbal assault, described above.

What's fascinating is that I've developed my own repertoire of gestures and facial expressions, and everyone seems to be adapting well to the new nonverbal lingo. Like a traffic cop, much of the time I control the bedlam by signaling with a few basic hand motions and am understood.

It's not all bad news, though. I must confess there are benefits to this condition. For starters, I can sleep on my good ear and snuff out all nighttime, noise-related activity. Granted, this would be remiss of me when my husband travels, but when he's in town, I plug the right ear up tightly and can sleep through a Fourth-of-July bash in my living room.

Another plus is while talking on the phone. Because my hearing ear is completely covered and muffled by the physical phone—this doesn't apply if the phone is set on speaker—I'm able to enjoy a quick chat, unmindful of the noisy, background anarchy.

I poke fun at it as I do with everything else that upsets my balance, but honestly, at times I exploit this hearing loss to salvage my own sanity. When my desire to listen to someone had faded, or I'm unable to continue processing the sound of one's voice, I inconspicuously shift my body to position that person to my left. At a dinner party, for example, whoever is seated to my left invariably gets ignored.

It's far too exerting to converse with those to my left. If it's really worth the trouble, I've got to turn my head 180 degrees much like the actress Linda Blair in the 1973 thriller, The Exorcist. Inevitably, this unnatural and freakish neck-twist encroaches on the person's personal space. And because exhaling directly into a stranger's nostrils is not only terribly invasive, but outright rude, I only do this with those dearest to me. If pressed, to avoid such undesired intimacy, I'll overtly snub the person. If he or she appears perturbed, I have my coined apology.

"Oh, were you (still) talking to me? I'm so sorry."

"But I haven't heard a word you've said for the past twenty-seven minutes," sad eyes lend additional credibility to the authentic-sounding script.

"You see, I got this deficit and suffer complete hearing loss on this side," I point to my left ear and smile coyly, "...ever since I had a monster brain tumor extracted a short while ago." Note the last bit of information is only tacked on if I meet resistance from a begrudged person or oversensitive one.

I've yet to have someone fail to concede and take it personally. Talk about a perfect batting average! Essentially, I've justified my bad manners and have been granted the license to perpetuate this boorish behavior. What's more, not only have I turned this individual around, now she pities me.

Can you imagine somebody feeling sorry for me after all that I've divulged?

The truth is that this handicap does have its perks.

Yet in all seriousness, what's most endearing is how my husband confidently claims the role of translator. Although he's a little overzealous at times. Because upon our arrival anywhere, he'll proclaim to anyone standing within a fifty-yard radius, "...you've got to speak loudly and only into her right ear." Most of the people he addresses don't know us and were never planning to approach us for conversation in the first place.

But just to be on the safe side, his pre-emptive strategy was born out of necessity. It all began, I suppose, one evening at Darna—a popular local kosher restaurant in Panamá—where we always bump into lots of people.

Yair was but a few weeks old and an acquaintance came rushing over to say hello. I'm told she spoke directly to me. However, the story according to Joaquín goes that I stared ahead unresponsive, and with a frozen grin plastered across my face. At this point, my diplomatic husband intervened on my behalf and broadcasted, "She didn't hear what you just said; she's deaf on that side now."

I do read lips, by the way, yet for purposes of marital harmony and to stroke his male ego, I acquiesce and allow him to play the protective-husband role.

Overall, this deficiency gives me an excuse to phase in and out of conversations at will. It is a rather impolite habit, I admit, but oftentimes, vital to stave off that forever-lurking migraine. I never really miss out on anything. Whatever salacious details I fail to hear during the event, are squeezed out of my husband once home later that night. It makes for great bedroom conversation and I get the bonus of the play-by-play commentary.

So there you have it, the naked truth.

My inner world is fraught with self-deception and trickery. What's mentioned are all but a few of the many games played and tactics depended upon for self-preservation. It's the path of least resistance. Because sometimes not even this feisty bitch has the gumption to say, "Can you please repeat that...again?"

Pearls of Wisdom...

- o   Always have a mission.
- o   Do what you must to make life manageable in light of added stress.

13. *Exercise Routine Interrupted*

After giving birth to Yair, my miracle boy, and waiting the mandated six-week quarantine period, I jump-started my exercise routine. I began with swimming. My balance was still that of a sloppy drunk and I needed to help my brain with all the re-wiring. My face was still noticeably asymmetrical. My left eye was disproportionately large and irritated all the time; it guzzled half a bottle of lubricating drops daily.

Eye make-up had become ancient history. Anything and everything caused me unbearable eye pain. Most of the time, I patched it to protect it from the atmosphere. Leaving it exposed for aesthetic reasons wasn't worth the trouble. Driving and exercising with one operational eye and one hearing ear made for an extraordinary experience.

But it didn't matter much. I fought hard to adapt to my changing circumstance.

By this time, I had converted from a stoic robot to an aggressive warrior. Liberating myself from this sickly, fragile body, I felt like a snake shedding its ill-fitting, dried-out skin. I was resolved to regain control over what I still could, namely my fitness, emotional well-being and intellectual pursuits.

I relinquished power over the recovery of my facial symmetry and loss of hearing, as I knew both were beyond my control. Impatient by nature, I surrendered and decided to let time take its course with my face, but knew my hearing was never coming back.

On a streak to prove I was the same tenacious woman as before, I worked diligently to reclaim optimal health and physical prowess. Each day I engaged in some activity: yoga, calisthenics, swimming, strength-training, cycling, walking or running. Determined and focused, I disregarded all sound and logical advice any pragmatic human being would heed after having undergone two operations within a span of three months.

I wanted to captain the household fleet again. My husband had assumed most of the childcare duties for months and months without uttering a sigh of complaint. Okay, maybe occasionally, but I wanted to take some pressure off him.

I turned a room of my big, old house into a gym and started a personal training business. I wasn't certified with ACE, or the American Council on Exercise, or boasted of any other American certifications, but through decades of self-study and having been a gym rat my whole life, knew what I was doing. I felt empowered by my good fortune, having cheated death and demise, and had emerged fiercer and feistier than ever.

Now it was time to pass on the proverbial torch of inspiration and encourage others to get fit. I called all my friends and told them about my new business. Joaquín made me business cards.

Soon enough, I had clients at all hours of the morning coming for private and group exercise classes. Beginning at six-o'-clock in the morning, I taught swimming classes, circuit training, interval training and weightlifting.

My clients affectionately nicknamed me "My General" and I was all business. Admittedly, I loved pushing them to their limits to show them how much they could endure both mentally and physically.

Things were going well and my new gig reinforced my commitment to my own personal recovery, physically, from the surgery and emotionally, from Adam's death. Being fit infused me with an abundance of energy—energy I needed to chase after all these spirited kids of mine.

As I endeavored out into the community after so much time in seclusion, people often greeted me with a combined expression of shock and confusion. It seemed nobody really had expected the baby and me to survive the surgery. Remember, many came by the house before we left for New York to say a dramatic, final goodbye.

"Wait a minute," they certainly thought, "didn't she just lose her brother?" I could almost read their minds and hear them remark to one another.

Frankly, I didn't understand myself why I wasn't all curled up in bed bawling my eyes out while watching novelas.

Why wasn't I gulping down anti-depressants by the half dozen? Shouldn't I be home licking my wounds? Was I wrong for forging ahead with my life? Was it unprincipled to neglect the negativity for a while? Did that mean I didn't love my brother enough? Am I an insensitive bitch?

As mentioned earlier, in our small town, gossip ran rampant and lives were unhealthily intertwined. Your business was not your own. I had spent the first few years making an effort to fit in, and become accepted by this exclusive and private club of self-important people. Quite honestly, the most interesting fact about several of them was the size of their bank accounts.

But now, after all this, I had earned my right to care no longer what anybody else thought. I had just regained my freedom, my sensibilities, and my life. I had been in death's ruthless grip and escaped. So what if I slogged around like a war veteran suffering from post-traumatic stress disorder?

Indeed, I was a survivor and wore that badge proudly.

Most of the people that knew of me, and my string of hardships were sympathetic and just blamed my strange, manic-military-like conduct on being a crazy gringa. That was okay by me; I earned my reputation and always embraced the non-conformist label—even for my dealing-with-pandemonium tactics.

One early-morning, I am in my home gym preparing for a training session with one my most beloved, delicate clients. To get through an hour with her, I have to be 150% focused on doing everything feasible to prevent her from experiencing a minimal amount of physical discomfort.

The temperature of the room has to be pleasant, the pitcher available with fresh, cold filtered water, the music carefully selected. If I fail to make her experience painless, at the first opportunity, she'll cry injury and forfeit the entire routine.

One technique I always use to motivate and distract her throughout the hour is to engage her in non-stop chitchat. So with this in mind, it makes perfect sense that I have no idea what's happening within my own body.

"C'mon, you can do it. You're going to look spectacular in that gown, I know it," I exclaim. Suddenly, I feel a discharge pour out from down below and hiss under my breath, oh great, perfect time for the arrival of my monthly visitor. Maybe if I sit down for a minute, I thought, cross my legs really tight and do Kegel exercises, it'll go away and come back after we finish the class.

But no, that isn't what destiny has in store for me. I squirm and I wriggle. I contract my inner thigh muscles, and squeeze them together like a vice grip, while continuing to dole out instructions in spite of my dampening underpants. But it proves useless. Nature is not only calling, it's pounding on the door like an angry landlord ready to evict his delinquent tenants.

"Excuse me just a moment," I mumble, annoyed to have to

leave her mid-set of bicep curls. "I have to use the bathroom. Be back in a sec."

I don't give her any other directives because I plan to return immediately. I race out of the gym. My body careens against the walls as I bounce—legs sealed together—like a pogo stick up the steps toward my bedroom where my tampons and pads are stocked under the bathroom sink. Thrusting open the door with my two open palms, I slide across the toilet seat and instantly hear a strange sound.

Whoosh......

Did Joaquín leave the faucet on? Within two seconds, I realize from where this sound emanates.

I look down into a sea of red.

I am hemorrhaging.

I had better get this mess under control quickly before she finishes with both arms and then gets back on her cell phone, I grumble to myself.

If I am not policing her, she'll do anything to avoid exercise. She is that sneaky.

But things do not go as planned and I can't quite manage the situation as I had hoped. I jump into the shower, still unable to take my mind off my client.

What is she doing? How do I let her know what's going on?

Suddenly, I find myself ankle-deep in blood. I'm not in any pain, but just the sight of so much blood pouring out of me makes me light-headed. Nobody knows what is happening because I am hemmed into this bathroom with no cell phone or intercom system.

The door is shut, window sealed, and there isn't a soul within earshot. The kids already left for school, and Joaquín is in the kitchen—far on the other side of the house, grabbing a quick bite en route to the front door. He is running late for work. And the housekeepers are scattered all around doing their thing with the local radio station blasting in the background.

The sequence of my reaction to the dilemma is off-putting. It doesn't register right away. My mind still frets over the other pending issue—namely, how to keep control of my client. My very first thought is: Oh no! I left her all alone. I hope she doesn't injure herself. How's she going to know when it's time to stop?

My second thought seeks to alleviate my initial worry: Of

course, she'll stop. As soon as it hurts a little, she'll sit down and start making calls to friends. But wait...then her heart rate will go way down, she'll lose her groove, get cold, bored, and then...injury!

Finally, my mind processes all else and is ready to take notice of the crisis-at-hand. So...what the hell is going on here with me? Are my internal organs disintegrating and emptying out?

Miraculously, at that very moment, I hear the bedroom door fly open. My husband re-enters to grab the sports jacket he left splayed on the bedspread.

He must take notice of the water running inside the master bathroom.

"Bye, Mi Amor. Have a great day. Call you later," he shouts.

"Mi Amor, wait. Don't go yet. Please come here for a second and take a look at this." I don't want to alarm him, yet know if I sound too accommodating or nonchalant, he'll shut me down and accuse me of "cramping his fast-paced style"—and out the door he'll be. That's my husband, my beloved dynamo who keeps me on my toes. Focused and strong-minded to the extreme, he's always in a hurry. When he's ready to go wherever he needs to go, he's already halfway out the door—leaving you in the dust.

I listen to him sigh aloud, clearly annoyed by my attempt to thwart his getaway-plan. I pay attention to the hurried footsteps as he approaches the bathroom door. The door barges open and Joaquín pokes his head inside.

He furrows his brows, confused. "Why are you taking a shower when your client is here in the gym and you are in the middle of...?"

Then he catches a glimpse of my reflection through the glass shower door and sees me standing there covered in blood.

"Holy shit! What happened? We got to get you to..."

After a brief exchange of rhetorical questions followed by a slew of profanities, we attempt to develop an action plan under pressure. But when we put our heads together, we fuse into total idiots and can't even figure out how to turn off the shower faucet—effectively, a good starting point toward solving this problem.

Once we overcome this first hurdle, I wobble out of the shower. He yanks every towel we own out of the linen closet—hand-trimmed lace guest towels included—and shoves the entire wad between my legs. Then we quickly remove the towels so we can squeeze the mammoth-sized pads left over from the hospital between them.

We find the largest maternity pants I own and shove my twitching limbs into them to help stabilize the giant pad and keep it from jerking around while I walk. Clutching onto his arm for support, we make our way toward the front entrance of the house.

Casually and with a sheepish grin, I inch toward the exit and wave goodbye to my client. "I'm so sorry, but I got to go," I apologize politely. "I'm hemorrhaging and Joaquín is taking me to the ER. I should be back in a few. It's probably nothing so just stay here and finish your routine."

Not sticking to the schedule and leaving work undone really throws me. Especially with this client-friend who, more than anything else, requires a tremendous effort on my part solely to convince her to not cancel in the first place.

My dear client stands there dumbfounded. I continue to belt out orders as my husband and the gardener carry me like a sack of potatoes to the car. My husband hops into the driver's seat and with a shaky hand, turns the key to start the car engine.

"Just stick around," I suggest. "Nobody will bother you. Finish the set, do another fifteen repetitions of overhead shoulder presses, like the way I taught you last week, and then walk for twenty minutes on the treadmill at 3.5 mph. I've got tons of CDs in the black case on top of the glass table... put on any music you'd like. If you need anything else, ask the housekeeper in the kitchen. Don't let my little ordeal interrupt your routine," I conclude, now completely reclined and chilling in the front seat of the car.

Above all else, she is a friend and a very dear friend indeed, so that does not go over well.

She glares at me as if I had two heads and were legally psychotic. Then begins firing away nervously.

"What is happening to you? Who should I call? Do you have other clients expected to arrive? What should I tell them? What can I do for you? What do we tell the children? Do you need me to go with you? Oh my God, what is it NOW?" Then a malicious gleam appears in her eyes and she sneers, "Qué diablos! Estás encinta de nuevo!"[37]

I had no idea. I was taking birth-control pills. Certainly, I could not have been pregnant. On our recent travels to Mexico City, where Joaquín and I escaped for five days on business, I was

---

37 What the hell?! You're pregnant again!

admitted to a local emergency room with a severe intestinal infection. Maybe the critters were reproducing.

It did seem unusually "heavy" for a menstruation, so what could it be? Whatever it was, life had already trained me to stay calm in the face of uncertainty.

Defying all traffic laws, Joaquín speeds to the place Yair was born, the nearby Hospital Punta Pacífica.

The car comes to a screeching halt exactly three minutes later outside of the Urgencias[38] entrance. Once admitted, several benevolent nurses help me disrobe and pull a hideous floral hospital gown over my head. Immediately, they settle me into one of the beds.

A technician appears within seconds and wheels a large ultrasound machine toward me. With the help of the two nurses, they manage to perform the ultrasound right away to determine what the heck is happening inside my abdominal cavity. Well, lo and behold, they detect that indeed I am pregnant and in the beginning stages of a miscarriage.

This perplexed me because I had been taking birth control pills regularly. After giving birth to four children in five years, the last one being born just three months after brain surgery, the farthest thing from my mind was getting pregnant. Not even I am that much of a masochist. Plus, I had been showcasing my new and improved hard body, and certainly, wasn't ready to give that up.

Not a chance.

What's more unusual is for me not to notice I'm pregnant. It is unheard of. Usually I'm overcome with nausea and dizziness just days after conception. In fact, when first pregnant with Yordana, back in 2000, a bizarre phenomenon occurred that never again repeated itself, thank God, in any of my subsequent pregnancies.

I remember feeling so ill that even certain sounds provoked a full-blown vomit attack. Unfortunately, one of those sounds was that of my new husband's voice. Poor soul. God do I love him, but at one point, I told him he had to begin whispering if he wanted to remain married. This was only six months into our marriage. He thought I was all melodrama, but being newlyweds and not knowing any better, acquiesced. Neither one of us had a clue what normal pregnancy sickness looked like.

---

38 Emergency hospital entrance

Now seven years later, during this surprise-pregnancy-abrupt-miscarriage fiasco, when my Ob-Gyn Dr. Carbone arrived, together we ruminated over my whereabouts, overall health, nutrition and late contraceptive practices. He knew that in the past I had been remiss, notoriously forgetting a pill or two and then panicked, would double or triple up on them as soon as I remembered.

As I mentioned, months earlier my husband and I had been in Mexico City. I ended up violently ill, contorting with stabbing abdominal pains and glued to the toilet seat.

After I'd been admitted to a local hospital and the IV drip was in place, Joaquín and I realized that the culprit was from the "one and only time" I neglected to say "sin hielo por favor"[39] in my glass of Evian.

The attending ER doctor in Mexico City prescribed me a super potent anti-parasite medication so that I'd cure up quickly before flying back home a couple of days later. He ordered me to take one of these mini-bombs each day for a month, essentially to annihilate anything and everything inside my body.

Reflecting on it all, I reasoned that if in reality I had screwed myself up so badly from this internal fumigation, it was better this miscarriage was happening now and not later. Nothing inside of me could have emerged alive after such a vicious assault. And had something indeed survived this holocaust, it certainly would've arrived in bad shape. Really bad shape.

Nevertheless, this rationale gave me peace-of-mind and serenity. I exhaled and allowed myself to be carried, once again, by life's currents.

They rolled my gurney into the operating room. Everything was familiar—the pungent smells of antiseptic cleansers, the white walls, the subtle hum of the IV drip, tool trays, the scrubs, the mundane chatter. It felt like a second home already. I enjoyed the high from the nitrous gas and drifted off into deep slumber.

Dr. Carbone and his staff performed the standard D&C procedure, or Dilation and Curettage, to cleanse me out of any and all non-expelled, retained products of pregnancy. Shortly after I awoke in the recovery room, I prattled on, trying to impress the nurses with my recent, two surgeries.

"This was nothing compared to my brain surgery and C-

---

39 Without ice, please.

section," I bragged.

"Thanks to a reliable old friend named anesthesia," I whispered so nobody would hear me.

During the following week of obligatory bed rest, Father's Day arrived. After a beautiful family day at home full of handcrafted gifts and cards, of singing quirky, improvised songs off-key and videotaping the whole precious ordeal, we put the children to bed. We felt like the richest people in the world.

Later that evening, Joaquín and I snuck out to the backyard and settled into a couple of lounge chairs. With a glass of red wine in hand, we inhaled the calming presence in the nighttime air. The sky was endlessly clear, simply sublime. Clusters of stars sparkled in the distance. I was mesmerized gazing out into infinity.

Finally, we were appreciating life, with all its ups and downs.

The radiant crescent moon cast a brilliant glow that reflected off the still waters, illuminating the entire three-quarter-acre of surrounding landscape. We sat in silence for several long minutes, sipped our wine and listened to the nocturnal sounds of the residential cicadas, crickets, owls, and bats. Joaquín, who grew up in Costa Rica and journeyed often into the rainforest, aided me in the identification of each species and its accompanying signature cry.

When he got to the part about rodents, I asked him to change the subject. I preferred to remain blissfully ignorant about the various types of rats and opossums that scuttled around the property at night while we slept.

Instead, my dear husband began another discourse. This time he waxed philosophy about the disguised message embedded within all of life's adversities—one of my favorite, most compelling subjects. "I think everything that just transpired in the hospital with the miscarriage and all was a direct message from God, Mi Amor. He's trying to tell us something. I mean, what are the chances that you bomb your entire insides while taking the birth control pill and you still get pregnant? Maybe we aren't finished having children yet. Think about it, what if another child is destined to be born?" he trailed off.

I sat there quietly, meditating on his hypothesis, yet said nothing. Truthfully, this spiritual logic spoke to me. For even as a little girl, I always searched for the meaning, for the signposts, buried deep within each one of life's obstacles. Heck, I even sought to interpret every frustrating traffic-jam as a sign that I wasn't meant to arrive on time to wherever I was headed. This, of course, never sat well with any of my former employers. I guess you could say we were on the same page, only that he recognized it and verbalized it first.

Two months later, my womb had a new boarder, Baby Number Five.

Pearls of Wisdom...

- o Venture outside your "comfort zone" for solace and understanding.
- o Focus only on what is in your own control.
- o Develop hard skin in response to hurtful criticism.
- o Ponder the deeper meaning of life events and seek to decode messages sent by the universe.

14. *Anniversary Rendezvous &*
Miscarriages of Justice

Yes, my womb had a new tenant and this fifth pregnancy, as all others that preceded it, advanced just as ordinary as its forerunners. Other than the accompaniment of the usual concoction of nausea, spontaneous puking, dizziness and bipolar-like mood-swings, I was fine. I really didn't remember what "normal" felt like anymore, and had developed my own peculiar barometer for measuring discomfort.

During the first trimester, I sought to maintain my strict workout schedule—my antidote for stress—but it became more difficult as my body expanded in all directions and grew sluggish.

I attempted to continue training clients, but because this breed demanded an unforgiving level of customer service, which sometimes seemed to include me performing the actual exercises for them, I had to wind the business down. It was hard for me to attune myself to the pregnancy and slow down.

My children, ready for good news, beamed with excitement with the prospect of having yet another baby to play with. My husband had realized his entrepreneurial dream. After successfully putting together a team of co-investors, loyal to his vision, he started his own company. His office recently opened to the public and he was ecstatic. No more stifling supervisors; he was in charge of his own gig.

He had prepared the business plan years ago and was ready to move forward with his agenda when unexpectedly, I came down with a brain tumor. My sickness foiled his plans and disrupted his timeline, as all his capital was diverted directly into my head. But now, I was better.

The miracle baby arrived full of good health. We had pried ourselves loose from the grip of misfortune that had us by the throat. Our hearts soared as we anticipated all the good things coming our way.

Finally, after two solid years of heartache.

Finally.

Despite circumstances, we always fought to stay optimistic. At first, we faked it. This coping skill was to help us maintain our own fleeting sanity. Yet, more importantly, as we took note of the rippling effect our moods had on the children, optimism became the default mindset. If nothing more, it was for them. We wanted to set the example; there were no pity parties at our house. We were rebuilding our lives and emerging stronger and wiser.

The months flew by as Joaquín skipped off to work each morning and I busied myself with the house and children and withering exercise business. Five weeks prior to the baby's delivery, we planned an overnight escapade to Isla Grande, a remote island off the Caribbean coast. We'd be celebrating our eight-year anniversary. Having experienced so much together, it felt as though we'd been married fifty years.

The logistics involved in planning for one night away were astounding. There were three housekeepers sharing the responsibility of watching over the four children. The eldest was six and the youngest, Miracle Boy, just seventeen months. We put the gardener in charge of Moishy and Izu, our two big dogs, and overall security of the farmhouse with its countless points of entry. In many countries throughout Latin America, when home-dwellers leave town, it becomes high risk for a break-in. Much of the time, thieves study a particular family's comings and goings. If they're tipped off that the owners are going away, they'll pull a crew of thugs together, and exploit the opportunity to burglarize the property.

We had the same dear friend, Tía Bonnie, come spend the night and oversee the small battalion. We never would've considered sleeping out had it not been for our trust and confidence in her. A little war-torn emotionally, Joaquín and I felt very protective of our children and home, and had to cover all our bases if we were to lose ourselves in a night of wanton bliss...

Morning breaks. We bid farewell to the children as they board their buses for school, and are history. We arrive to the Pacific coast after a bumpy four-hour stretch of rutted dirt road punctuated by giant potholes and stones the size of baseballs.

We park the car in the designated ferry parking lot. It seems like an abandoned lot with nothing more a few stray roosters and chickens patrolling the area. After unloading our bags and locking the car, we walk down to the water's edge.

A small, dilapidated dock wafts in the shallow waves. A

battered canoe tied by a rope floats next to it with the word "Ferry" hand-painted on one side. The pungent smell of low tide is intoxicating. The air is crisp and rays of sunshine shoot down like laser beams from between the late-morning clouds.

We board the ferry and the captain, a thirty-something local with tanned muscles and a calming presence, paddles us across a gorgeous bay surrounded by a lush mountainous landscape. Rowing our way around several remote islands that seem to erupt spontaneously from the ocean floor, we finally arrive to a quiet and relatively uninhabited larger island thirty minutes from the mainland. On this semi-private island are two hotels, an old abandoned building and ours.

The captain beeps the makeshift horn as we approach the shoreline and a couple of hotel employees rush out to greet us and extend a hand as we lift ourselves out of the canoe. After we check in, we follow the hotel attendant up the steep steps that take us to our spacious room outfitted with authentic, rustic furniture and locally-made ornaments. We toss our bags onto the bed and rapidly change into our adventure gear. We plan to do some hiking around the island.

We fill up one large knapsack and a fanny pack with water bottles, snacks, cameras, extra garments, first aid supplies and toilet paper. Just in case.

I hold up pretty well during the three-hour trek, and keep pace with my husband despite my ballooning abdomen and urge to urinate with every step.

Returning to the hotel property sweaty and bruised from a few minor falls, we plunge into the property's impressive pool and indulge in a refreshing swim. Emerging re-energized, we're ravenous and ready to feast on anything they serve us, dead or alive.

The waiter arrives with two orders of grilled Sea Bass with lemon and drizzled butter. Mouths watering, we relish the tropical lunch and suck down the obligatory piña coladas that accompany the meal, and take notice of the exotic birds flying freely about this paradise.

The soft gentle breeze blows off the placid ocean waters and it doesn't seem real.

With each breath, we inflate with peace and tranquility, practically communing with our wooden chairs as the rum seeps into our bloodstream. We toast to capturing this serenity forever, and vow to return home and change the negative vibration that had orbited around us for years.

It is the dawning of a new era, a promising new start and I am certain we are on our way back up. Our new business is gaining momentum. I haven't seen my husband this content in years.

With a fierce determination to realign ourselves and improve our circumstances, we giggle about gearing up for another round of parenthood: diapers, nighttime feedings, chronic sleep deprivation—the whole kit and caboodle. The presence of an additional child will be undetectable, we decide. Because quite frankly, once you run out of hands and lap-space, three, four, five— it's all the same.

Climbing back up to our room cleverly built into the side of a small cliff, we collapse onto the bed, and doze on and off, tired from the drive, hike and spiked cocktails. We stare out the window and witness a magnificent sunset and catch sight of the sun as it dips beneath the ocean horizon for the night. I pull out the bottle of champagne that miraculously survived the treacherous journey here and we toast to eight years of marriage.

True to our initial vows, in such a short stint of time, indeed we had stayed together through "thick and thin." We revisit each anniversary, one by one, and reminisce how we celebrated—what we ate, what gifts were exchanged and how many children were born or about to be born at the time.

After a warm bath and a little time "vegging-out" in front of the television, we pass out.

I don't recall what time we fell asleep, but I do remember the sickening phone call that startled us awake. It was 11:37 pm. One of our closest friends, Loyra, the sister of Tía Bonnie, tells us something unconscionable.

There had been a break-in, an armed robbery, and all the adults in our house had been tied up and gagged at gunpoint.

Without catching her breath, Loyra immediately relays that by a miracle of God, the children remained unharmed.

They slept through the entire incident.

I assume Loyra doesn't want to tell us too much. She actually calls my husband's cell phone directly. Unbeknownst to her, I overhear her prep Joaquín, as she dictates word-for-word what he should relay to me.

Clearly, she fears I'll lose my mind and go into labor. His mincing of words does not make one hell of a difference. I read the anguish on his familiar face from the minute he answers the phone.

After a minute, he passes me the phone. Loyra wants to speak to me directly. Stunned and breathing consciously, I hold the phone in my sweaty palm and listen. As she speaks, my mind wanders, unable to focus. I glare out the large window onto a pitch-black ocean, and shiver as she reiterates the most critical piece of information, in the quiet eeriness of this frightful night.

"Darah, escúchame, póngame atención ahora. Los niños no fueron tocados y se quedaron totalmente dormidos durante todo el robo. Todos los cuatro están bien y todavía dormidos. No supieron nada de esto. Me entiendes, Darah? Darah, me entiendes?"[40]

I mutter out a breathless "sí."[41] She then confesses that the thieves had kicked in our bedroom door and swiped every piece of jewelry I owned—indeed, my entire stock. Plus, they pilfered many other irreplaceable, sentimental items, she says.

I took nothing but my simple wedding band on this adventure trip and left all else openly displayed above my dresser in an unlocked wooden jewelry chest. The only thing missing was a sign that read: "Welcome, please serve yourself." My hard-working husband had purchased the entire collection for me, little by little, over the last eight years.

When we married, I had no nice jewelry because ironically, years before we met, while vacationing in Key West with a friend, I lost it all. Foolishly, I had brought a satiny pouch with all my good, sentimental jewelry to the beach, unsure which pieces would combine best with my trendy, new sundresses.

Our first afternoon there, while sunbathing by the hotel pool, someone snuck into our room and snatched my pretty sack, visible atop the bathroom counter.

Am I just a magnet for good fortune, or what? What are the odds that something like this happens twice?

But this time was markedly different. This time I wouldn't

---

40 Darah, listen to me, pay attention to me now. The children weren't touched and they stayed totally asleep during the entire robbery. All four of them are fine and still asleep. They didn't find out anything about this. Do you understand me, Darah? Darah, do you understand me?

41 Yes

suffer much over the loss of these goods.

A gigantic exhalation of air escapes my lungs upon hearing the news. A single tear courses down my cheek. My extremities begin to tingle, and suddenly, I feel much, much lighter. I slip into a transcendental state. So much for material possessions, every molecule of my body chimes in unison. Instantly and willingly, I detach from all objects in exchange for the safety of my four precious children. A mysterious stillness settles over me.

Nothing else matters. And at that very moment, I comprehend Deepak Chopra's Law of Detachment on a cellular level. I get it.

Yet a little while later when my not-so-spiritual senses return, a flood of sadness washes over me. What really hurts the most are the captured family memories that we'll never recover because, according to Loyra, the crooks snatched our still cameras, video cameras and laptops. This pain is incalculable.

Here I am again, very pregnant and unable to hurl myself onto the floor recklessly or drown my sorrows in a bottle of vodka. Distressed and on the brink of a nervous breakdown, my body is ready to collapse. But once again, it's still not the right time.

When can I fall apart?

Helpless, we can't get off the island until the first canoe-ferry arrives at eight-o'-clock the following morning.

Joaquín tries to remain cool-headed and reassuring as we cling to each other during what forever will be remembered as the longest, most torturous sleepless night of our lives. We lay awake the entire night imagining the terrifying scene over and over again, re-enacting how it all went down.

The next morning we gather our things and set off at dawn, standing by the shoreline, waiting for the canoe captain to come for us. Our stooped shoulders and sullen faces mirror the heaviness we carry in our hearts. The hotel staffers are the same locals that had smiled upon us as we toasted in celebration the day before. Without uttering a single word, everyone senses something devastating has occurred. Not one of them dares to ask what it is.

We begin our voyage at sea at precisely eight in the morning and although we are rushed to arrive home, once back in the car, have to drive at a snail's pace as the potholes have transformed into muddy craters after last night's rains. Being eight months pregnant and already experiencing random contractions, we can't risk me going into premature labor here, in the middle of nowhere. First, we have to confront this behemoth awaiting us back home.

I don't know if I have it in me to face another calamity. I'm afraid to go home.

Pulling into the driveway hours later, we are received by a terrified staff of domestic help, a shell-shocked friend, a small posse of law enforcement officers and insurance adjusters. Astonishingly, the nannies successfully managed to get all four kids dressed and out the door for school so they were gone when we stepped inside.

They had distracted the children to the point that not one of the kids had noticed my beaten down bedroom door, muddy boot-prints or grimy handprints smeared all over the walls.

Kudos to these women who spent the entire night wide-awake, consumed with terror, having suffered severe physical pain from being thrown down, gagged, and bound with heavy rope. How they were able to feed the children breakfast, get them dressed and off to school was one performance worthy of an Oscar. No doubt.

As we pass through the threshold of our home, I shiver, sensing the ghoulish realism of last night's disturbance. Aside from the obvious traces of the robbery—the dirty handprints, filthy tile and overall disarray of the furniture and wall hangings—the house atmosphere feels violated.

That day I speak privately with everyone—one by one. Something doesn't feel right. One of the housekeepers, an easily distracted, seventeen-year-old city girl, who just started working for us three months ago, seems unusually calm and composed in stark contrast to the frazzled mental state of the others. Not only are the housekeepers prepared to quit on the spot, they also will require extensive therapy for their PSTD, or post-traumatic stress disorder; rightfully so, they are traumatized.

As we listen to each person's version of how the robbers entered freely and without force, because the house alarm had yet to be activated by that time of night—which it habitually is—it starts to smell like an inside job. If this is in fact the case, the mere thought of having a paid enemy sleeping under our roof and caring for our most treasured assets, our children, makes me sick to my stomach.

Who is accountable for this? I resolve to find out. I want blood.

My hunches inform me that this young kid has more street-smarts than she cares to reveal, or admit. She is very cool and poised indeed, wearing a silly grin while the others are visibly panic-stricken. Apparently, she was the only one, aside from the dogs, that slept soundly through the entire night after the burglars left.

The police officers and investigators on the scene had interrogated everyone that same night, in an attempt to determine how the intruders entered since there were no signs of forced entry. Everyone's accounts of how the break-in transpired proved incongruous. Learning of this amplifies our suspicions.

The nanny spins a sensational tale. She claims that when the doorbell rang—which curiously, nobody else seemed to hear—she cracked open the door to convey the message that we weren't home.

What? What a cockamamie story! Even my preschoolers know never to open the door or tell an outsider that Mommy and Daddy aren't home. Why didn't she just talk through the closed door?

We quickly discover that this theatrical performer made a quick phone call from my house phone, minutes before the thieves arrived. Immediately after the hooligans dashed off with the spoils, we'd been notified, she scurried off to make another hushed call.

The next day, three of the domestic workers, in addition to Tía Bonnie, are summoned down to police headquarters to give a formal statement—their version of what actually happened. Cooperating with the lead detective's recommendation, I discharge the live-ins one at a time, as they dart out in intervals. When one arrives, the other departs; it is a relay race of sorts. We prevent everyone from communicating with one another during this time for fear of conspiracy.

We trust no one and we have good reason.

I decide to send the young girl the day after all the others testify. I spring the news on her as soon as she awakens—fresh out of bed. With no time to think or scheme, I tell her to leave right away, denying her both breakfast and coffee. Thinking like a seasoned interrogator, I reason that by mid-morning, this famished teen will be singing like a canary to assuage the pangs of starvation and succumb to her caffeine craving.

I also know she hasn't a dime on her, so the plausibility of purchasing a quick snack is out of the question. Hunger will be a powerful motivator, I assume, based on the empirical data gathered from my daily observations—observing her wolf down food like a savage in my own home for three months.

As soon as she hurries off, when nobody is looking, I creep into her bedroom. A large mound of soiled clothing bulges out from under her bed. The stale air reeks of body odor and almost knocks me against the wall. A thick film of dirt, dust and grime covers everything in the room. Instinctively, I cover my mouth to keep from vomiting.

Soon enough, I stumble upon a small notepad buried under the heap of dirty laundry. Upon closer examination, I decipher her sloppy penmanship and leaf through her diary-type entries, lists of phone numbers and information about her love interest—her beloved, incarcerated boyfriend. I nervously rip out the pages crammed with scribbles, smuggle them back into my bedroom and pore over the papers.

At eleven that morning, I receive a phone call from the head detective, a woman who also smelled a rat from the minute she arrived at my house two nights earlier to investigate the crime scene and speak with all witnesses.

She tells me the girl, stomach rumbling and wiggling around uncomfortably, had implicated herself as the mastermind behind the felony. I thank her and tell her I will be coming down to the station that afternoon to show her some papers I confiscated that most certainly, will be instrumental to her conviction. She is delighted and says that with the girl's written confession, this case will be easy to close.

In a proper court of law, everything I found would've been enough evidence to convict her, at the very least, of being an accomplice to first-degree armed robbery. It's revolting that she volunteered to put my four innocent children in harm's way.

The kids trusted her. They snuggled up to her while watching movies at night. She had made beautiful braids in their hair. They even had entrusted her to help care for their pet turtle Rainbow that curiously, died the morning after the nanny presumably only changed the tank water.

Things start to coalesce. The muffled cell phone calls she continuously received for weeks prior to our departure, and the quick errands she always had to run spontaneously. Looking back, I remember always noticing her survey everything in the house, as though she had been taking notes. She'd retained a mental inventory of all our belongings including the respective locations of the goods.

Anytime anything went missing, she knew exactly where it was.

Many times, I'd catch her "cleaning" in areas of the house that weren't part of her assigned responsibilities. Her response was always the same: "Pensé que podría ayudar aquí tambien así que ya terminé con lo mio."[42]

It is a closed case. Of this, I am certain.

However, one small problem threatens to sabotage her almost guaranteed conviction. Despite the overwhelming evidence and un-coerced confession, the law is on her side in more ways that I could ever imagine.

We live in a third world country, her country.

Relatively backwards and overtly corrupt, Panamá's legal system and politics are a mess. It is powered by a host of self-indulgent, what's-in-it-for-me políticos and lawyers who interpret laws to best fill their pockets and befit those they care most about. Nepotism figures prominently in this game, a game of jockeying for power and wealth.

I gravely underestimated this girl when first hired. Her broken Spanish and dearth of academics belied an impressive depth of knowledge of the laws that protected her rights as a minor, knowledge that would rival that of any savvy lawyer. To her good fortune, apparently the judges—who thought more with their pockets than with sagely wisdom—concluded that not even a full confession could put this guilty under-aged felon in prison, or juvenile detention.

That's right. Despite her complete admission, her guilty plea, and the submission of incriminating personal records, the nanny swaggers out of the police station a free bird. She was a few months shy of eighteen and well aware that her government did not allocate funds for rehabilitation. This shrewd teen timed the offense well; her age and employment status, along with her imprisoned boyfriend's unfaltering guidance all converged to create the perfect crime.

I try earnestly and in vain to challenge the system and turn over additional evidence including records of the calls she made from my personal landline. At the very least, I want her held responsible for the injustice that invariably will disrupt and haunt

---

42 I thought I could help out here also because I already finished with my stuff.

many people's lives for months and perhaps years to come.

Then it hits me. We are the foreigners. Victims no less, this system will not protect us. The judges that heard the case had resolved to dismiss her entire confession because of her tender age. Moreover, once she's advised to present in a juvenile court, the assigned public defender convinces her to remain mute and not incriminate herself. She does, and gets a slap on the wrist with a breezy, two-day spree at the juvenile detention center.

The names and information of the four adult gunmen that she'd disclosed during her voluntary confession were obliterated once she was processed through the juvenile system. With the lead detective's hands tied, unable to prosecute this star suspect any further, the entire matter dies, right along with my sense of justice and desire to continue living in this Godforsaken country.

People tell me it is illegal for the two judicial branches of government to share notes, despite her glaring culpability.

I am enraged with this miscarriage of justice and feelings of powerlessness swallow me whole. I vow to take the law into my own hands. After all, the law failed us miserably. To add insult to injury, the so-called statute stipulates that even if she were convicted on charges of theft or child abuse—and let go, for example—I'd still have to pay her severance and liquidation.

My legal counsel consists of a few lawyer friends. They get straight to the point and forewarn me that any pursuit of justice will be exasperating and useless. The domestic employee, forever destined the victim, is assumed to suffer endlessly at the hands of the slave-driving, rich and ruthless employer.

This is a much deeper and ageless conflict than I ever could imagine—a real-life Pandora's Box.

The robbery is irrelevant.

It is a War of Classes.

Two days after her statement, her errant mother calls me. She doesn't ask about the shaken family or offer any help. Nor does she thank me for employing her inexperienced, reference-less daughter. The purpose of her call is to demand payment of her daughter's outstanding wages.

I unleash my wrath. "First she has to return my jewelry and other personal belongings," I threaten, "and only then, will I consider paying her the fifty bucks." Not surprisingly, her mother, totally disinterested and unapologetic unabashedly restates her hardworking daughter's rights to the remaining fifty dollars.

I slam down the phone and decide to take my chances, knowing very well that this irreverent reaction, my refusal to comply, could provoke the revocation of my residency, get me arrested or worse yet, hunted down by her other gangster chums.

I come to the realization that it's futile to care anymore.

The weeks following the break-in are eternal and not only are Joaquín and I unable to sleep, but also our three live-in employees find themselves awake at all hours of the night. Because of all the dysfunctional sleep patterns, the mood in the house degenerates into one of mistrust and I sense a total bailout. I know my people and the motto by which they live is: when things get tough, it's time to split.

Nevertheless, I play the game and listen attentively to their histrionics about why it isn't safe to continue working with "us people." After each one concludes his or her monologue, I successfully convince each person to stay until the next quincena, or two-week pay period. I also allude to a bonus for doing so, which in plain terms is no less than a flat-out bribe designed to entice them into not abandoning us just yet.

As if this is not enough to deal with twenty-six days before my delivery date, Joaquín and I talk about moving again.

After eight years of fighting the conventional system that dictates people "of society" ought to live in guarded high-rises, now we are prepared to exchange our acre lot for a life of apartment confinement.

Security has become the overriding priority. Our countryside dream, shelved for now. Reality is this house is old, dilapidated and at present, termite-infested. It lacks many security basics; it has too many off-track sliding glass doors, windows with broken or missing panes and rusted, inoperable locks unable to stymie the entrance of intruders. It is also missing the tall, imposing fence that usually runs the perimeter of a huge property in Latin America, serving to demarcate the space and safeguard it from wary street-side onlookers.

Another problem we face is an overrepresentation of construction workers that prowl the neighborhood at all hours as low-rise apartment buildings spring up around us. A by-product of local municipal corruption is that the zoning laws existing on the books rarely are enforced; in no time, buildings will surround our home. Many times over the past several months, I caught these guys shamelessly peering into our property as they gulped down lunch perched atop an adjacent, unfinished building. Perpetually under the microscope, we feel exposed. It's terrifying.

Additionally, we'll have to seek out alternate homes for the two huge dogs we brought as puppies from Costa Rica and have been raising since 2000. Letting go of them is not going to be easy, especially for Joaquín.

Nonetheless, once again, we are on the move and hustling to make last minute, life-altering decisions.

Pearls of Wisdom...

- o Fake optimism until you really feel it.
- o Use anger to fuel your actions in a positive direction.
- o When all else fails, know when to walk away.

15. *Goodbye Dogs, Welcome Baby Dalia*
& Hello Apartment Living

Spring, 2008

Here we are in the first week of April—just three weeks away from the due date of our fifth child. We decided to move again. Fate was pulling us in this direction—it was not of our own choosing, I assure you. I loved this house and the lifestyle it represented. We would've nixed the idea, but in light of the recent break-in robbery and deterioration of the house itself, we elected to bite the bullet, conform, and move into the ghetto—the Jewish ghetto in Punta Paitilla.

Thanks to my colloquial Spanish, psychology background, and knack for monetary enticements, a.k.a. bribery, I was able to convince the housekeepers to stay put right on through the programmed move, scheduled for two weeks—give or take a few days—after the birth of our final baby.

Joaquín and I roamed the streets of Panama City daily during lunchtime, with and without realtors, in search of the perfect apartment or condo for a family with an aversion to apartment living. Fun!

Because of the anticipated living arrangements, we knew our two beloved canines would be unwelcome and unfit for such a sedentary, enclosed lifestyle. They had grown accustomed to patrolling a sizeable garden since we adopted them both, and were confirmed outdoor pets.

Joaquín put ads in the local newspaper announcing that we were looking for a good home for our "canine-boys." He was determined to interview the prospective dog owners in our home to see how they'd interact with our guys. We weren't accepting money or payment of any kind for the dogs; we only were interested in finding good people that would treat them well.

I disliked the newspaper idea at first, not wanting to introduce strangers into our home, but he assured me that he'd screen them extensively via phone first before inviting them over.

The dogs had to exhibit interest in a potential new owner, too. And nobody can sniff out goodness like a dog. They have a sixth sense, I believe.

I remember the last time I relied upon the local paper for a business transaction. It was the only time I sought to purchase this way in Panamá. Just like my ill-fated trip to Ecuador, once again, I trusted my instincts and heeded to my body language, and avoided real trouble. Although it didn't start out too well, everything ended alright. It was only the in-between time that nearly cost me a great deal of collateral damage—mainly, my life.

It is early July 2001. With a newborn in tow, and promising new career for Joaquín, we just moved to Panamá from Escazú, Costa Rica. I have a month's practice driving the first of many roving battleships—a stunning grey Range Rover—and am in the process of familiarizing myself with the hostile roads and lawlessness of driving on them.

We need a desk. Everything we see at the local boutique furniture stores is too posh and delicate or too drab and befitting for an office, not for the home. We peruse the newspapers and classified sections. There's an advertisement for used desks —old school desks, doctors' office desks, and all sorts of solid wood, practical desks. The ad states that the owner had a warehouse full that he'd purchased from businesses that went belly up.

Interested, I call for directions. A young girl answers the phone and makes the appointment.

The following day I set out for the office, feeling proud of my burgeoning independence as I cover unfamiliar terrain in this new land. When I arrive to the office, I have to park street-side and duck my head to enter the office through an oddly low-hanging storefront door frame.

Everything is dreary and brown. Dated brown paneling canvases the walls, the flooring is a tattered brown carpet and there is no air conditioning—just a couple of dingy pedestal fans that keep the hot, muggy air circulating.

The so-called receptionist sits on a swivel chair behind an old teacher's desk. Three objects sit atop the counter, positioned in a linear formation: an old-fashioned rotary phone, a pen and a notepad. Nothing more. Strange, I think, but nonetheless, ask her the whereabouts of the collection of desks.

She takes my name then up and leaves to look for the man selling the desks. A few minutes later, she returns and introduces me to a tall, husky figure, a middle-aged man clad in cheap office attire wearing a mischievous grin. "Come with me outside," he says. "We can talk better there." I trail him outside and he points to his car. "You can ride with me and we'll go together to the warehouse."

I politely refuse, insisting on taking my own car.

The building is just a few blocks away near the center of town. I follow him into the empty lot. The building's façade looks weathered, yet its colonial trimmings remain somewhat charming. The man inserts a long key into the keyhole then pushes open the heavy metal door. The hinges cry out in protest as if they're awakened for the first time in years.

I follow him into this dark, dank chamber. He flips on an industrial sized switch that does little to illuminate this vast, almost windowless space—with the exception of a single high window—bordered by thick concrete walls. No drywall construction here, I notice.

We are unmistakably alone.

"Where are the desks?" I ask. My heart pounds inside my chest. My palms and underarms instantly soak with perspiration and my hair stands on end. As he answers me, another region of my brain powers on. The hypothalamus, in close association with the limbic system of the brain, activates the sympathetic nervous system—more commonly known as the flight-or-flight mechanism. It serves as an early warning system. My senses acute, my eyes hone in on the lock inside the door. It is one of those heavy security doors I only have seen outside of the Unites States—one that you need a key to enter and a key to exit. He inserted his key into the interior side of the keyhole after we entered.

It hangs there.

Still.

And captures my attention.

"Venga por aquí arriba c-o-n-m-i-g-o. Allá están todos los escritorios,"[43] with an outstretched arm he motions toward the creepy stairwell encrusted in cobwebs in the back of the room.

At that moment, my body screams, "Now or never!" I could almost read tomorrow morning's lurid headlines: Naïve Gringa Follows Serial Rapist into Abandoned Building.

"No thanks. I must go now," I race toward the exit, turn the

---

43 Come with me upstairs, this way. Over there are all the desks.

thick key, thrust open the cumbersome door and bolt to my car. Fumbling for the car keys, I manage to find them quickly and turn on the ignition. I peel out of there, tires screeching, and catch a glimpse of him in the rear view mirror—palms turned up toward the sky and brows furrowed in consternation.

Breathless, I phone my husband and relate what had happened. "I'm glad you're okay, Mi Amor. You have to be careful. We just will ask the local carpenter that's making our office furniture to build something you like."

Joaquín was working and had that I'm-not-taking-you-seriously voice. Surely, he thought I was overreacting. But that didn't matter.

Because had I not listened to that inner voice, a foreign voice that seemed to come from a deep, hollow cavern far, far away, most certainly, I wouldn't be here right now, writing this book.

With that in mind, of course you can understand why the whole notion of placing an ad in the newspaper distressed me. Even though we were the advertisers, it was arguably just as risky because of our willingness to receive people in our home.

My husband was visibly heart-broken that Spring of 2008; better yet, he was distraught. Each time he glanced in the dogs' direction, he'd sigh loudly and shake his head back and forth, knowing that at any moment they'd cease to be part of our family. These dogs were his life. While I was busy having babies and caring for them, Joaquín stayed devoted to the dogs, consciously spending quality time with them each evening after work "because Mama," he'd say, "is simply too busy to care anymore."

His level of commitment was admirable. I never had seen anyone so attached to an animal. He was accosted by guilt, feeling he was abandoning them. Yet there was no alternative. Two active eighty-pound watchdogs that passed the day chasing squirrels and iguanas couldn't be cooped up indoors all day long. It wouldn't be fair to them.

Nonetheless, the first parental prospect for one of our sons was a big-breasted, aspiring model that came to the house specifically to meet Izu—our gorgeous and energetic white American Labrador Retriever. She fell in love with him instantly and the feeling was mutual. Because Izu lacks discretion and is won over by anyone with food, we knew he would not suffer much separation anxiety provided she had a stocked fridge. Indeed, she assured us that her favorite pastime was staying home and renting movies. When she did, she liked to nosh next to her pet curled up on the couch. Score for Izu.

The other dog, our treasured Moishy, was the one we had rescued first-married in Playa Jacó, Costa Rica from a dilapidated shack inhabited by a posse of crack heads. He was already up there in years and predictably, wouldn't be an easy "sell."

Moishy was not royalty. He didn't have any papers or an authenticity chip demonstrating his pedigree like Izu had. Moishy was a callejero, a mutt. A curious fact about Moishy is that his testicles never descended, and therefore he was often mistaken for a female. But this never rattled his self-confidence; he was braver and nobler than the biggest-balled male I ever met. Dogs included.

Despite his righteous character, as we'd anticipated, Moishy was unadoptable. The only person willing to take him, because he knew the heart of this animal, was Virgilio, the live-in male worker. Virgilio lived at our house six days a week and was very poor. He admitted that Moishy would be tied up all day, tethered to a tree. His large, un-fenced-in property was home to many venomous snakes, aggressive geese and countless rodents. And although he wasn't a killer, Moishy liked to hunt for sport. With us, he'd been sheltered from such dangers and free to roam, unleashed, in our well-maintained yard.

However, time was not on our side, and we had an entire house to pack, with much to sell and donate. We were pressed to turn our patio furniture, backyard and pool supplies into cold, hard cash.

So we paid Virgilio a handsome severance including monies to hopefully spend on Moishy's food and visits to the veterinarian, thanked a most gracious Moishy for years of good times—of protecting our family—and wished for the best.

Over the years, Joaquín and I spent much time musing about the interactions between our two faithful companions. We laughed ceaselessly as we mimicked them with our contrived doggie-voices. Most of the time, we knew exactly what they were thinking. We studied and analyzed their behaviors like two geeks in a psych lab and came to understand them, as a parent instinctively knows his or her child.

Now it was time to say goodbye. For good. This long chapter of our lives as dog-owners was coming to an end. My heart sank and I feared for my husband's fragile state of mind. He had grown way too emotionally attached over the years and without much time to prepare mentally, his original "boys" soon would disappear into the past.

Dalia was born on April 29, 2008. Mom flew in just after the birth. I had insisted on a VBAC, vaginal birth after Cesarean, and Dr. Carbone knew my body would be able to withstand it. Fortunately, the recuperation was fast and easy and just seven days after delivery, I was home packing up our closets. With Mom's help, and nursing newborn Dalia in tow, we made several daily trips to the apartment to set up the kitchen and all the closets—the five kids', our own, and the two linen closets.

We worked non-stop for eight consecutive days, before contractually having to move out of the house. We jetted back and forth between the house and the apartment to pack, unpack, and meet potential buyers interested in what we had for sale. The baby lay asleep in her infant carrier during most of this time, and I only took her out to breastfeed, burp her and change diapers.

The apartment building, called the Mirage, was luxurious with an exquisite all-marble entranceway. The unit we rented was approximately 4,500 square feet, and boasted of four bedrooms, four and a half bathrooms, in addition to the maids' quarters. After signing the contract, we discovered that the present owner of the apartment, a Cuban-American named Guido with loose ties to Panamá and Colombia, was on Interpol's Most Wanted list. Fabulous.

Everything was hush-hush and the specifics were hard to come by. Nobody was talking. Thus, we weren't quite sure for what criminal activity he was internationally hunted. What most stood out in my mind, though, was the introductory two-hour phone conversation he and I had, where he blathered on about his ingenuous, intricate system of locks and bolts and hidden cameras and monitors.

Apparently, the realtor conveyed that we had suffered a break-in robbery recently. Maybe he was trying to reassure me. Instead of feeling safe, the entire time he yapped about his $100,000 investment in security upgrades, I wondered what compelled him to erect such a fortress.

Who is after this guy? Will they come after us, too once moved-in?

He lived in Miami, under the same roof as his alleged soon-to-be ex-wife, who proved to be a real piece of work. This Colombian woman almost foiled the entire move four short days before our scheduled move-in date. Seemed that she had caught wind of the impending occupancy late in the game, and one evening fired off a slew of threatening emails to my husband. She claimed that the apartment was in her name and hers alone and forbade us to live there.

"You and your family dare not step foot inside, or I'll contact the authorities," she threatened.

Panicked, we immediately contacted Guido. He never lost his cool—perhaps the sign of a career crook?—and brushed it off, cavalierly assuring my husband that his wife had no legal recourse and alluded to some obscure mental illness. Who knew what we were getting ourselves into, our lives intersecting with these convicts?

Joaquín and I were both freaked out, but by this time were halfway settled into the apartment and the new tenants were days away from moving into the farmhouse. We had no choice but to take Guido's word. Because God knows, if push came to shove, we couldn't entrust our safety to the powers that be. In spite of the established property laws and our legal rights as tenants, we knew better than to expect the system to uphold them. If anything would need to be resolved, it'd have to be through other means, outside the scope of the law and due process.

Fortunately, we never had to exploit such extralegal pursuits of justice.

The lifestyle we led once converted to apartment dwellers was excruciatingly public. No more privacy. No more anonymity. No more personal outdoor space.

Is this how the Jews in all these buildings live out here?

Everything was shared, communal property. The on-premises gym was outfitted with state-of-the-art equipment, and the other facilities such as the racquetball court and pool area were top notch. But that never impressed me.

Several times the kids goofed off and got lost riding up and down the elevators. Each time they wanted to play outside in the fresh air or inside the kids' activity room, an adult had to accompany them to the area social.[44]

I was nursing and busy at home with my last of kin, my infant daughter, and the nannies were the ones that typically escorted the children to the play area. Soon enough a pattern emerged and they wouldn't bring the kids back for hours. Not only did I not get to see my kids much after school—eventually I schlepped the baby to the communal social area to nurse her out in the open so I could keep an eye on the others—big problems surfaced from the daily nanny-to-nanny encounters.

For starters, there was no bona fide supervision of or interaction with the children going on during these three-to-four-hour sabbaticals, I quickly realized. Because soon enough, the nannies discovered that the super-wealthy neighbors, who also owned beachside chalets or cabins high up in the mountains, paid higher wages than we did. And from that moment on, not one day passed that our trying-to-blackmail-us housekeepers failed to remind us of their colleagues' employment benefits and bonuses that included extensive travel.

We couldn't compete with that and didn't even try. Guido was already pressing to renegotiate for more rent money—perhaps to pay off lawyers or hit men?—and soon enough, we were doused with the reality that we were in over our heads with this whole upscale apartment living.

I continued to pander to the housekeepers to keep them returning after their days off, and remained positive because Joaquín's new venture was promising and the future looked bright.

After all, we'd put in our entire net worth and the investors had poured loads of cash into Joaquín's creation. They undoubtedly loved him, so what could possibly go wrong?

Pearls of Wisdom...

- o When out of your element, modify your ways to blend in.
- o Listen to your body when it alerts you that something is not right.

---

44 Social area: the floor that contained the building's pool, play and exercises quarters.

16. *Dreams Devoured & Looking for Home*

Stupid girl. Lots can happen.

It's September 2008, and we've been living in La Mirage since the fifteenth of May of this same year. Joaquín's business—a financial supermarket—opened eleven months ago in October 2007. Without warning, Mark Joe Ferrari sent in his wrecking crew to dissolve the company and kidnap the brainchild Joaquín painstakingly delivered alongside his less-visible, technical partner.

I'll never forget the paranoia that snatched Joaquín's sense of reason. He wasn't himself. One evening, he comes home flustered and while pacing up and down the bedroom, maniacally rattles off numbers of accounts and life-insurance information should Mark Joe choose to come after him with a squad of wayward cops. He is convinced they'll sequester him off the streets mid-day and throw him in jail.

But this was simply illogical thinking. My husband did nothing wrong. He started up a legitimate business with the backing of a wildly successful national bank, and worked long hours to launch it out of the red as quickly as possible. And he was almost there. Just about to break even.

That's it.

But it seems that this rookie was in the line of fire. Intimidated by his influential uncles, Mark Joe desperately needed a scapegoat. So he went amuck to clip the wings of a thriving business just as it had begun to soar.

In retrospect, the business was not foundering. It was a new endeavor, yes, and about to break even. Prior to its spontaneous dissolution, there had been no forewarning, no meetings called, and no call to action. Absolutely no strategies were implemented to avoid this sudden death. In fact, no conversation existed at all between my husband, the CEO, and the investors.

Barely eleven months had lapsed since its inception, and the young rookie panicked. Period. Regrettably, he was the one with the deep pockets, and the one with the least amount of experience in making the big league decisions. But he was born into the right family, a very rich and very powerful Syrian Jewish family, so he scored the coveted job of general manager, a.k.a. funds-dispenser.

The story goes that his uncle, the boss, grilled him during that notorious Board of Directors meeting—a meeting that resembled little more than a family reunion—about the new business rookie-boy chose to sponsor. Yet instead of defending his decision to fund Joaquín's business idea, this neophyte sheepishly called it quits, cowering like a scolded child before the probing panelists.

Most definitely, it didn't help that he knew next to nothing of the day-to-day business operations and therefore, was incapable of delivering explanations as to what was evidently no more than the normal growth pattern of a start-up. He also neglected to tip off my husband in the process. Joaquín not only wasn't invited to partake in these closed-door meetings, he never was made privy to any of the information exchanged during them after the fact.

Had Mark Joe paid attention to the operational details, he would've understood the complexities of this enterprise. It just was beginning to take off, and skyrocket out of the red zone. However, Mark Joe never did take anything other than a superficial interest in the business enterprise. So his fear-based decision made impulsively and under duress, was the catalyst for our own personal financial devastation.

We had nearly emptied our bank accounts, investing our entire net worth into our dream. And to this day, not one red cent of our money ever was returned to us.

Curiously, Joaquín had anticipated this rift since Mark Joe first neglected to return his calls. The systematic breakdown of communication began weeks before.

"The guy is just overwhelmed by his other managerial responsibilities. You're being paranoid, Mi Amor," I dismissed my husband's concerns.

I was clinging onto one defining statement, and one only, that Mark Joe had made at the very beginning, before they solidified the actual business plans.

"I don't need to understand any details about the business, Joaquín; I'm betting on (you) the horse," he had assured Joaquín, verbatim, months before, when he agreed to help fund the project.

Mark Joe had shown staunch support for Joaquín from the get-go. They seemed to have taken a mutual liking to one another. In my state of blissful naïveté, that was enough to seal the deal and make it work.

Man was I mistaken.

And in the two months that followed that notorious Board of Directors exchange, our lives were altered forever. Our living expenses devoured the rest of our humble savings. Eight years of diligence and hard work and all we had to show for it vanished. We fell into bankruptcy and had no choice but to find our way back to my native United States.

In the immediate aftermath, our options were limited. There was nowhere to go in this small town. We couldn't stop the bleeding, even with a modest, but steady stipend from our wonderful and supportive rabbi who rallied funds together to help keep us afloat and out of the streets until Joaquín found another income stream.

However, it was too late. When Bogota[45] fell through, for no apparent reason after a seemingly triumphant interview with the company's founder and CEO, intuitively we knew Joaquín had been slandered—his professional reputation stained. Right away, it seemed as though the rich and powerful Ferraris who run things in the banking industry surreptitiously blacklisted Joaquín.

Our collective angst reached a fever pitch.

"Go out and tell your side of the story, Mi Amor," I urged my husband time and again, my fists clenched and ready to do battle for him. "You have nothing to be ashamed of; if you don't protect your good character, nobody will do it for you and people will believe whatever they hear."

Yet my deflated husband's good standing plummeted in a matter of weeks. His self-esteem took a big hit. Nobody likes to feel intimidated. We were dealing with a sprawling and highly influential family who had high-ranking government officials tucked inside their deep back pockets. These people were connected, loaded, unscrupulous, and had presence everywhere around the world. We hesitated because we didn't quite understand the reach of their power.

Moreover, because their surname carried so much weight, when Mark Joe originally decided to co-invest in the business, we believed we hit the jackpot. Ironically, we felt protected by that very last name that came to haunt us during the remainder of our

---

45 More on this to come.

days in Panamá.

To this day, we question whether we should've done things differently. Should we have been brazen and publicly defended ourselves against this family, this immoderately influential machine, that knew far better than we did how to navigate (and manipulate) the system? Who knows? At the time, we were dispirited, caught off-guard and humiliated, and chose to suffer quietly. We knew our place. Once again, we were the foreigners, the pariahs.

Nonetheless, I think if we could go back and do it differently, we would. Because at the end of the day, when excessive opulence and intemperate power subsides into moderation, or fades away entirely, all we have is our word. If we cannot speak our truth even amongst those too closed to listen, and despite our own fear of rejection, we'll never achieve anything—most specifically, peace of mind.

Thankfully, a single ray of sunshine penetrated through this acrid cloud of desperation and eventually, emotionally outweighed the ill will, and we took umbrage in it: our clean conscience. Not once did we compromise our sound ethics, and believe me, many times, we were tempted.

We fled Panamá disheartened, unable to save our tanking reputation and afraid for our future, for our lives.

That is the lone, untainted truth.

I abhorred the pressure these titans silently exerted over my husband's career, over the scope of our livelihood. Witnessing the slow demise of Joaquín's now-shattered dream, and the resulting plunge of his self-confidence tore me up inside.

There was no elixir to cure me of my indignation. Too much irreparable damage had been done.

Once things turned sour, I knew we no longer belonged. Panamá suddenly became claustrophobic. Reinventing ourselves would have been impossible in this fishbowl.

I wanted out. Joaquín did, too.

It was time to pack up and go home.

So tell me, where's home now?

Pearls of Wisdom...

- o If something seems too good to be true, it is.
- o Get out of it (the job, relationship, situation, etc) before temptation gets the best of you and you compromise your ethics.

17. *A Family Flees*
& My Journey Through Hell

In September 2008, Joaquín's business, Money Solutions, nose-dived as soon as they pulled the plug. Instantly, life as we knew it disappeared. As mentioned before, we didn't know where to land.

Friends and family discouraged us from relocating to the US. The country was in the throes of a full-blown recession and Florida, specifically South Florida, bemoaned one of the highest unemployment rates in the nation.

Yet sadly, we had nowhere else to turn. We ran out of money and had to be out of our pricey apartment by the thirteenth of November. We couldn't last another month biding our time to see if something else popped up.

So with no more than a few weeks' notice, less than two months after the disintegration of the business, we decided to uproot ourselves. We sold some stuff, donated a bunch, packed up a few suitcases and stowed the rest in a rented storage unit. We withdrew the kids from school, made copies of all their medical, dental and academic records.

And fled.

November 13, 2008, is the life-altering date forever engraved in my mind. Early that morning, we set out to start life anew, anonymously and far away. We headed to a vast, yet familiar land, to a place we had refused to call "home" for many years.

We migrated all the way to the front doorstep of my mother and her husband Warren's small town home, to reside indefinitely. We arrived like modern-day refugees coming to the free, new world in search of a brighter future. But at that moment, we felt demoralized; our future was painted black. And this blackness grew even darker and thicker the second I boarded the airplane with my three youngest children.

Looks of disdain come at us from all directions—even before we take off. "Sit down. Look through here," I toss my purse at my two-year-old son. Another twenty minutes on the runway plus three hours in the air. I repeat my mantra: *God I love my kids. God I love my kids. God I f-u-c-k-i-n-g love my kids.* I clench my fists. My jaw tightens. Sweat pours out of me. One hour in and already, this journey is more exhausting than that mini-triathlon I completed in 1998.

"Ma'am, they're blocking the aisles."

"Sorry," I snarl in a barely audible whisper, "I have to change his diaper."

I latch onto the soft forearm of the two-year-old gyrating at my side and yank him into the bathroom, attempting to squeeze all four of us inside. Hold my baby. Give my four-year-old a cracker. Dammit people. Do something.

Nothing. I am on my own. Stay cool, Darah. Grace. Grace, under pressure. My face is frozen and void of expression. I fight back tears and the desire to send everyone to hell. Yet without flinching, I disguise my despair and silent rage behind a mask of stoicism.

Weighing in at barely 105 pounds, a darkness that cannot be erased by a couple nights of good sleep encircles my dry, bloodshot eyes. In fact, these shadows are so black and embedded into my skin, it looks as though my skin were stained with permanent ink, like one of those trendy make-up tattoos. My brows appear knitted together from the constant furrowing and my hands quiver from too much coffee and a lack of food. My life just crashed to the ground a few days ago.

It is November 13, 2008, and I am on an American Airlines international flight from Panamá destined for Miami. Each time I took this unpleasant flight in the past, without fail, I subsequently swore off American Airlines for good. The flight attendants on this particular route seem to have grown increasingly inattentive and embittered over the years.

Good customer service has become some vestige of the past. Somehow though, through our credit card affiliations, we remain roped into a dysfunctional marriage with them, wedded together by a points program from which we cannot divorce ourselves. Nonetheless, we reluctantly travel on this airline time and again, and consistently encounter crews of burnt-out, apathetic people that make flying a most miserable experience.

November is a gorgeous time of the year to be in South Florida. It's sunny, breezy and temperatures typically hover around the low seventies. It's the change-of-seasons time when the streets and beaches burst with visitors from the cold-weather north. Everywhere people are exercising outdoors and the approaching holiday excitement is palpable. The entire metropolis pulses with electricity.

Unfortunately, we aren't in the right mindset to appreciate such seasonal enthusiasm or climate-related pleasures.

We are in hell.

Joaquín is on another flight, on another airline, and traveling with our eldest children—two girls, ages five and seven. We had to cash in on six frequent flyer tickets before they expired. There was no option but to split the family up. He is on the Central American airline, Taca, where the customer service never declined in direct correlation with the floundering economy. I was supposed to travel with the girls. They have self-control; the little ones do not, and we had agreed that my frazzled state of mind was unsuitable to keep three babies in check.

I messed up big time. A nervous wreck making the flight arrangements a few weeks earlier, my shuddering fingers inadvertently typed in the names of the two boys along with my own. After clicking "enter," I immediately realized the colossal mistake I'd made. Frantic attempts to call and email the airline customer service department and re-do my reservations were in vain.

This trip to Miami marked the beginning of what we erroneously assumed to be the end of a litany of catastrophes that had befallen us for years—catastrophes that, as you've read, challenged our ethics, toyed with our sanity and seized our senses. Relentlessly.

Returning to the moment, as we begin to deplane, the nightmare continues. Controlling the three rambunctious kids—ages four, two, and six months—while I scoop up all the bags, almost sends me into a tailspin. With my baby girl perched on my bony hip, I wiggle my way through the narrow aisles. While deplaning, I drag my two little boys behind me. We stand just outside the entrance for a good ten minutes waiting for the double-stroller to ascend from the plane's storage area. The kids are antsy and the same nasty flight attendant eyes us and unleashes more of his wrath.

"Why do you people travel with young children in the first place?" he hisses.

I can feel the adrenaline pumping through my veins. My heart races and my face turns crimson and hot. If I were traveling alone, perhaps in another time or place, I'd pounce all over this insensitive, antagonistic misery like a tigress defending her cubs. Yet thoughts of intimidating cops and glistening handcuffs flash through my mind and hold me back, and keep me from acting on impulse.

You people? Who is "you people?" Since when is it illegal to travel by air with young children? Should I have sedated or muzzled them beforehand? Maybe I should have put them up for adoption before leaving. Better yet, we should have opted to drive through the treacherous terrains of Central America, Mexico and entire continental United States. Yeah, we could have made it here easily months later, provided we weren't robbed, kidnapped, or killed first.

Prick.

Once through customs, my overloaded cart careens recklessly towards the large, sliding glass exit doors. Piled up high are backpacks, totes, duffels, diaper bags, and six oversized suitcases. My cranky four-year-old grips onto the right side of this metal mule. The flesh on his chubby, little knuckles turns white as he strains not to fall off. With my left hand, I drag the other two kids, facing backward, strapped tightly into the side-by-side double-stroller. What's in front of me is a mystery. My entire visual field is blocked.

"Ouch! Watch it, would ya lady?"

"So sorry, sir," I apologize after jamming into the heels of some unsuspecting and intolerant power suit.

Trudging forward, I catch a glimpse of my mother's redheaded reflection through the glass wall that separates the waiting area from the customs mishigas.[46] My breathing escalates. My chest begins to heave and I feel the lump in my throat rise.

I cannot believe we are here.

My tired eyes swell with tears—tears I ferociously held back for months, with the resistance of a heavily fortified retaining wall that keeps a raging river from flooding a nearby town.

"Oh my God, there she is, Warren. Help her! Why isn't anybody helping?" my mother shrieks after taking one look at her

---

46 Yiddish for stupidity, craziness, irresponsible behavior.

daughter-on-the-verge-of-a-nervous-breakdown. Mom is a fiery natural redhead, an outspoken, quick-witted Jewish woman who suffers from bouts of anxiety. Evidently, her symptoms escalated after everything that happened with Adam and me in the summer of 2006.

Certainly, our current reality has brought all her dormant neuroses, once again, to the fore.

She reads the situation well. My defeated expression and slovenly appearance says it all.

We scamper out of the high-traffic greeting area and deftly navigate around the pockets of confused people congregated by the doors. We embrace and exchange awkward grins and bow our heads in resignation. The kids barely acknowledge their grandparents' presence and I'm too spent to scold them for poor etiquette. They're irritable and hungry from their exhausting journey that began at five this morning.

We step foot outside the building and the air blackens from car exhaust. We weave our way across three lanes of internal airport traffic and continue directly into the short-term parking garage. My mother's shocking red BMW, parked just within eyesight, practically jumps out and greets me.

Something inside is triggered. I start to hyperventilate. My knees buckle and I grab onto the stroller handle for support. Without warning, I sob pathetically and all hell breaks loose. Powerless, I fold into my mother's arms.

I'm done.

Warren pulls me off Mom and holds me. His soft, burly body feels warm and smells familiar. I regress to a pre-verbal state and with my chin, motion toward the children. Without missing a beat, they assume control and unbuckle the straps, lifting the two little ones out of the stroller. Puzzled looks appear across the kids' sleepy faces while their mommy languishes in a mental breakdown.

My shoulders and neck loosen a little. The crippling tension that had been rippling through my limbs, for weeks now, begins to subside.

It feels good to fall apart. Finally.

Pearls of Wisdom...

o   Hold yourself together until it is safe to let go.

18. *Reality Sets In*

Mom and Warren bring two cars to the airport—both equipped with car seats borrowed from friends and family. They both drive small sedans so all the luggage and car seats consume most of the space. I ride shotgun with Mom in her signature BMW and the baby's infant seat is rear facing, and secured into the backseat. The two boys climb into the toddler seats strapped into the back of Grandpa Warren's Honda Accord. We pull out of the parking garage and follow the street signs to head north on I-95. Destination: Hollywood, Florida.

At 7:00 pm, just forty minutes later, we arrive to the town house development.

We made it.

I remember that the kids haven't eaten in hours and must be famished. Since leaving Panamá that morning, I'd been shoveling sugary snacks and salty chips into their mouths to keep them quiet, distracted and less annoying to fellow passengers.

We pull into Mom and Warren's front driveway. I cringe as chills creep up my spine. Stay cool, Darah. Keep it together. It's the beginning of better times—a new chapter—I repeat in an effort to brainwash myself.

I catch my breath, realizing that this small townhouse is now our official "home." We freaking live here.

No more fancy apartment.

No more old, country home with the pool and trampoline.

No more space of our own.

No more space.

Period.

Oh God, help us...

In this three-bedroom, two-story home, all nine of us will cram in and reside for God knows how long. The thought of it all is overwhelming. I know my kids' unremitting energy and relentlessly inquisitive natures will erode anyone's patience—even the kindest, most loving childcare expert. It's going to be an enormous challenge for an older couple like Mom and Warren—a couple used to a lot of downtime, privacy and silence—to share space with our rowdy bunch.

Oh boy.

Before departing on this journey, Joaquín and I had come up with an exit plan. Like military generals preparing for combat, we drew up blueprints, precisely mapping out how we all would squeeze into such tight quarters—where we'd hide the kids' toys, position the baby's changing table, hang everyone's clothes, store toiletries—addressing every last detail.

We agreed on the importance of staying out of our hosts' way. With two toddlers in diapers full-time and another at night only, I knew I would need to be super-organized, tidy and parent differently than I had back in Panamá.

Never a nervous mother, my laissez-faire style undoubtedly, would clash with the prevalent helicopter-moms hovering over this community, quick to belittle a free-range mom like me.

In Panamá, I was lucky. *Really* lucky. I had several sets of eyes and hands assisting me, day in and day out, with most of the childrearing duties. Parenting five kids was less taxing. Here, help is unaffordable.

I am overcome with gratitude for Warren. He is very good to Mom, as he is to us. He genuinely cares about our kids, our welfare, and us. He is the only maternal grandfather they have known. He's been with Mom since long before Yordana was born. Mom was blessed to find such a caring and patient man many years ago, and to have stayed together this long.

We realize this is a lot to ask of him. We are not his blood relatives and let's be honest, they lead a tranquil and comfortable life. Realistically, our presence is about to throw that all off-kilter.

What sickens me most is that we have no plans to ever leave, at least not until we get back on our feet financially.

We walk through the front door. I traipse over to the kitchen, not in any mindset to cook; I'd rather wallow in my breakdown. But I'm still these kids' mom and they have to eat a hot meal at some point. Stuck in a fog, I mindlessly pull open the familiar whitewashed cupboard to grab a frying pan and then pull out a handful of eggs shelved on the fridge door. For a moment before closing the door, I stare pensively and feel myself get sucked inside this cold vacuum, and transported back in time—to our last visit.

I always loved coming to visit and then loved going back home to my own charmed life. We were the radical family members living far off in the exotic, third world with "all the live-in help." Now, this is my world and this is my home. I stare blankly into the refrigerator, overwhelmed by emotion and by mom's vastly obscure synthetic food collection.

Nothing has changed.

Snapping myself back to the moment, I shamble across the kitchen to the stove, scramble up the eggs and serve them with buttered white toast. All is ready in three minutes. To their hearts' delight, the kids gobble up every morsel. The baby fends for herself and manages to gum it down as her checked-out mom escapes off to the bathroom.

I return after splashing my face with cold water and force a smile now that bellies are full. We trek upstairs and I corral the kids together and plunk them down into Mom's giant Jacuzzi. I open the faucet and the tub fills up with about a foot of warm water while I pour half a bottle of bubble-bath gel into the stream. The white foam begins to rise up to their skinny necks and the children squeal in delight as they paint one another with it.

Then suddenly, as if frozen in time, I catch a glimpse of all of us reflected in the giant wall mirror that hangs behind the bathtub. There we are, standing in formation, and motionless. We're grinning instinctively, totally amused by the kids' giggling and playfulness.

This moment seems to lighten up the palpable heaviness that hangs over the house like a dark storm cloud—ever since we officially moved in two hours ago. I suppose this is a good thing. Because we all seem to relax—just a little.

After bath time, I rake through an endless torrent of bags to find the kids' favorite things: bottles, sippy cups, pacifiers, special blankets, stuffed animals—stuff that reminds them of their sleep-time routine at "home." The four eldest kids will share the computer room. Three inflatable mattresses sprawl across the carpet and form an L-shape. They surround the daybed like a moat, where Yordana will sleep. Mattresses, pillows and blankets all cram together and cover the entire bedroom floor. There's no walking room. At least if one little body rolls off the mattress, it'll crash land on someone else's bed. Maybe it could be worse.

I lay each of the boys down to sleep with a big hug and smother them with kisses. Together, we recite the Shema, the Hebrew prayer that asserts our faith in the oneness and sovereignty of God. Then we automatically rattle off a rote list of things for which we are grateful.

What follows is an equally long, if not longer, list of things we graciously want bestowed upon us. I encourage the kids to be happy because we're on a long camping adventure at Mimi and Grandpa's house and they think that's cool.

Just before my four-year-old son falls asleep, he mumbles, "In how many days are we going home, Mama? I miss my friend, Eli already."

My heart sinks. I sigh deeply and pause contemplatively before answering.

"It's a big surprise and only God knows," I whisper, then tiptoe out of the room.

Two down.

Now it's the baby's turn to go to bed. She will share a room with us. Her portable crib is rammed up against the frame of our full-sized bed. She's a good baby, and doesn't fuss unless she's got a valid reason. Besides, she's tired so she goes down easily with a couple soothing taps on the rear.

Having sex and watching television will be tricky under these ideal conditions.

At 11:30pm Warren returns from his second consecutive airport run with Joaquín and the two big girls in tow—drained and famished from their twelve-hour journey. They were obliged to deplane twice, and wade through the heat and the airport crowds in two third world airports.

They make a beeline for the kitchen, crank open the fridge and ravage Mom and Warren's leftovers from last night's dinner out. With happy tummies, they skip off to bed. All four of us adults let out a giant exhale and collapse onto the couch.

"So, listen," I begin, going straight to the point, "we will pay for all our food and gas and keep our two rooms tidy and the bathroom we use clean."

We had planned to address it all at the very beginning, so that Mom and Warren wouldn't fret, feel exploited, or taken for granted. We wanted to avoid future resentments. That's why right out of the gate, I am all business and outline our responsibilities and financial contributions. Joaquín assures them that we'll be super conscientious about controlling the noise, clutter, water use and respect their privacy and space.

I hope we're not over-promising on what we can actually

deliver, I reflect.

With sad, compassionate eyes, they insist that such a conversation isn't "necessary."

We know better.

After a mere few days, the novelty of our "visit" will fade, and it is best to broach all loaded topics from the get-go.

"This is going to be an experiment to see who loses their sanity first," I jest, already on the brink of losing my own.

Joaquín grins awkwardly and nods in acknowledgment.

"In this gloomy economy with no job leads in the pipeline," I tease, "we'll have better luck inviting a camera crew in to film a reality show. Right, Mi Amor? Why not expose our bad situation and take advantage of this American obsession? Certainly, many with similar experiences will relate."

I attempt, despite feeling sick to my stomach, to maintain a sense of humor.

As the days drag on, sometimes Joaquín is up and I feel down. When one of us is in really bad mental shape, the other always makes an extra effort to stay positive, to keep things balanced. The tables are always turning, like a wheel of fortune. We cannot allow ourselves to plunge into an emotional tailspin, as tempting and imminent as it is.

Yet after the sun sets, it's a whole different story. Something about the dark, about the night. In the wee hours of the night, when the house is silent and everyone is fast asleep and breathing heavy, demons come out to haunt the two of us. They keep us awake, suspended in a state of fright. We lay there tormented by ghost memories of a life that just vanished.

Our eyes bulge with fear, as we're petrified of the future.

We quietly encourage (and lie) to one another. "Don't worry, Mi Amor, things can only get better from here," I remember Joaquín tried to soothe me that first night then turned away toward the wall, to conceal the crushed look on his face.

Deep in my heart, I know a sign of hope yet has to appear on the horizon. We have to feign an optimistic attitude until our fate changes and until things come full circle. Whenever that will be.

The first few weeks at Mom's are unbearable. I feel like I'm free falling into a dark abyss, with no safety net. The future looks bleak, if not outright terrifying. There is no job to wake up to, nowhere to go, nothing to cleave to aside from the daily drudgery of keeping the house tidy. Thank God for that. I battle with myself constantly to embody that quintessential warrior spirit I had somehow adapted years before, but now seems to have escaped me.

I spend most of my waking hours talking to myself, and fight not to lose faith in the cycle of life.

I am a consummate performer, a master of deception, masking my true feelings all day and night, for the sake of the children's (relative) stability.

Scores of friends and family stop by or call daily and question us relentlessly about our so-called plans; they insist on a play-by-play of the grim events that ultimately brought us back here. Each time I appease my rapt audience and begrudgingly revisit the past, it evokes a chilling sensation of being trapped in a bad dream.

Could it be that at any moment I can simply choose to wake up, pack up our things and go home?

My sprightly kids see life differently. They are aroused by this new experience—an arousal I artificially stimulated weeks before our arrival.

"Yay! We're going on a long trip to the United States, to see family and friends and stay with Mimi and Grandpa Warren," I cheered daily, hoping it would eventually sink into their tender minds. "Aren't we lucky?"

Now, I conclude, is not a good time to ruefully reveal my budding hypocrisy and expose this masquerade. Instead, my hapless face mirrors their pixelated excitement about this indefinitely sanctioned "camping" adventure.

Internally, however, I'm dissolving into a basket case. My faith has been shattered, my heart, hardened. I am aggrieved with the world and feel like giving up.

Nevertheless, the charade continues and my academy award-winning performance is fueled by a mother's fierce desire to protect her children from emotional scarring—at all costs. In retrospect, it is undeniable that I was clinically depressed. And yet, despite my implacable longing to spend the day wallowing in bed, curled up in a fetal position, or worse yet, abandon ship, I remained strangely efficient and resourceful—a high-functioning mess. Ha! I fooled them all.

Nobody ever suspected how much I flirted with insanity...

I need a project to re-direct this mounting anxiety into a productive and positive vein. Fortuitously, one materializes immediately and I latch onto it with the verve of a nursing infant. By law, I have to enroll my kids in school before too many days lapse, as it could, from what I'm told, compromise their current grade status. Somewhat reanimated, I invoke my graduate-school diligence and immerse myself in the study of Florida's educational system.

When the kids are watching television or fast asleep, I pore over pages and pages of digital information regarding standardized tests, score implications and attendance policy. Like a detective on a mission to solve a case, I search to identify the most befitting scholastic environment for my kids. Together, we visit all nearby public and private schools, and collect mounds of applications required for admission.

The school calendar in Panamá runs from March to December, and the age cut-offs for each grade differ than those mandated by Florida's educational system. Some of the kids will need to linger on in the same grade level for more than a year, and others, because of their birth month, will jump ahead. All qualify as ESOL students, or English as a second language, because despite always speaking English at home, they have greater fluency in Spanish.

This is an important annotation on the admission forms and permanent records and frankly, there is no disservice in my conscious choice forever to "label" my kids Hispanic and ESOL students. After much analysis, I know the system well enough to recognize this as a de-facto advantage. Faculty and school administrators are patently sympathetic to the disadvantages minorities' face—even if merely to fill a state or county-mandated quota, or appear politically-correct.

I meticulously sort through all the children's medical records, birth certificates, social security information, and former report cards and make appointments for additional vaccinations. This task keeps me busy and purposeful—less disheartened. Anyway, it's almost two weeks since we first arrived and the kids are antsy, craving routine.

They really assumed to be on vacation. Maybe kids in general just have that uncanny ability to detach from reality and escape into their rich imagination, simultaneously operating in two parallel worlds. Most certainly, an enviable and admirable survival tactic that if demonstrated past a pre-determined age, undoubtedly, would qualify you for psychiatric evaluation.

Nonetheless, the kids never seemed to realize that we hit rock bottom and lost everything. Yet, conversely, we never confided that our move to the United States was the consolation prize. Nor did we divulge that they probably would never see their friends again. They knew all our furniture and most of their belongings were still in a storage unit in Panamá; we had disclosed that much.

But they held onto the belief that we'd be returning after our "trip"—no matter how long it took. We even told our friends the same thing—perhaps in an unconscious effort to avoid saying goodbye. And we sincerely wished for the same.

Truthfully, we had not a clue if or when we would be back. It was a tacit, yet viable option, and the most logical one, too; all of our business contacts and personal connections were in Panamá and Latin America. My husband had made a name for himself; he was a Big Fish. Because of this, we couldn't foreclose on the possibility to return. For years, we remained flexible, in a constant state of "stand-by," leaving the proverbial door cracked open, waiting for a change of tides.

The good news was that the kids were adapting well culturally and emotionally, and for the very first time, surrounded by the love and warmth of so much extended family. Their English-speaking skills improved rapidly. I inundated them with English-speaking educational television programs and exposed them to most genres of American music—rock oldies we almost never listened to in Panamá because remember, we were entrenched in most every aspect of Panamanian culture, including the music. When I dive into something, it's all or nothing.

Because we noticed early on that indeed they were thriving, we decided there was no need for them to partake in the details of our dismal dilemma. Not only would it have added no value, but also, it would have triggered a landslide of stress and anxiety. Consequently, conveying such weighty information only would have magnified our own worries, as we would be trying to assuage our children's shifting emotions while trying to reconcile our own.

The kids never asked for their lives to be turned upside down. We wholeheartedly believed we were doing the right thing. Being on a need-to-know basis was best for them. We fed them easily digestible smatterings of information at a time, information they'd be able to swallow without disrupting this delicate transition.

Look, despite the apparent ease of their new world acclimation, inwardly, I knew our hasty insertion into this other life befuddled them. They were grappling with a new culture, a semi-new language, a different school, unfamiliar people—a totally foreign lifestyle. They missed their friends and the familiar routines that filled their lives with a kind of satisfying and reassuring stability. I know because each day, all day long, they would converse among themselves, "When we get back to Panamá, I'm going to...I can't wait to tell my friends (fill in the blank) that I..."

What's a mom to do? I only wanted them to be kids, to play blithely and be blissfully happy. And being so little and naïve, I felt my childrearing imperative was to shield them from the harsh realities of adult-life. My logic dictated: they live with a houseful of loving family, have plenty of food to eat and take a warm shower or bath each evening.

What else do they need to know?

However, inside, my heart was engaged in battle, a tug-of-war. My faith was withering and being replaced with a rising embitterment. Deep inside, there was a dark place where sinister thoughts lingered in the crevices of my mind like street corner thugs. A festering fungus, that I was too ashamed to admit to anyone, ate me alive.

Because despite everyone's assertions that I still had much to be thankful for, I felt like a complete failure as a woman, as a mother, and as a daughter—forced to start life over at middle age when most people I knew—my inner circle of friends and family and even acquaintances—relished comfortably established lives.

Shamefully, envy, the green-eyed monster, consumed me and kept me awake at night. I secretly hated everyone who suffered less than we did, and was incapable of experiencing genuine happiness for other people's successes. Even people I loved.

I was losing my soul.

It has only been a few weeks, and I miss my life. I miss my friends. God do I miss the help. I am so damn tired all the time. Life has become a burden. Joyless.

Throughout the years, friends, family and even people we hardly knew brazenly asked why we continued to stay in Panamá, a (relatively) corrupt third world country with an unbearably dank climate. Why not return to a more efficient US and be closer to family? That was the million-dollar question. After all, we had not one blood relative in Panamá. During the Jewish holidays, a time when it tends to get lonely for transplants like ourselves, thankfully, we were "adopted" by local friends and their families—so our kids wouldn't feel marginalized and left out of the experience of intimate, family gatherings.

Moreover, during the last seven years, we consciously cast off opportunities to return to the United States. With five young children, Latin America was the best option for us at this stage in our lives. The help was affordable, and the lifestyle simpler and less encumbered by rigorous, civil legalities. Some folks still closed business deals with a handshake.

The country air was fresh, rugged terrain untainted, and many parts were left to be discovered. This always appealed to the explorer in me. Additionally, the "economic perks" inherent in Panamá living were noteworthy and kept us somewhat tethered, despite the insufferable heat. For example, the flexible, forgiving and easily manipulated tax structure enabled many people to net a greater portion of their salaries.

Companies were extremely accommodating and for a high-level executive, the company accounting department would report his or her earnings as hovering around $1,500 a month. This way employees would pay little to no taxes based upon the fictitious wages. Most every business operated this way and it was no secret.

In Panamá—and many cities and small towns throughout the world—there are limits. Limits breed structure. If you want to enroll your child in art class, for example, there are at best, three reputable studios close by from which to choose. If tennis is your sport, there are perhaps, four sets of well-maintained courts, and a handful of qualified coaches to provide lessons. It's easier to make decisions when you aren't inundated with an overabundance of equally competitive alternatives.

In general, we always found that Latin America offered our family a simpler and more holistic lifestyle, void of the excesses to which most Americans are exposed. America's legendary culture of materialism and gluttony was a reality we fought hard to avoid.

A by-product of life in the land of opportunity, it is both America's blessing and her curse. I liked that the supermarket did not stock a hundred varieties of cereal. Ironically, it made life easier to know there were only twenty-five from which to choose. It made me feel strangely safe and insulated from the culture of consumerism back in the United States—a culture that'd swallow me whole.

Furthermore, from a pragmatic optic, as the woman of the house, I depended a great deal on the plethora of domestic help available for hire. We weren't millionaires by any stretch of the imagination—not even close—yet live-in help is a perk accessible to most lower-to-upper middle-class families. It certainly mitigated the overwhelming workload and pressure inherent in the care of a houseful of small children, two large, rambunctious dogs and one gigantic, rickety old country home. Additionally, I was more apt to entertain and host dinner parties and gatherings in my home.

We always planned to make the revolutionary move when the kids were older and more self-reliant. Definitely, we'd encourage them to attend college in the United States. But destiny had something else in store for us. Because in a sudden twist of fate, life took an abrupt turn. And in spite of our desires not to raise them in this post-9/11 terrorist-obsessed, warmonger society beset by distrust and economic panic, we ended up here.

After living off American soil for many years, I was unprepared to juggle it all and reluctant to expose my small-town kids to this rapacious society. I was passively anti-establishment and pained that external circumstances had imposed a lifestyle upon us I fundamentally didn't believe in anymore.

Our contained little world in Panamá was easy to manage, and we were bent on keeping things copasetic.

I questioned my own competency and readiness to devote myself unequivocally—and to the exclusion of all else—to my children day and night. Essentially, I'd need to prepare them, boot camp style, to bring them up-to-speed culturally and academically. Nothing less than full immersion would cut it. The job set before me was daunting.

It'd be my career, and mine alone. Mom and Warren leave early for work each morning. Joaquín's checked-out; he spends most of his time mirthlessly prospecting for work and cannot be derailed. Bereft of ambition and determination he is not, and his remarkable work ethic, albeit unemployed, is nothing less than enviable.

I have to do everything possible to keep him decidedly focused on bringing in money. The onus falls on me.

How will I muster up the strength and desire? Like most

American mothers, I suppose.

However, operating with an unsettled, fragmented mind, I'm unequipped for the job. How can I realistically provide emotional stability for the kids when my own mind is unhealthy?

And when will I squeeze in me-time to exhale and re-group? While sleeping?

In Panamá, the pace was distinctly slower. Existential matters of life purpose and balance that frequently plague modern, multi-tasking American moms don't exist in the collective consciousness, if at all. All the literature I've read both online and in print about women's perpetual struggle for that well-adjusted life that successfully incorporates work, family and a thriving social life is uniquely American.

Perhaps it resonates with European and Asian women. Maybe Nordic and African women as well. As a wife and mother, I only have resided in Latin America and can testify confidently that the ubiquitous "seeking balance" is not a pervasive problem here.

Having children did not mean we had to deny ourselves a romantic weekend getaway or lunch out with friends. Thus, it goes without saying that in Panamá, I benefited from a life of my own—as a woman, as a friend, small business owner, and as a wife.

My husband and I invested time in our marriage; we fled the home-front premises bi-weekly on dates, dashing off to catch dinner and a movie or on a balmy evening, we'd challenge each other to a set of tennis or wander around the open-air touristy areas brimming with restaurants, bars and local music attractions. We were able to relax, catch up, and explore, knowing explicitly that our children were safe at home.

Having a life outside the confines of motherhood was a tacit prerogative for women in my social circle. None of us were mired in domesticity. Because of the live-in help, I enjoyed periodic reprieves from domestic life to nourish friendships, attend classes, or indulge in some self-grooming service. My friends and I called such escapes "disconnects" because we had the luxury simply to detach from life-as-we-knew-it, even if only for an hour or two.

In addition, at the end of the day, there was never any mommy-guilt baggage because effectively, I was the one who routinely read my children their bedtime stories, tucked them in, reminded them to say their prayers, and checked for monsters under the bed. I taught them how to brush teeth, wash hands, practice proper table manners and social etiquette. I showed them how to tie their shoes, and each afternoon, assisted with homework assignments.

Personally, I took excellent care of myself as well. Unless I had been on a kamikaze mission to self-destruct, it made absolutely no sense not to. It was a financial no-brainer and the perfect pick-me-up after being drooled on and used as a tissue to wipe clean runny noses. My self-care routine consisted of a bi-weekly manicure and pedicure that set me back a total of fifteen dollars, tip included. The monthly massage in my own home put me out another ten bucks.

The intangible rewards reaped were priceless. In short: life was balanced and now I am scared to death. "Balance" in this fast-paced, cutthroat, do-it-yourself, stressed-out, multitasking land is elusive and mythical. Despite the hype and surplus of books claiming otherwise, let's be honest: it doesn't exist.

Thus, the unyielding hunt for a suitable school continues and I reminisce...

Four of the children had attended private school in Panamá since age two. They grew used to a homogenous environment with all Jewish kids from the surrounding neighborhoods. Classroom sizes were small and the instructors often called home to check up on an absent or sick student.

My kids embraced this warm atmosphere and greeted their teachers with a hug each morning. Maybe it was a derivative of the Panamanian society or a by-product of a Latin culture, or a Caribbean influence. Who knows? Regardless of its origins, my kids thrived from it.

Here in Hollywood, Florida, although our district school is an A-rated, five-star school, it is simply too large, too impersonal, and too regimented for my sheltered bunch. My woeful first impression was hard to shake off—despite many a parents' raving reviews, and the countless symbols of scholastic achievement swathed all over the school building walls.

The school grounds are well-manicured, cheerful and inviting. A wildcat mascot is painted adjacent to a myriad of motivational phrases on an exterior wall of one of the main buildings. The campus sprawls across twelve acres and appears much larger than the neighboring elementary school I attended thirty years ago.

After pulling into the south-facing parking lot, I enter the administrative office. Nobody bothers to look up to greet me. The administrators seem aloof and austere.

Oh, shit. This whole place reeks of red tape.

I clear my throat in an effort to capture a staffer's attention. Nobody stirs. "Hello?" I half-heartedly announce aloud to no one in particular, hoping to elicit a response. "I'm interested in enrolling my children here." One artificially tanned woman seated in the opposite corner of this wide-open, shared office space momentarily glances up from her computer screen. Without removing her ruddy hands from the keyboard, she grimaces and grudgingly watches me.

She is visibly annoyed for having been disturbed. I toss her a wan grin and introduce myself, and hurriedly rattle off an abbreviated version of the kids' academic background. When I notice that indeed I got her undivided attention, I go on to explain our precarious living situation, which inadvertently compels me to relive the recent painful past. Inevitably, my eyes fill with tears as I confess to having no residence of our own. "...and that's why we live with my mother for now," I conclude my spiel.

In response to my monologue, this sun-kissed, pink-acrylic-nailed woman rolls her eyes, reluctantly lifts herself out of her desk chair and shuffles over. In complete disregard of my performance, of my emotional candor, she mechanically hands me several application packets. She then threatens me grimly with the legal repercussions of address falsification, "...so if anything seems suspicious, we will notify the School Board of Broward County to follow up and your children will be transferred to the designated school for that zone."

"Sorry, ma'am, but now I've a lot of work to do. Once you have all your papers in order, you can return," she orders, and shoos me away.

Are these people even human? I am homeless and penniless, dammit!

No way in hell.

My callow kids weren't prepared to infiltrate this callous world. Frankly, I didn't even know how I would manage to survive in it. That afternoon I bunkered down and began calling all over both Broward and Dade county, in search of a familiar scholastic setting—a small, private Jewish school.

Yet with no cash, no credit and nothing in the pipeline, it was downright impractical, if not outright irresponsible and most certainly, an unrealistic, unattainable goal. No matter, I was hell-bent and not willing to compromise. I had seen the alternative.

*"It is our choices that show what we truly are,
far more than our abilities".*

– JK Rowling

Pearls of Wisdom...

- o Focus on the love you have for your children, pets, spouse, plants—or whatever wills you out of bed each morning.
- o Be a performer to keep life running as smoothly as possible for the kids' sake.
- o Feed small children age-appropriate bits of information about difficult situations.
- o Be clear and driven about what you want trusting that the universe will align to bring it about.

19. *Culture Shock, Missing the Third World & Achieving the Impossible*

During that first year back in the United States, I painfully realized just how much my American identity had disappeared. Compelled to adapt as the ground shifted below my feet, I felt alone, disconnected from the world and beset with culture shock.

Converting into an "American" again, albeit online from Panamá, was one onerous task. The cultural mores already felt foreign to me—even months before I stepped foot back on American soil. Thus, in anticipation of this impending culture shock, I had begun my due diligences back in September of 2008, two months before our official migration. I got the ball rolling the morning after a disenchanted man came home that fateful night, expressing his worst fears—fears that, at the time, were still unfounded.

In addition to following the stipulated return-to-America track, I simultaneously pursued another option: the stay-in-Latin-America alternative; thereby, working the predicament from two opposite angles, and staying flexible to whichever panned out in the end.

True to my sojourner nature, I remember bursting with hope that should Joaquín's so-called suspicions come to fruition, we would relocate to Bogotá, Colombia, where we would be received with a high-paying, executive job. This carrot was a galvanizing force that kept both of us aglow with faith in spite of the degeneration of Joaquín's relationship with Mark Joe.

Proactive as he is, when Joaquín first sensed the beginning of the end—after the initial communication breakdown between Mark Joe Ferrari and himself—the owner of a prominent bank in Bogotá quietly interviewed my husband for a general manager position. Immediately, we set out to do some undercover work—conversing with Colombian friends to inquire about the realities of life in this culturally rich and dangerous capital city.

We thought we had it in the bag. And full of wanderlust and unequivocal faith in my husband's irrefutable knack to win over even the most intimidating of power suits, I was more than eager to embark on another adventure. Panamá was becoming too small anyway—too familiar, and too intellectually and culturally stifling. It was time to move on.

Nonetheless, playing it safe, I had dutifully submitted all required information via email to qualify us for Florida Medicaid. Thankfully, I calculated the processing time well, so by the time we eventually did arrive to Miami, we were on our way to having medical coverage. Joaquín and I renewed our Florida driver licenses online from Panamá. If plans for Bogotá didn't turn out like we had hoped, we'd need current Florida licenses to attain local auto insurance, build lines of credit—as we had none—prove residency for the school district, and qualify for a myriad of random, resident discounts.

In the end, Bogotá fell through and although all our US paperwork was in order, the realities that shook me once we arrived in Miami were unfamiliar and unanticipated. Despite being American born and bred, it soon became evident that I was inexperienced and unprepared for life here. I had been away and disconnected far too long. A foreigner in my own country, I never had resided here with kids and would be in for a rude awakening.

Those first dreadful weeks of November 2008, in South Florida, were marked by frequent interactions with uptight, short-wicked state officials—and frankly, people everywhere. It seemed that the entire welfare institution was designed to discourage people from attaining their goal: government assistance.

After that first phone conversation—when a skeptical representative railed against me with accusations and interrogations for over an hour—I remember having to dig deep inside to muster up the desperation-inspired patience to return willingly to the rink for another round, in pursuit of my objective.

Nevertheless, hours of phone calls later, slashing through the tangle of red tape, our victory was that much sweeter when we received that coveted, welcoming letter by mail. It indicated that our personal data was processed and we were accepted members of the state's welfare program. Hallelujah!

Immediately, in one giant exhale, I released pent-up frustrations that had ruthlessly marked my face with worry lines. The worry lines, however, never did disappear.

Feelings of gratitude toward this inefficient, sluggish system that eventually came through for us replaced those of frustration. I was a champion and had navigated successfully through an exasperating and intimidating system.

But man did it suck the life out of me.

Apparently, I had grown used to Panamá's trademark inefficiency. Many times, the enforcement of regulations or obligatory procedures was subject to the discretion and interpretation of the authority figure in question—be it a police officer, store manager, Department of Transportation administrator or bank executive. Despite the disorganization and subjective unfairness of it all, I was well adapted to a place where many, many times, rules were enforced arbitrarily. Remember the lab techs administering my MRI?

It was a forgiving culture. People ran it, not machines. Therefore, interactions with individuals of power oftentimes meant that that person's perception or good mood would influence the decree, and make your life easier or more difficult as a result. It both comforted and empowered me to know that with a sincere compliment, innocent question, sad face or five-dollar bill, I could swing the verdict in my favor—much of the time.

I missed terribly the small-town Panamanian society. Yes, the predictably incompetent system, fraught with moral turpitude was the one I pined for. Go figure.

Lumbering away in this dense, bureaucratic US forest to facilitate our changeover into confirmed Floridians requires hours of focused study each night. Additionally, it is that much more challenging because it seems I've developed some degree of adult ADD—my mind adrift, perhaps resulting from prolonged exposure to extreme stress coupled with chronic sleep deprivation, and exacerbated by an undiagnosed depression.

I have a hell of a time concentrating on any task and cannot follow through on anything. Furthermore, because my inquisitive children consume all of my patience, there's nothing left over to negotiate through automated phone systems or reason with obstinate government workers about why we don't qualify for unemployment.

Night after night, sleep eludes me. The tumultuous waters of the mind don't settle down when I lay my head down for the night. Sleep is a battlefield.

To worsen matters, my daytime experiences are equally unpleasant as I struggle to acclimate to this new, ideological milieu.

Most every face-to-face encounter I have with intolerant others—administrators, cashiers, office clerks—is cold or confrontational.

I miss that endearing way Panamanians refer to one other, with a warm vitality and familiarity. "Claro que sí, mi reina. Venga conmigo por aquí linda, yo te enseño..."[47]

Regardless of what ground we cover, that hackneyed reproach wafts in the background like dreary elevator music: "Watch your kids. Ma'am, don't let her climb up there. Don't touch that, you can get hurt. Keep your kid next to you at all times. No playing on the stairs. Be careful. You must wait in line like everyone else. Children aren't allowed...."

Ugh!

I know, I want to shout aloud. I'm their fucking mom. Nobody cares about the kids' safety more than me!

But I don't expose these comments for what they truly are, clad in insincerity and spewed out mechanically as if read from a telemarketing script. I've matured enough finally to practice the dazzling art of political correctness. So I wince and nod in acknowledgement, and wear my best fake grin. Because clearly, they don't genuinely care about my children's well-being; it's merely symptomatic of an epidemic I call "lawsuit paranoia."

It's hardened people here. Fearful of being sued, folks have withdrawn their hearts from personal interactions. I never noticed this maddening phenomenon before, but now I sure do and totally resent it, particularly as a mom. Nonetheless, I bite my lip and press on, my eye on the prize: a natural and painless transition for the kids and for my husband.

My culture shock carries on and surfaces unpredictably, in the strangest of ways.

Human nature is a mixed bag, I suppose. Not only do you never truly come to know someone fully, I believe, but also your own erratic responses, set off by the simplest of experiences, can shock you. Even something as ordinary as a trip to the Post Office to mail a letter.

Walking distance from Mom's townhouse development is a local holistic pharmacy that rents space to the United States Postal Service. They occupy a counter in the back of the store with two attending clerks and there's always a line. One afternoon I pop in

---

47 Yes of course, my queen. Come with me over here pretty lady; I'll show you.

around three; I have a few letters to send overseas. I almost have to pick my jaw up off the ground after entering through the automatic, sliding glass door.

What's going on here? The clerks aren't sneaking off for their sacred coffee breaks at the precise moment the queue grows. Each attendant seems to dole out helpful advice about how best to send various classifications of correspondence. They even have the authority to resolve customers' dilemmas.

These postal employees speak cheerfully while interacting with customers. They aren't clowning around with co-workers or cupping their hands over the phone while whispering sweet-nothings to their lover on the other end of the line. These people are professionals, and resolutely focused on servicing the customer.

That's right my friends; the operative word here is customer. They pay attention to the client and do the best they can to be helpful. Efficient. Competent. Reliable. Pleasant.

Let's face it: I'm shocked. Without warning, I break down crying once I climb back into the van after my own satisfying and drama-free interaction. For the first time since we arrived, I feel a sense of relief, and appreciate this place—a place where routine tasks don't collapse into wild goose chases.

In Panamá, most habitual errands are, in short: a pain in the ass. Mailing a letter to the United States through the regular domestic system—not through a personal account with a private company that assigns each customer a private Miami-based P.O. Box—is an endeavor that requires a hefty investment of time and patience.

Before I got smart and paid the exorbitant fees to rent my own monthly P.O. Box with a Miami-based address, my entire day often would revolve around accomplishing this one errand—sending correspondence to the US, where we still had monthly payment obligations, long before digital payments became ubiquitous.

The self-righteous, impatiently-demanding-superb-customer-service American attitude I had proudly practiced in the US, quickly vanished when I first arrived to Playa Jacó, Costa Rica to reside as a new bride, back in April of 2000. With each consecutive interaction where I, the customer, happened upon a retail outfit, restaurant, auto repair garage, Telecommunications Company—wherever—my expectations continued to fall to the ground. Right away, I learned to appreciate the slightest degree of know-how and smidgen of decent customer assistance.

Disclaimer: this is not to say that one cannot find unparalleled customer service in these countries. On the contrary, you can, but it is going to cost you. Big time. March into any expensive restaurant, private health clinic, or strut into a fancy hotel lobby dressed to kill and undeniably, you'll be treated like royalty.

Back then, at the turn of the century, we just were starting out, and despite an occasional visit to such high-end places, we sought to blend in, and live like the hardworking locals. Because that's what we were. I had two options: bemoan the lack of customer service and country-wide operational inefficiency, or take deep breaths and transform into a Zen-like creature, toting around a self-help book whenever I had to accomplish something.

Face-to-face exchanges with employees of governmental agencies, banks and city regulatory bodies were by far, the most infuriating and mentally taxing encounters I underwent, and paradoxically, the ones where I strained to put my meditative techniques and affirmative mantras into practice. Workers simply don't want/care to help. Most of these underpaid, underappreciated employees lack any real decision-making authority.

Their quincena[48] arrives regardless, and because most employers can't be bothered or don't bother to get involved, it's almost unheard of to fire an employee for delivering bad customer service. In these parts, "the clerk is always right." Never the customer. Thus, the incentive to perform well doesn't exist.

Within a month of the birth of each one of our children, we dutifully visited the US Embassy to register the child's citizenship and simultaneously, apply for the baby's US passport. We did it once in Costa Rica with the birth of Yordana in May 2001, and subsequently in Panamá, with the other four children.

When everything went smoothly, we would make it out of the Embassy compound in less than four hours and the sensation was nothing less than exhilarating. From what I've heard, comparable to winning the lottery. The elating sense of accomplishment would surge through us as we ever-so-gently cradled the coveted document that read: Consular Report of Birth Abroad—knowing good and well we had beaten the odds.

More often than not, an unknown variable would foil the best

---

48 Bi-weekly paycheck

of plans, and result in the abject failure of the mission. You just never knew if official transactions or procedures would go as planned—even something as mindless as returning a garment to a department store would nose-dive into a three-hour nightmare. At the last minute, something would "pop up" and ultimately, the customer would have to pay the price; the currency was his time, energy, patience, and oftentimes, money.

The office or department store would shut down abruptly or more frequently, the only person—usually the highest-ranking male—who was empowered with the authority to resolve that problem, your problem, had wandered off minutes ago to lunch or to a "meeting" (in bed with his secretary at the push-button[49] around the corner.) Or, he just dashed out for the consecrated, ritualistic coffee break, and let me tell you this: these coffee breaks were guarded and protected with a vengeance. Nothing less than a building up in flames will interrupt or terminate them. Nothing.

"Sorry, for the 'inconvenience,' but please return another time," was the stock reply sputtered out of a disinterested co-worker's mouth. "He's on (coffee) break."

"Ohhh, I see..." I mockingly would bob my head in reverence of the sacrosanct coffee break.

"When is a good time to return? When will Mr. Boss-man be back on the premises? I need this document signed immediately," I cautiously pressured, trying to obtain a concrete answer. There was no reliability or accountability though, and most everything promised was in vain, and designed to keep customers contently gullible. Therefore, the ambiguous, "come back tomorrow or next week," (because either way we don't give a shit and still get our paychecks), was the standard, careless comeback.

Nonetheless, because we are creatures of habit that gradually adapt to our surroundings, albeit flagrantly dysfunctional, my initial shock and exasperation with the ineptness of it all, eventually gave way to complacency. I grew to expect it and planned accordingly. I too stopped caring at some point.

Yet aside from the natural aggravations that oftentimes transformed routine activities into inefficient, time-laden witch-hunts, we never experienced social problems with our kids behaving like kids. In this regard, I found the Panamanian culture

---

49 Discreet rent-by-the-hour motels outfitted with private individual parking garages scattered throughout Panama.

very kid-friendly, broad-minded and neighborly.

What's most troubling here, in our town home development in Hollywood, Florida, is that the kids' constant impulse to dart in and out of the house, wander and explore, is frowned upon. No space near the house seems suitable. Days after our arrival, it becomes apparent that the children's desire to play freely is at variance with several of the kid-unfriendly neighbors who wish to avoid contact with them at all costs.

"Your kids cannot play near my driveway or walk on our lawn; it's not safe for them here. I'm nervous about them playing near the street. Do you know your kids are riding bikes with no helmets?"

"They're too loud and are making the dog nervous," intolerant elders scold almost daily, lips pursed in disapproval.

Gimme a freaking break.

In the neighborhoods within which we mingled in Panamá, kids of all ages played together in local parks and open spaces. An odd-looking person or stranger loitering on the premises would stand out. The paranoia of predators and pedophiles lurking around every street corner is practically nonexistent. Nobody put his or her guard down completely, yet life was predictable, routine. Neighbors frequented the same places and exchanged long-winded greetings. That's how it was.

Whoever saw a helmet-less kid fall off his bike and bump his head would extend support. That caregiver wouldn't lash out to rebuke or blame the child's parent for disregarding the recently revised county bike-helmet ordinance. Everyone more or less looked out for each other's kids.

Without the platform Lenore Skenazy already had back in April of 2008, when she published her controversial column that stated how she permit her nine-year-old son to ride the New York City subway home alone—yay Lenore! —which incidentally, further enflamed the ongoing battle between the helicopter moms and their free-range counterparts, I had not a leg to stand on with my unpopular just-let-them-scrap-their-knees philosophy. I wasn't yet blogging and had no creative outlet to vent my free-ranging frustrations. And frankly, being on the continuous verge of a nervous breakdown, for the first time in my life, I hadn't the strength to fight the world.

Changing strategies, I steer the kids away from the grumbling neighbors and shuttle them to county parks, public libraries, and recreational areas in the vicinity. Like a shepherd tending to the needs of its herd, I lead them to fertile pastures—places where they can roam free, sweat, get dirty and stay out of everyone's sacred front yard.

We make our way to the beach; it's a straight shot four miles east. Our time spent outside invigorates the kids and rejuvenates me. The sea breeze is clean and crisp, and the sweet scent of freedom perfumes the atmosphere.

Fortunately, beautiful Hollywood Beach with its bustling Boardwalk is just a ten-minute drive from home. The kids love rolling around in the sand. Public funds in Panamá rarely made it to their designated coastal destination, so many of the nearby, public beaches remained littered with shards of glass, debris and animal excrement. All of which made this visceral need to "roll in the sand" impossible.

I spread out a giant sheet and plop myself down near the water's edge where the kids are busy making sandcastles.

I stare out into the endless ocean horizon, imagining where life will next take us. Anything seems possible right now.

Growing up, we visited the beach often. My friends and I would literally roast in the sun, slathering dangerous quantities of Crisco oil all over our tender skin, then diligently turn over at exact intervals when the buzzer sounded—in pursuit of the most even, perfect tan.

We'd grab a gigantic slice of cheese pizza at our beloved Anthony's Pizzeria, and scurry back to the car every so often to deposit more coins in the meter. Incidentally, I never appreciated this majestic place as I do now, in this pleasantly cool month of December, with five young spirits in tow.

And wouldn't you know it, my reverse cultural shock surfaces again. Who would've imagined because I've memorized every square-foot of this spot, recalling names and locations of longstanding businesses with uncanny precision. Yet, many action-packed years have elapsed, and I'm different now.

Having lived on foreign soil for many years has left me disjointed from precious childhood memories I now struggle to claim as my own. Definitely, the fact that so many local, loved ones have passed away since I first left town in 2000, heightens this unsettling awareness.

I'm completely estranged from my past American life in

suburbia and cannot connect the dots to the wife and mother I am today. It's troubling, as though my memory were blocked resulting from some horrific childhood tragedy.

However, that's not the case. Nothing unspeakable occurred to evoke this fragmented feeling. Conceivably, I've acclimated to another lifestyle so much so that the comfortably neurotic childhood I had loved has become unrecognizable as my own.

Who knows? Maybe it's a normal by-product of aging. On the other hand, perhaps, it's symptomatic of the early-onset of mental illness.

I peer at it all through new lens, and I'm not quite sure what to think of it all: the free open-air concerts, the well-run beach chair rental gig, the certified lifeguards stationed in well-stocked huts, the impeccably-manicured playgrounds; it is all so damn...textbook. The brightly-lit parking structures, efficient digital parking meters, seamlessly-paved paddleball courts, clean, well-stocked public restrooms. Holy shit. Obviously, someone's channeling the public funds in the right direction. What a novelty.

Again, the logic of my reaction escapes me, and the infinite sea bears witness to my emotional outburst as I bury my face in my hands and bawl my eyes out.

Am I home? Is this where I live now?

I'm not the only one undergoing strange reactions, either. My kids are going through their own, unique assimilation process, yet in a more light-hearted way, I suppose. Two weeks into our new life, when we first arrived, I remember an enchanting and funny incident that reveals just how "foreign" my children were.

We are out running errands when my kids spot some local gardeners zooming by. They're perched atop a couple of sophisticated, motorized mowers. Bandanas pulled around their heads and necks to protect them from the scorching mid-day sun, the men are busy grooming a large property on the corner of a residential intersection. The kids are astounded; they think it's some sort of carnival ride.

I brake at the red stop sign. The three eldest kids crane their little necks and shout out in broken English through the open car window, "Hey Señor, can we ride it when you're finished?" The men do not hear a thing. The deafening din from the lawn-motors keeps them conveniently unaware and unsuspecting of those around them. My kids cry in earnest for me to stop the car so they can wait their turn and hop on next.

On another occasion, the kids were frolicking about in the front yard. Suddenly, an underground sprinkler system motors on and catches them by surprise. Water sprays out in all directions and soaks them right through to their undergarments. They are delighted and convinced that the affable residential maintenance man, José, adjusted the timer of this "neighborhood water game" just for them.

"Mama," my drenched four-year-old boy bounces toward me, "José put the water spouts on for us again. Can we change into our bathing suits and play a little longer?"

My little immigrants refused to believe my practical explanation that this was no game but an underground irrigation system, set up at timed-intervals to keep the lawn pretty and green. Thereafter, each time they'd see a bemused José cruising around on his golf cart, they'd beg him ruthlessly to recalibrate the clock so that this time they could play for a longer stretch.

In Panamá, it was simple. During the dry season, we'd water the grass and surrounding foliage with a plain garden hose, or at most, a lightweight contraption secured into the hose's nozzle and in a fan-like display, it would send the water spraying back and forth between two designated areas.

Consequently, these unsophisticated plastic devices were tough to anchor down, especially to our uneven terrain, so they'd topple over with a strong breeze or be knocked down by our mischievous canines. Ultimately, it was less of a hassle to simply press one's thumb just so in order to change the direction and pressure of the water's stream, rather than invest in a piece of equipment destined to break down. The live-in male worker watered the garden while the kids jumped around on the trampoline.

Admittedly, I was impressed with all the ingenuity around me. We visited the United States many, many times over the years, but I hadn't functioned in society, as a resident, in eight long years. And during those years, I fancied myself a visitor, a "foreigner," and the more I immersed myself in Panamanian life and culture, the more my American identity seemed to fade away.

During the South Florida living adaptation process, I developed a galloping fear of highway driving. Even senior citizens cursed me out with a chorus of horn-honking while I white-knuckled it at exactly fifty-five miles per hour.

After each treacherous voyage on the monotonous Florida Turnpike or I-95, I'd totter out of the vehicle, nauseous and inconsolable. My preoccupied husband wasn't the least bit concerned I'd wrap the van around a tree and get us killed. He dismissed my concerns as frivolous and irrational.

"Mi Amor, with practice you'll regain your confidence. Your reaction-time is still a little slow," he remarked nonchalantly more than once.

However, no amount of patronizing or placating helped calm my frayed nerves. Worse yet, I found myself dozing off during the daily four forty-five-minute commutes to and from the kids' school we'd found in Margate. (In a few pages, I'll explain how and why this school.)

Driving was not the "sport" it had been in Panamá; here it was a chore. The driving I did in Panamá, and Costa Rica years before, was the antithesis of monotonous. It was a stimulating undertaking that required a sharp set of technical skills, indomitable concentration, and an unflappable will to survive. Eight years of driving on roads punctuated by mammoth-sized potholes or single lane gravel roads that snaked through mountainous terrain, and navigating unmarked roadwork areas or unfinished construction sites was what I had learned to do. Always on guard, the notion of "falling asleep at the wheel" was absurd.

In Panamá, it had taken me six months of "driving boot camp" to achieve this high level of proficiency. My rigorous training included a few—okay, many—fender-benders and unforeseen collisions with thick, cement columns poorly placed in dimly-lit parking garages throughout the city. Of course, having a husband enamored with tough, oversized cars, I always sported some obnoxious roving battleship.

Problem was that I was set up for failure from the minute I climbed up into the vehicle. For starters, my line of vision barely cleared the steering wheel—I'm 5'1"—and I flaunted thick prescription lenses that fogged up from humidity the minute I shut the car door. Therefore, I was routinely blind the first three-four minutes of driving time.

Almost daily, those first six months, I'd return home with eyes cast down like a juvenile delinquent in confession before a punitive judge, and appear in front of a most aggravated man who'd pontificate self-righteously about what a bad driver I was.

Joaquín routinely came home Monday through Thursday for lunch—the big family meal. I'd return from the gym and errand-running within minutes of his arrival. Predictably, there he'd be, standing on the front porch, greeting and petting the dogs. Yet the dogs were mere decoys. In reality, he was killing time so he could watch me pull into the driveway and initiate the vehicle inspection. After a cursory greeting and peck on the lips, already he had identified the most recent ding, scratch, or dent.

So fueled by a desire to placate my husband and dispel the myth that women are bad drivers, my abilities improved dramatically. No longer was I a victim of other drivers' aggression, but had become an irrefutable menace on these Panamanian free-for-all-roads, where drivers were little more than cruising manifestations of Charles Darwin's Survival of the Fittest theory. Consequently, my husband refused to let me drive on family outings, preferring to fall asleep at the wheel instead.

Note: In the event that you plan on driving while traveling throughout Panamá, a word of advice—don't. If you choose to do so anyway, please familiarize yourself with a few facts. For starters, to cut other drivers off is commonplace. No need to apologize or pretend you didn't notice. Going in the opposite direction on a one-way road is okay if traffic is light. Traffic "authorities" oftentimes overlook such violations if you shrug your shoulders and grin coyly while driving past them.

Seatbelts are optional; most people buckle only while approaching the highway. Prolific horn-honking is considered another dialect—it's how vehicles communicate with one another and with pedestrians. And take note: sometimes—okay, many times—a police officer's willingness to issue a ticket diminishes the second he becomes distracted by a voluptuous passerby or quite frankly, anyone with a vagina.

Because many officers are on the take, once pulled over, a neatly folded, crisp five-dollar bill inconspicuously wedged between your license and vehicle registration card will seal the deal and get you out of trouble.

"All they really want," I was advised by a close friend during my first year in Panamá, "is enough cash to buy a burger, fries and coke or a six-pack when their shift ends."

Fair enough, I thought. Sure as hell beats the lofty price of a traffic ticket or puttering away long hours in driving school.

Thus, with that sage advice, I figured that any attempt to make this overtly crooked system straight would be fruitless.

So I put into practice the "If you can't be 'em, join 'em" approach and never looked back.

As 2009 gets underway, Joaquín travels back and forth between Panamá and Costa Rica in search of a job, or at the very least, a gig.

Finding a school to accept my spirited bunch is my full-time job. I will not be derailed—not even by the same five kids that tote around with me, badgering my lone hearing ear with unrelenting noise and whiny chatter. Our decision to slip the kids into the private school sector makes no sense financially and everybody unabashedly flaps their tongues, commenting about the absurdity of it all.

"You are in the US now," friends and family advise. "You have no money and must lower your expectations. The public schools here are excellent and the kids will adapt."

Screw that. They all mean well but I'm the mom and know what is best for my kids.

Nonetheless, the hunt is on for a private, religious school that will give us a hefty break—like a seventy-five percent discount. Ha! Good luck with that. The average monthly cost for just one student is the equivalent of a large car payment. I want to enroll four. Am I out of my mind? Instead of trying to make sense of it, I let my heart dictate what's best for the kids. I have faith that somehow, later, we'll work out the financial kinks.

My God, with the exception of their immediate family, everything the kids have come to know and love was torn from their lives. Overnight. I must do this for them.

Alas, many phone calls, emails, and days later, I find the Hebrew Academy Community School in Margate, a solid forty-five minutes from the house, heading north on the Florida Turnpike. Although it is a religious school run by Ultra-Orthodox Jews, it embraces students coming from backgrounds that reflect all levels of observance. That is important since we are slowly falling more in line with a Conservative lifestyle than an Orthodox one. (More on this later.)

The admissions director, Rabbi Lichy, goes above and beyond the realms of "help" to accommodate us. He expresses a genuine concern for the children's adjustment and well-being, and sensing my own anxiety and apprehension, like a mathematical wizard, devises a creative way to work out the numbers. Through a combination of scholarships, grants, discounts and volunteer work, we make it happen. Like us, he, too wants to see my puzzled children thrive in their new surroundings. For him, we are eternally grateful and cannot praise him enough.

Touring the school's corridors, my eyes twinkle and quietly rejoice in the numerous Hispanics I hear and see shuffling around—both students and faculty. Because right now my kids are more fluent in Spanish than English, this is an invaluable selling point. At least they can socialize in their native tongue.

I sigh with relief.

I arrange with Rabbi Lichy to pay whatever we can afford; he is well-acquainted with our precarious living situation and knows we cannot commit to a specific, monthly amount without a steady, reliable income. A compassionate man, a good soul, this is just what we need right now. He is a Godsend, my personal Moses. And because of his benevolence and authentic caring, a glimmer of hope appears on the horizon and the sadness dissipates a little.

Hope runs through my veins. Hooray! The kids have found a school!

Explaining to the kids why they're attending school while "on vacation" is tricky and rather comedic as I spew out a lot of nonsense, in an effort to deflect the truth. In the end, I concede just enough for them to consider it temporary and part of their "American adventure," and thus, avoid outright lying.

Soon, when they're a little older and can understand, I'll tell them the whole story...

Nonetheless, despite my chilling fear of the unknown, and not knowing where this road was taking us, this trying stretch emboldened me to press on.

Finally, I was learning to let go and recognize that certain things were beyond my control. That lesson penetrated much like the slow erosion of a rock over ages—the rock, my head, and the eroding matter, the perpetual drip of reality.

Pearls of Wisdom...

- o Grant yourself a grace period to experience intensity of emotions. Then move on.
- o Embrace uncertainty while remaining clear and steadfast about what you want.

20. *Almost Smothered*

Wouldn't you know it? When you actually let go of the reins and let fate guide you, things start happening.

As planned and almost to the day, we lasted exactly three months at Mom and Grandpa Warren's house, moving out on February 15, 2009. I think we got out just in time without causing any permanent damage to the already-strained relationships or to the house for that matter.

Joaquín and I had decided, in advance, that three months would be our limit. We knew, unmistakably, that after ninety days, things could turn sour. So regardless of whatever employment/financial situation we'd find ourselves in, we would find somewhere else to go.

The last thing we wanted to do was overstay our welcome and ruin the tenuous web of relationships evolving between all of us. Since birth, all five of our children had grown up outside of the United States and without frequent exposure to family. For the first time in their lives, they were in close and constant contact with blood-relatives. And that wasn't the only novelty for these kids.

Right out of the gate, the children were compelled to master English—reading, writing and speaking. Despite always conversing in English at home in Panamá, they were more comfortable with Spanish—it was their native tongue—and the one they'd used to speak with friends, teachers, nannies, and each other. For the first six weeks at Mom's place, nobody understood the mishmash of words spoken by the three youngest children—the baby still had yet to say her first real word.

Their puzzled minds were conjuring up a convoluted form of Spanglish, as they regularly shifted between the two languages mid-sentence. I found myself on high-alert, translating even the simplest of greetings as technicians or neighbors knocked on the door.

Many times, for example, I'd strain my hearing ear and eavesdrop on a confused exchange between Mom and one of the kids upstairs. In a rescue attempt, I'd shout out a few key words to help Mom decipher my struggling child's need to be understood.

Oftentimes, he was trying to share something about his day, or more urgently, was asking for help in the bathroom. Switching gears, I'd return to the rolling conversation downstairs between Grandpa Warren and another child who was inquiring about the garden.

Those first three months, I worked ceaselessly to buffer this communication gap. My goal was to facilitate the rapid development of repertoire between the children and their grandparents, an essential building block of a strong and healthy relationship.

My eldest would assist me with the translations if she felt up to it, and I encouraged the children to watch hours of educational programs in English, to expedite the process. With a one-track mind, I prodded my kids along, to help them assimilate into this culture and to this lifestyle, as quickly as possible. I didn't want them stigmatized or worse yet, bullied by their school peers for speaking improperly, or for being clueless about American stuff.

At this time, two were in diapers, and a third only at night. Undeniably, the terrible two-year-old boy was unbearable most of the time he was awake.

The kids were holding out well with the current household logistics, and I continued to chauffeur them almost daily, to open spaces to play and let loose.

Joaquín traveled often in pursuit of employment opportunities throughout Latin America. When in town, he locked himself away on the computer following up with contacts or preparing documents for consulting gigs he occasionally scored.

Consequently, I was on my own with the kids most of the time. Now that the four oldest were in school and struggled to catch up to their classmates—having dropped in mid-semester—I had to tutor them.

Apparently, the expensive, private bilingual school they attended in Panamá, El Instituto Alberto Einstein, was not on academic par with the schools in the US, despite claiming otherwise.

The leading problem was that I couldn't do it all at once: supervise the two active boys playing outside, oversee the now-crawling baby nearing the stairwell, and assist the two older girls with their English and Hebrew homework. They weren't only studying English, but being a religious school, were required to read, write and speak in Hebrew. In addition, the eldest was expected to translate biblical passages from Aramaic or Hebrew to English.

These after school be-witching hours were dizzying; it was a three-ring circus and I was manic, racing between all three rings. The girls had homework and required my help, the boys needed to unwind in the outdoor air, but tended to gravitate toward the street, and all five were starving.

Day after day, I only offer the kids chicken nuggets, mac-and-cheese, or hot dogs for dinner. Who has the desire or time to cook? I can barely eat at all...

Additionally, I set out to tidy up our tiny living quarters before Mom and Warren returned from work at 6:00 pm. Because clearly, an implicit part of this arrangement was that the house ought to be kept up as if all seven of us "weren't really living here." More my obsession than theirs, I grew fanatical about covering our tracks and kept my senses on high-alert to any brewing undercurrents of resentment stemming from our prolonged stay.

I had a lot to accomplish and needed help. My physical and mental health was in jeopardy. My neck, shoulders and upper back were constantly overwrought and I could barely turn my head. I tossed back an average of five cups of coffee a day to keep myself going and doing, and avoid nodding off during my daily four forty-five-minute commutes.

Busy rebuilding our lives, every couple of weeks, I'd become mentally distraught, and break down, weeping silently in bed, careful not to awaken the baby in the crib pegged to my side of the mattress.

Seeing me gaunt, pale and stiff, Mom and Warren suggested hiring help for those critical few hours after the children returned from school until they ate, bathed and were ready for bed. They saw it as an investment in my sanity, and consequential mental health of the children, Joaquín and even their own.

They offered to finance it, and everyone agreed that while Joaquín was away traveling, it was paramount to my survival. No longer could I play hero. I was disavowed of the quixotic ideal of having transformed into a do-it-all-by-myself American mom. Because the truth was that I was at the end of my rope, and could barely cope.

Nonetheless, I accepted their generous offer.

Having been down this road countless times in Panamá, I

confidently went about interviewing several young Colombian women that had come recommended. Finally, I chose one young woman that seemed a good fit. Lacking many basic domestic skills, and not yet a mother herself, she ended up helping mostly with the baby and laundry; the boys were too restless and too draining. The older girls' homework was beyond her grasp, and besides, that was my responsibility.

Sadly, after a few weeks she left, claiming she was getting married and her new, unemployed fiancé didn't want her working anymore. I knew how to read between the lines. Panamá had been a good training ground for this enigmatic talk. And despite all the constant hiring, firing, training and resigning drama, I still missed it terribly.

It seemed like ions ago that we'd been living a full life, a balanced life and an enjoyable life—free from these kinds of existential worries. We were rotting in a jaded existence and going nowhere fast. I felt something had to change.

Nonetheless, this misery was a growing force that undoubtedly, soon would become a catalyst for change. By now, I understood the undulations of life's currents, cycling up, then down, then up again. We were down, close to rock bottom, so trusting in the natural vicissitudes, I knew we'd be hurled back up eventually. It was a matter of time; something I could not force or control.

During the past two months, the house adjacent to Mom's was sold and being restored. Apparently, a couple well into their eighties had lived there for almost forty years and passed away within days of each other.

Their surviving children sold the property shortly thereafter and the new owner, a general contractor, was in the process of renovating it. I didn't pay that much attention to the work they were doing, but it was impossible not to notice the procession of workers parading in and out of the property all day. In fact, many parked in our spot.

My friendly kids often would encounter the painters, plumbers and electricians working day and night. I was on-guard to ensure that the children didn't wander into this perilous area fraught with dangling electrical wires and exposed toxins.

One time, I trailed my fast-footed two-year-old in through the open garage. That is how I met the owner. He was working alongside a crew to transform this dated, dilapidated abode into a bland, but clean, functional home. He equipped it with new, mid-quality appliances and neutral-colored finishings. All looked straight out of a Home Depot catalogue.

Between us, Joaquín and I joked privately about being next-door neighbors with Mom and Warren. We had no money and no income so it was all hypothetical.

"Wouldn't that be the ultimate poetic justice?" I chided him. "All these years, Mom always complained that we live so far away and she never gets a chance to see her grandchildren, or really get to know them. Can you imagine being that close?"

It's true. For years, Mom had hemmed and hawed about the heartache of having her grandchildren in another country and not understanding their language. She hated that she was not an integral part of their lives.

Hmmmm... be careful what you wish for, I remembered thinking on November 13, 2008, that fateful evening when we arrived to live very, very close indeed.

A few days later, after the chasing-curious-two-year-old incident, Joaquín and I were standing in Mom's front driveway, watching the kids play outside and conversing nonchalantly about their progress at school. Suddenly, the owner of the home emerges from inside and approaches us.

"How's it going?" my husband inquires. "Have you made much progress with the renovations?"

"Why don't you guys come in a take a look?" he encourages, motioning for us to follow him inside through the open, garage door.

Joaquín and I exchange a quizzical glance and I mumble, "Why not? Just call the kids so they're with us and not left out here alone."

The owner takes us on a walk-through, proudly and painstakingly pointing out each upgrade, improvement, and repair. He did a good job.

It is fine, small and plain and certainly not an option for us. A three bedroom, two bathroom, 1,600 square-foot home is far too small for a family of seven. More decisively, we're broke.

We thank him for the tour and congratulate him on a job well-done.

"So, what do you guys think?" he trails us outside. "What would you pay to rent a place like this?" he questions, catching us off-guard.

"I...ah...really don't know," my husband responds cavalierly. "Like around $1800 a month, I guess," Joaquín throws out a random number. Evidently, he and I are both oblivious as to where this is headed and what we unwittingly may be getting ourselves lassoed into.

"Okay, great," he chirps. "Let me talk to my wife and I'll get back to you by say, tomorrow. You guys going to be around? If we all agree, you can move in as soon as the fifteenth of this month."

Gasp. What just happened?

The next morning Joaquín leaves for Panamá and plans to stay a few weeks. He is striving to close a deal for a sizeable consulting job. Once he does, we'll know precisely what money we have to coast on for the next month or so, depending on our expenses.

"What was all that about, Mi Amor?" I ask him, flabbergasted and uncertain whether we just had made an official offer to rent a house.

"What should I tell him when he calls me tomorrow? Obviously this guy is very forthright about getting tenants in there right away."

"Just wait and see what he says tomorrow after he talks to his wife, Mi Amor, and we'll take it from there."

"O-k-a-y. But are we crazy?" I ramble on breathlessly. "You don't have a stable income. We have no money saved for a deposit or for the required first month's and last month's rent, and we have no credit. And you know, here in the US, everything is so regimented with contracts and lawyers and you can't just..."

"Shush. Let's not get ahead of ourselves. Just wait and see. Tranquila."[50]

Clearly, we hadn't planned for this. Joaquín didn't have a full-time job and therefore, no reliable income to count on. From time to time, he'd land a gig, and that would manage to keep us afloat to pay for food, gas, the kids' school, and other household necessities. But getting entangled in a lease, a legal contract, under our current unstable situation, would be totally irresponsible on our part.

But furtively, despite voicing concerns, I'd scheme to make it happen. This "carpe diem-ish" philosophy of seize opportunities as they arise and work out the specifics later, was one we'd been living

---

50 Relax

by for years.

However, my personal life philosophy was ethereal; it reached far beyond even that. It was about developing a sensitization to the intangible signs the universe continuously presents, and trusting in my ability to de-codify these frequently cryptic messages. And then adjust my sails accordingly.

I call it being in a constant state of stand-by—attached to nothing and ready for anything. To practice this, you must be relentlessly intrepid, possess a high tolerance for risk and be willing to accept whatever outcome ensues. Most important, you must never look back or never second-guess a decision already made.

Let's face it: we needed a change of environment, and at Mom's, the breathing room was thin. I felt smothered. The kids couldn't spread their wings. It was time for something else.

Besides, there were photos plastered all over the walls, and in our closet. On the garage shelves sat labeled boxes full of his stuff.

In fact, everything here reminded me of Adam.

Pearls of Wisdom...

- o Discomfort is the cue that it's time for change.
- o Surrender control of the details and fate will guide you.
- o Attune yourself to the signs the universe puts in front of you, then take action.

21. *Hand to Mouth, Religious Honesty & A Writer is Born*

Everything in life is relative. We all have heard that worn-out cliché a million times, but I never comprehended its meaning as much as I do now. We migrated to South Florida three months ago with nothing. And aside from our material impoverishment, as a family and as a couple, we lacked privacy and space. So when we took the leap of faith and moved next door to this 1,600 square-foot town home in February 2009, it felt like a mansion.

The owner cleaned it up nicely and discarded most evidence of the almost ninety-year-old couple that had occupied it for close to four decades without once updating a single fixture. The walls were plain vanilla, the popcorn ceiling, plastic vertical blinds, and many bathroom furnishings were still in working-condition so they stayed—mediocre and dated—in all their characterless glory.

All the furniture and stuff we slowly acquired either came to us by way of donations or purchased for pennies off Craig's List. Our house was functional, a legitimate "working house," and one where the monotonous hubbub of the washer, drier or dishwasher was heard at all hours of the day.

Most significantly, we loved having so much space and privacy.

In hindsight, I realize we never really expected to stay there more than a year. There was always something coming down the pike, supposedly. I held onto the fantasy that Joaquín would find a prestigious and lucrative job and that at any moment, we'd move back "home" to Latin America.

Because of my stubborn hope and resolve to live by the Law of Attraction, I believed I could will circumstances to change sooner than later. That's why I never bothered putting any personal touches into the place. Never hung a painting, picture frame, or bought a plant. I kept one foot out the door, and waited for serendipity to move us out of South Florida and back up in status.

That is, until April 10, 2011, when I found myself face-down in the middle of the road, eating dirt. And then indeed quickly after that, pictures went up and everything changed. (More on this in the next chapter.)

The kids' resilience is wondrous. I never imagined them such adaptable creatures. They grow far more self-sufficient than they had been in Panamá. There they relied on the help like a crutch, which consequently stunted their growth in the self-reliance category.

Their adaptation to these new surroundings has been natural and relatively effortless, much more so than predicted. It took under a year to Americanize them.

We helped prod them along, encouraging them to read a lot, interact with neighborhood children, extended family, and we continuously rewarded them for behaviors that reflected a burgeoning autonomy.

I was still commuting forty-five minutes twice a day to the kids' school and running errands, cooking, and cleaning during the handful of hours in between drop off and pick up time. The frenetic pace took a toll on my mental acuity as I battled fatigue at the wheel almost daily.

In fact, I found myself ending each day with bone-weary fatigue, a class of subdued narcolepsy where you fall asleep mid-sentence as soon as you eye-ball your pillow. Oftentimes, the reply to my husband's late-night come-ons was, "Yes, Mi Amor, but please let me sleep right on through it."

My baby was just seven months old when I began tearing her from her crib, deep in slumber, to embark on the forty-five-minute commute to school. What bad luck she had. Despite my efforts to adjust her overall routine, specifically her sleep patterns, each day she'd fall asleep merely minutes before we had to leave the house to pick up the other kids. Thus, her afternoon naps were constantly sabotaged, unless she'd been particularly tired that day and pass out again in her car seat once back on the road.

But she was a good sport, and never fussed much. She ate most of her meals during one or more of the four daily commutes. When she still lacked the dexterity and coordination to feed herself, we'd stop at a rest stop off the Florida Turnpike. I'd crouch down at her side in the infant seat and feed her from a pre-packed lunch box in the parking lot. Alternatively, sometimes instead of letting the van idle and waste gas, we'd go into one of the plaza restaurants, and I'd order a coffee and get us a table.

We were like gypsies, she and I, and spent more time on the

road than at home. It saddened me that I couldn't provide her with stability, a calming atmosphere to nap and eat and play at home now that we finally had this huge place all to ourselves. But at the end of the day, it was my choice; I was the one who lobbied hard for that school, and committed myself to do whatever it took to keep the kids there once accepted.

When I began spending my volunteer hours to help care for the babies in the school nursery, it worked out well. I took Dalia in with me and she interacted with the other little ones her age, surrounded by toys, familiar faces and Mommy. At several junctures over the course of fourteen months, we considered moving northwest, up to Margate, to rent a small place closer to the school.

However, after an honest reassessment of the big picture, being neighbors with Mom and Warren was a bigger payoff; the tug-of-war between Mom and I had improved immeasurably since we moved out, and the kids were growing progressively closer to them as well.

They were the only set of grandparents the kids had known and interacted with on an ongoing basis. They met and visited with their paternal grandparents a couple of times over a span of many years, but had little memory of them beyond their names and the biting, squawking geese that roamed their vast property in Ciudad Colón, Costa Rica.

The days were long. I began long before dawn and carried on past midnight, tidying up and folding heaps of laundry. Nonetheless, the kids seemed to both rely on and thrive from the structure this rigorous schedule provided.

Attending a religious school had its advantages and disadvantages. One of the rewards of this homogenous, religious environment was that the kids retained a strong connection to their faith. The pride they exhibited celebrating holidays and in their overall Jewish identity, stemmed directly from this strong influence.

Yet, most of the kids' classmates lived far away and closer to the institution so play dates or sleepovers were usually out of the question. Most importantly, even for those select few friends that lived nearby, their families were markedly more religious than we were so we couldn't invite them over to our home due to the stringent level of Kashrut[51] they practiced.

At first, we tried to maintain the same level of observance and dietary restrictions as we had in Panamá, where a booming, religious Jewish community buffered us from the nonreligious world. But in reality, Kosher food is expensive, and so is missing work because of all the holiday restrictions—especially when you're barely working and need to take whatever you can get.

Paying each month's bills was a nerve-racking mystery. For two and a half years we lived in a perpetual state of unease, as one by one, each new job lead we eagerly and diligently pursued led us down a road to nowhere. The economy was suffering, especially the financial industry, and more so in South Florida than in many other remote parts of the nation.

Friends, family and people we'd meet in the community always took a liking to Joaquín. When he'd follow up with them, many would meet with him or take him to lunch and toss him a name or two. Some went a little further and made calls on his behalf to get him a meeting, or if an actual position were available, an interview.

Nothing ever panned out. Nothing. For two and a half years. It was soul-destroying and wrecked havoc on his self-esteem.

Yet somehow, each month, through resourceful thinking and continued downsizing, we pawned what little assets we had left and turned them into liquid cash. This is how we responsibly met our financial obligations.

Our five kids qualified for Medicaid for each consecutive year after our initial induction, although as a family they denied us food stamps and cash assistance. Apparently, we owned too many assets—that being, a tiny fraction of the principle of one used car. At least the kids had medical coverage and received all their check-ups and annual shots on time.

Joaquín and I were not—for some illogical reason—granted medical coverage even though our children repeatedly met the criteria. For years, we both failed to consult with a doctor. I went three years without a pap-smear, mammogram or comprehensive examination. Nor did we see a dentist.

I never could wrap my head around that one. How could the system find our children eligible, but the parents who are incapable of paying don't meet the requirements? As their primary caretakers,

51 Kosher-ness

shouldn't we need to stay healthy, too in order to best care for them? Wouldn't that make the most sense? I grew tired of calling, trying to persuade these irreverent representatives of my rationale. My letters all went unanswered as well.

Instead, we tried not to get sick.

In January of 2010, we reached a crossroads. The children were excelling in school, and had caught up to their peers linguistically; the kids' English reading and writing skills had shown a striking improvement, which bolstered their self-esteem noticeably.

Gradually, as a family, our level of religious observance began to whittle down, influenced by both economic and pragmatic factors, but most importantly, resulting from recent spiritual enlightenments.

We no longer needed to wear our beliefs like articles of clothing for the world to see. Privately, we could believe and practice whatever we wanted to without having to announce it publicly.

This epiphany liberated us from the chains of our own dogmatic thinking. Because our core beliefs were solid and unshakable, we were open, finally, to a spectrum of choices regarding both the practice of our faith and the children's academic environment—more than ever before. No longer did it have to be one extreme or the other. The kids were now prepared to enter that school—that five-star, award-winning public and free one located just around the corner from our house. The one reigned in part by the eye-rolling, acrylic-nailed lady.

To Rabbi Lichy's disappointment, I pulled the kids out of the Jewish school after winter break and inserted them into the public school system mid-year. I communicated frequently with their new teachers to help smooth the transition to this new, diverse more-bureaucratic environment.

But I was still troubled...

During those long years, my parenting style had become that of a sergeant. I felt beleaguered and combative. Uptight and yelling at the kids all the time, I rushed around, trying to do it all. My anxiety was not reflective of a deteriorating situation per se, but rather this residual stress seeped out of me in small, steady increments now that circumstances, although perpetually unstable, had improved somewhat.

The dam that had kept me stoic, robotic, a machine, was

beginning to collapse. The emotions I'd stifled for years weren't going to dissolve, much to my dismay. They were very much alive and ran like blood through my veins. I still needed an outlet, a reliable system to decompress.

One day, after an energizing workout—yes, gym membership was a priority despite our lack of disposable income—I came home to a familiar scene: my husband glued to the computer. Either he was pruning his resume, applying for positions all around the globe, or studying for his state exams. Always learning something and always innovating.

"Mi Amor, since you're constantly scribbling all over the house, on old receipts, the kids' school papers, the bills, why not start something called a blog? It's like an online diary. This way you can put your diarrhea of thoughts"—yes, he chose that word to describe it—"to good use, and into some semblance of order."

I liked his idea.

It piqued my interest.

Joaquín, forever the practical one, had tried in vain for years to organize me. Each time he'd return home inspired, having purchased Palm Pilots, fancy-schmancy rawhide agenda books, engraved notepads and smartphones. Yet repeatedly, I'd gravitate back to my consistently unreliable and archaic system: pen and paper.

When an idea popped into my head, I read a word I liked or experienced an awakening, I'd grab the closest thing to me, which was sometimes a napkin, and jot it down with the nail-biting urgency of a teenager. Nothing would stop me from scrawling upon the back of our tax return if it were within reach. Nothing.

Instead of seeking to stifle my desire to express myself through writing, or squash my spirit, he sensed my need and aspired to help me channel this bundle of unbridled creative energy—and unquestionable need for a therapist—in a positive direction.

He introduced me to Blogger, and that very moment, snapped an impromptu, unflattering picture of me with the webcam. My sweaty head was swathed in a red bandana and I looked like a wiry gangster. This is how it all began, how I was introduced officially to the world of writing.

The name for my blog came intuitively: Warrior Mom - Straight Talk from the Heart. I wrote almost daily about marriage, the funny things kids say and do, and about overcoming roadblocks. Mostly, I liked to reflect on my interminable quest to adjust to this estranged society and to our new, imposed lifestyle.

Since then I have trademarked the name. Every pore in my body oozes the essence of warrior and straight talk. And although external conditions have not been so dire as of late, thank God, the warrior-spirit stuck. After all this time, my demeanor, my DNA, my internal hardware, has changed. Forever.

That same year, 2010, when Hanukah rolled around, Joaquín endeavored to reignite one of my long-forsaken passions—biking. One day he surprised me with a faux-mountain bike from Target. In Panamá, I never had the opportunity to ride, a lifelong favorite pastime. Most neighborhoods lacked paved sidewalks and city parks were crammed with dog-walkers, strollers, and joggers. The only real spaces to pedal were either far off in isolated terrain or at Amador, a bustling waterfront area outfitted with a couple of bike-rental gigs unfavorable for hardcore road-biking. Sometimes, clusters of road-warriors braved the city highways, Corredor Norte and Corredor Sur. But biking alongside reckless drivers was unadvisable if you valued your life.

The day after I received this most-cherished gift, I started up again. And braved the same journey I'd weathered hundreds of times before since adolescence. For over a year, I set off alone near dawn on weekend mornings, and rode like the wind for a two-hour sprint to the beach and back home.

Until the time I fell and didn't make it back.

Pearls of Wisdom...

- o Rejoice in kids' natural resilience.
- o Compare your life's progress with only that of your own life.
- o Avoid extreme thinking. Live in the gray-zone.
- o Find healthy outlets for stress before you fall into unhealthy ones.

22. *Sunday Evening Blues*

April 10, 2011

The last thing I remember is taking a photo of the soft contrast between the dark blue tones of the ocean waters and pastels of the clear, late-afternoon sky. Breathtaking. The sea, calm. The breeze, crisp and gentle. Uploading a magnificent photo on Facebook and Twitter, it's appropriately titled: Sunday Evening Blues.

South Florida weather in April is a dream. And I'm on my mountain bike. Doesn't get any better than this, I thought, smiling to myself. Yet, unbeknownst to me, this euphoric sensation is about to end. And the ubiquitous melancholy associated with the word "blues," is about to take on a whole new meaning.

Hubby is home alone with the five kids and dinner is the next activity scheduled on the family agenda. Inhaling the fresh ocean air one last time, I gaze out dreamily onto the endless sea, bid the water farewell and hop back on my bike. I head west. Twilight is fast approaching and I have no reflectors. I know the kids are starved and getting antsy. I'm attuned to them and can feel it. The Sunday evening, back-to-school transition is a challenge for all of us, especially after a fun-filled, relaxing weekend.

Heart pounding, the back of my shirt instantly soaks with perspiration. I love it. I feel so damn alive. I lap up the salt from the beads of sweat as they drip off my nose and slide into my mouth. And dare not wipe them away.

Vehicles maneuvered by distracted drivers thread carelessly through the many narrow beachside streets. Coursing my way through, my gloved hands maintain a tight-grip on the knobby, rubber handles. Finally, I snake my way out and attempt to bolt across A1A, the coastal highway, without dismounting or slowing down. The sidewalk narrows and a jutting, cement bench seizes more than half my riding space. But I'm unfazed. I've done it countless times since my high school glory days.

However, balancing inside this tight passageway is tricky, a real crapshoot. And truthfully, I'm not nearly as agile and steady-on-my-feet as I was before 2006, before brain surgery.

In an instant, all five physical senses switch on to high-alert and become acutely aware of the close proximity to the bordering busy street. Code red.

Suddenly, my cock-eyed confidence collapses into breath-holding fear.

I lose total control.

Instantly, I go flying off the bike and am rocketed into the busy intersection. Crash-landing face-first, my chin takes the entire brunt of the fall and smashes into the burning asphalt. My head then ricochets off the road and comes hurtling back down onto the left side of the face.

Whack.

I lay there motionless.

Time crawls in slow motion. I hear the eerie sound of bones cracking and feel the internal shrill of my skull vibrating. Sprawled out flat on the road, my eyes open tentatively to the devastating aftermath. Tiny fragments of what appear to be teeth float in a large puddle of blood.

Oh shit. Are those my teeth?

I run my tongue over the jagged ridges of what used to be my trademark overbite trying to ascertain how many teeth are gone.

Should I edge over there and pick them up?

The thought crosses my mind and quickly disappears. My listless brain suddenly rouses out of its stupor to assess the damage. Am I alive? How did I get here?

I hear a voice.

MOVE IT! NOW!

Fueled by adrenaline and raw instinct, I slither out of the road and drag my body to the sidewalk. Tiny cuts open up and down my limbs as I slink across the rugged asphalt. I don't feel it, though. Arriving to my destination, the sidewalk, I collapse onto my back exhausted and surrender to fate—to whatever comes next.

People instantly converge and fire questions at me from all directions but I cannot answer.

Thank God somebody saw. Thank God people are coming to help. Voices blend. Small pools of blood quickly form around me painting the white sidewalk red. Pain consumes me.

My face is broken. And who knows what else .

Thoughts of the heartache I just unduly caused my unsuspecting family—home, happy, finishing homework and awaiting my arrival—occupy my brain. Silhouettes of strangers come and go; images of my children appear and quickly vanish.

Muffled whispers, car engines, horns and sirens surround and deafen me. What's going on? The scorching sun blinds me but I dare not close my eyes. I must pay attention. A man walks over to me and assumes I'm unconscious. He calls the paramedics.

"Do you have a name? Are you alone?" No answer.

My jaw is fractured; both the right and left condyles have splintered off from the rest of the mandible. I'm in bad shape. Really freaking bad shape. Somehow, I manage to press redial and hand my cell phone to this man. He glares at me quizzically then nods compassionately. His eyes reflect pity as he wistfully takes in my appearance.

I must look like a bloody train wreck. "Your husband is on his way, dear," a tall woman standing alongside the take-charge man assures, and then whispers something to him. He hesitantly hands me back my cell phone and I tuck it securely back into my tattered fanny-pack with my torn, gloved hand.

A few minutes elapse before the ambulance arrives. Everything is surreal, and still moves in slow motion. My mind begins to wander, trying to recall how this all happened. But I cannot process the information in any logical sequence; the smack to my head has distorted my thinking. In fact, I cannot think at all.

The intensity of the pain transports me to another realm of consciousness, one that precedes panic. It is a heightened state of awareness. I am stunned. My body feels weightless and I experience the sensation of floating. My weary head is dazed and baffled. I feel hyper-alive, and uncommonly calm. My jaw is locked in a creepy, half-open position and my mouth bears a frightening, catatonic expression.

My lids grow heavier and heavier. I'm sleepy. Drift off to sleep. Everyone will take care of you, my head belies. My comprehension wanes, but I listen intently to all jumbled words uttered between the growing crowd and team of paramedics. It takes an unfathomable amount of energy not to doze off. However, being at the mercy of strangers who are making determinations about my very life compels me to stay awake and alert. That's the priority, no matter what. I must participate—as much as possible—in these decisions.

I fight to pay attention, to capture every detail. I know I'll be writing about it later. I cling on to that one thought like a life raft and it keeps me from checking out.

If not for my expressive eyes darting about the crowd trying to communicate with those few taking control of the situation, lucidity would be impossible to determine. With a combination of aggressive eye contact, brow furrowing and hand gesturing, I maintain a sense of responsibility and control over my well-being. Through tenacity and grit, I avert the paramedics' attempts to shove my broken face into a snug-fitting neck brace, which undoubtedly, would have further displaced my broken bones.

They load me into the ambulance. Within seconds, my beloved Joaquín arrives. I see his approaching car through the corner of my eye and heave a sigh of relief as he pulls up next to the idling emergency vehicle.

He's always there for me. God, what would I do without him?

He steps out of his car and just as he approaches the ambulance, a police officer ushers him back into his car with a dismissive flick of the wrist, and leads him far away from the gory accident scene. Far away from me.

Inside the ambulance, the paramedics buzz about, communicating via radio with the awaiting emergency team at the hospital. Several huddle around me and fuss over my vitals while the others communicate via radio with the hospital crew. A member of the team informs me that my injuries are brutal and many. "You're in really bad shape, lady," he sighs.

Strangely, the acknowledgement of this engenders a feeling of surrender.

Sigh. I'm helpless. It's out of my hands.

My husband races behind us to the hospital. He still knows nothing of my condition. The kids are waiting for his imminent return.

"Mommy got a flat tire and I have to go pick her up. Be right back," he later told me he had said to the kids when he left them all at home alone, expecting to return just minutes later.

Worry and despair overtake me once my mind achieves a moment of clarity. I lay in my reproach.

You just fucked up a beautiful Sunday for the entire family.

How do you expect to make it home in time to help Yordana prepare for her FCAT tomorrow? You promised her. You must keep your word no matter what. It's all you got left.

This curveball changes everything.

My life hangs in the balance.

Screw that, though. I ain't going down this time. Either.

Pearls of Wisdom...

- o Find a purpose—no matter how frivolous or ridiculous—to stay engaged and lucid during moments of bodily trauma.
- o Fight like hell to stay alive.

23. *Broken Face*

Crazy what goes through your mind when you're hanging on for dear life. Feeling like the hapless protagonist of a made-for-television drama, I envisioned myself writing about it all, once recovered.

The whole drive to the hospital and subsequent days awaiting surgery, these thoughts alone rescued me from despondency.

Instead of focusing on the pain, I severed myself from it and fixated my attention on everything else, principally the retention of every detail. If nothing more, let me fight through this one wide-awake and come out a pillar of strength for my family, I reasoned, stuck inside my head for too many hours.

That's the interesting thing about breaking your face, and losing your ability to speak. You spend inordinate amounts of time locked inside your own probing mind, alone with your uncontested—and after the admission of narcotics—twisted thoughts. And you come to believe them as gospel because they remain undisputed...

They unload me from the ambulance and wheel me into the operating room where a team of doctors, nurses and other trained personnel takes my vitals, disrobes me and captures images of every square-inch of my body. I feel like an artifact recently dug up, after decades of failed excavations.

Unable to speak, I rely on my fingers and eyebrows to disclose critical information about my age, marital status, medical history, allergies and discomfort level. I carry no identification and nobody bothers to realize that my husband is standing outside in the waiting area, eager to inform and be informed.

I'm enraged when they cut off my brand new designer cycling shorts with a swift motion of the surgical scissors. Because despite my insistence that I am not pregnant, and have my period at that very moment, they shove a catheter deep inside me to gather a urine sample and determine for themselves.

I felt downright humiliated when they manipulated me so brusquely and to this day, denounce the head ER doctor for his negligence, as he led these boorish and inhumane explorations of my body. His bedside manner was unapologetic and callous. I get it; there was a sense of urgency and a battery of tests to conduct immediately. However, extending dignity is everything when you're a patient lying helpless atop an examination table, descended upon by groping strangers.

After the technicians administer the MRI and CT Scans, my sustained injuries are confirmed: shattered chin, fractured jaw, and left side base of skull fracture.

I catch a sideways glimpse of Joaquín for the first time since the fall after the tests conclude and they roll me back into the corridor.

"Hi, Mi Amor," he stutters, "y..y..you're...you're gonna be okay. It's not that bad."

But I know my husband, and his false bravado is unveiled as soon as I look up into his glistening eyes.

"Your wife is losing a great amount of blood through her left ear resulting from a base of skull fracture she suffered during the fall. There's a high probability that she busted her eardrum and will lose all hearing on that side," the same insensitive ER doctor reported, Joaquín later told me, hours after I'd been admitted.

"Well, then I suppose it's a good thing it wasn't the right side," my husband had responded, "because she's already deaf on the left."

When he told this to me, I shivered. I knew a miracle had emerged from this tragedy.

After the quick exchange with Joaquín, another scrub grabs hold of my gurney and wheels it into a large room. Finally, someone rinses my blood-soaked hair and with some antiseptic wipes, swabs my asphalt-dusted face. An old man with a shock of white hair and a heavy European accent comes at me with a needle and sews several sutures into my face to close the one-and-a-half-inch gash under my chin.

A man in a white lab coat enters the room. Without introducing himself, he wraps my neck with a stiff plastic brace, forcing my hanging, unhinged jaw to close—thereby further escalating the immense jaw pain. At this point, they still haven't pumped me with pain medication.

Focus, D. Focus on the details. Detach from the body's pain...

Prepped and pretty as a picture, I'm whisked into the intensive care unit—ready to be seen by visitors. The results of the MRI are as of yet, unconfirmed, and my case is considered high-risk because of the base of skull fracture.

The whole unit churns with frenetic energy and unmistakably, is short-staffed. The ICU nurse rushes in, breathless, and asks about the pain level while poking me with a syringe to get an IV drip started. My husband is now at my side and able to help answer many questions for me.

"Are you in pain?"

I wiggle my finger yes.

"A lot of pain?"

I toss a vacant, feeble stare in my husband's direction. "She's overwhelmed with pain, you can see it in her eyes," he translates.

"Okay, let's see... how much do you weigh again? Um...I can't seem to find it here on the chart..."

She quickly prepares an entire cocktail that includes antibiotics, steroids for the inflammation, hydration fluids and Dilaudid. Ouch. Just saying that word provokes a knee-jerk reaction of wanting to puke my guts up.

Because apparently, this poor scatterbrain didn't pay close attention to the dosage she administered—she was overseeing too many patients—so each time I fluttered my finger that "it still hurts," she pumped more "D" into my veins.

Days later, when they were ready to operate, I would pay the price for her carelessness.

The kids don't come. I don't want them to see me like this. And I look pretty damn scary. They are home with Grandpa Warren and he tries to minimize the severity of the accident so they stay calm.

The eldest has her big, serious statewide exam tomorrow morning. The FCAT, a parent's nemesis, is the student's ultimate litmus test—the moment of truth. The student body's collective score is one of the barometers used to determine and grade a given school's overall, scholastic success. Additionally, a student's ascent to the subsequent grade is based upon this one, defining exam. Yordana has been preparing for the FCAT since the school year began eight months ago and needs her rest.

The other four kids simply go along with what they are told as Warren successfully distracts them with his antics and box of donuts.

Mom rushes into the ICU later that evening to see me.

Disheveled and visibly distraught, mascara tracks heavily mark her tear-stained cheeks. She just flew in from a fun-filled weekend in Georgia, where she was visiting my brother and sister-in-law and their two adorable daughters. She was informed of my accident moments before boarding the plane, and had been misinformed; she assumed I'd been hit by a car and didn't know if she'd find me dead or alive.

Poor mom. She sobbed inconsolably the entire flight, fearing the worst. What she's had to go through...

Late in the night, once my base of skull fracture is deemed not life-threatening, I am moved to a regular room.

The next day, after school lets out, the kids pay me a visit. They wrote poems, made drawings and said prayers.

Yet nobody prepared them to see me. Not like this.

I am missing my two upper front teeth and the adjacent incisors are chipped and jagged resembling sharp claws. Several of my back upper and lower molars are broken and tiny shards of teeth continue to crumble out for days, and even months, after the accident. My unsightly jaw dangles way low—think Jay Leno—and my misshapen chin is black and crusty. Traces of asphalt and other tiny particles of street-side debris have embedded into my cheeks and forehead. A frizzy, tangled mop of blood-soaked hair drapes over my head.

I didn't smell like roses, either.

My eldest, Yordana, almost ten at the time, keeps her composure as she walks in. She hugs me and tells me all about her big, scary exam, confident that she did well. Miraculously, it seems her performance was unimpaired by my mishap. She told her teacher, whom I adore, about my biking accident before the test began and was showered with love and support.

My second girl, Leah, is equally mature and smiles sweetly when she first sees me. Her seven-year-old eyes reflect not even a flicker of sadness, fear or rejection for her mother in such a slovenly state. God bless her.

Natan, my authentic and emotional then six-year-old boy, cups his hands over his eyes and breaks down sobbing the instant he steps foot inside the room. He had misbehaved minutes before I took off on my wondrous-turned-ill-fated bike ride the day before and most certainly, this weighs heavily on his conscious. I summon him to my side and begrudging, he gives me a stiff hug—his lean little body tries to wrangle itself free from his mother's grip. He loves me too much to look into my eyes.

My four-year-old miracle boy Yair—the one who survived the last hospital stint with me in utero five years before in New York City—struts in as if he owns the place. His eyes go directly to a pretty floral arrangement placed atop the nightstand. "Who gave you those beautiful flowers, Mommy?" he innocently cheers. He kisses me like he saw me five minutes ago—like nothing was out of place—and dutifully hands me the drawing he made in school and turns toward my mother.

"Mimi, can we now go downstairs to McDonalds for chicken nuggets?"

Dalia Adina,[52] my gentle flower, hesitates at the hanging partition that separates me from my roommate. She takes teeny, deliberate steps inside my half of the room located in the back near the window. Noticing her hesitation, Joaquín swoops her up and brings her to me. She is almost three and this big girl stuff is too much for her to do on her own.

We've been together a very long time. Unlike the others who were enrolled in school as soon as they could walk, Dalia never left my side. She is my longest travel companion and the one I always say will take care of me when I'm old. At a year, she was already trailing her absentminded mom throughout the house, scolding me for leaving my cell phone, keys and purse in random areas.

At first, Dalia buries her head in her Papi's chest, and then after a little prodding, diligently hands me her scribbled paper. Afraid to approach me for a kiss, she then spins around on her heels to join the ranks of Yair, who is already halfway out the door, pestering Mimi *(Mom)* to take him downstairs to the on-premises McDonalds.

It's okay. They're only kids, and I can only imagine how hard it must be for them to see their strong mom looking so very broken.

By the third day, the head maxillofacial surgeon, Dr. McNichol, informs us that he put me on the roster to operate two days later. He wants the facial swelling to go down first. What he doesn't know however, is that I have been completely overwrought with nausea and vomiting for days—ever since my Dilaudid overdose in ICU. Due to that initial blunder, I haven't been able to keep

---

52 The name Dalia in Hebrew means "flower" and Adina means "gentle."

anything down. And oddly, I've developed a Pavlonian type of involuntary reaction; each time someone new comes to visit, I grab the bucket and throw up.

This is how I greet friends.

Dr. McNichol reiterates many times over the course of my stay that he needs me well-nourished. This will increase my chances of withstanding the operation and bolster my strength for the lengthy recovery period. My jaw is going to be wired shut for four-six weeks post-op, and I'm expected to lose a lot of weight. He urges me to consume whatever I can up until the designated twelve-hour fasting time before the administration of anesthesia.

Too late.

I go into surgery rail-thin—five pounds lighter than when admitted four days earlier—with my skin chapped and chafed from dehydration.

The operation lasts six hours. Dr. McNichol and his team successfully reconstruct my shattered chin and reconnect the dislocated mandible hinges. Hours after surgery a panoramic x-ray reveals a shocking amount of titanium holding the whole mess together.

The first twenty-four hours post-op, the pain pierces through my skull, face, neck, and trickles down the inside of my throat. By the next day, the IV drip of strong narcotics takes effect and a large portion of my discomfort subsides. Temporarily.

Nevertheless, the problem is that my inner claustrophobic doesn't adjust well to the jaw-wiring situation. Indeed, it takes a lot of meditating and willing myself free from my body to avoid entering a full-blown panic attack. In addition, they keep this ghastly intubation—a sore-throat-causing hose—inserted deep into my nostrils that snakes its way down my bony throat.

It is left in place overnight in case I vomit, the shift nurse tells me, so I won't asphyxiate. But my scrawny throat is bone-dry so this foreign material rubs the interior lining with every breath. It feels terribly invasive, and I choke on it throughout the night.

Affixed to the wall with heavy tape and in plain view is an emergency pair of sheers. They serve as a powerful reminder that in the event I have an irresistible urge to throw up, all I need to do is snip the wires fastening my jaw together. Once accomplished, this would allow the mouth to crank open and expel all gastric juices.

Scary thought. I stare wistfully at those scissors day after day.

They serve as a dark omen of what might happen if I don't stay cool and keep my jittery limbs and wandering mind in check.

Thus, I do what I always do, and set myself on a course of faith. I study the big, round-faced clock high on the wall, trusting that with the passage of time, my condition will improve.

The following morning at precisely eight-o'-clock, in waltzes the surgical crew and student-residents tagging behind. I point to the tubes that had raped me all night long and insist on their removal. "I will not vomit. Promise!" I scribble on a notepad before they have a chance to refuse me.

What relief! Once out, I consider coating my throat with a beverage or some liquid meal replacement drink. A few bottles of Ensure are parked on top of the adjacent nightstand, still unopened.

Lips pressed together manually, I have to suck hard through a thick straw if I want to quiet my now-rumbling tummy. Fortunately, that vacant space where my two front teeth popped out serves an invaluable purpose: insert straw here.

My sister-in-law flies in from Houston to help me with the kids and house days after I'm discharged from the hospital. Mom takes a few days off work and so does Joaquín, but shortly thereafter, everyone has to resume with his or her lives.

Sandri stays over a week and proves a tremendous help with the house and kids. And for me, serves as a distraction from the pain. My kids, thrilled to spend time with their tía, drill her about growing up in Costa Rica with their father—the adventure-seeking and risk-taking, Quincho.[53] My next door neighbor, Mom—the chronic insomniac who's been on a diet for the last forty-five years—selflessly devotes all her spare time blending shakes and juices, making organic soups from scratch and checking up on me. Joaquín, as he did in 2006 before and after my brain surgery, rises to the challenge and does all the physical work required to keep house. I never realized how proficient he was at this domestic stuff.

The kids are happy to have me home, yet unsure how to assess my fragile condition. They require constant reminding and monitoring to avoid inadvertently impaling me with their sharp-angled body parts.

---

53 Popular Costa Rican nickname for Joaquín. Additionally, night after night, Joaquín tells the kids Quincho bedtime stories, referring to himself in the third-person, and sharing his adventures about growing up in Costa Rica.

Unable to stay quiet, I learn to speak without moving my lips. Before long, I have a promising future as a ventriloquist. In fact, scores of friends I speak with over the phone in the weeks ahead once my vocal chords are stronger, ask me why the wires were removed so soon.

They were not. I'm simply doing the best I can to adapt to the new normal.

Press through it, D. Warrior-style. Nothing less will do.

During this meditative time of recovery, I experience a rollercoaster of emotions. I feel saddened for my husband's prolonged bad fortune—namely, his inability to find a respectable job commensurate with his level of expertise. I mourn my own vanity and wonder what the hidden message is behind me always disfiguring my face and hindering my ability to communicate verbally.

Is there some cosmic reason behind this? Was I an evil and vain shrew in a past life and am now paying for past-life sins with a slow erosion of my former good looks? Did I use my tongue for lashon hara?[54] Is my retribution a loss of ability to speak coherently?

Always, I'm searching for the signs—the deeper meaning of it all. To make sense of it, I need to feel a mystical level of certitude, and only once I have sorted through this supernatural logic, can I begin to chip away at my many, many flaws.

Time and again, the lyrics to U2's song, *Stuck in a Moment*, a lifelong favorite of mine, plays in my head.

It speaks to me more than ever before...

I never thought you were a fool
But darling, look at you. Ooh.
You gotta stand up straight, carry your own weight
'Cause tears are going nowhere baby

You've got to get yourself together
You've got stuck in a moment
And now you can't get out of it
Don't say that later will be better
Now you're stuck in a moment

---

54 Hebrew for "bad tongue"— literally meaning to gossip and slander.

And you can't get out of it

You are such a fool
To worry like you do.. Oh
I know it's tough
And you can never get enough
Of what you don't really need now
My, oh my...

...Oh love, look at you now
You've got yourself stuck in a moment
And you can't get out of it

...I wasn't jumping, for me it was a fall
It's a long way down to nothing at all

And if the night runs over
And if the day won't last
And if your way should falter
Along this stony pass

It's just a moment
This time will pass

It's just another test. Please don't despair, I keep telling myself each day, as I encounter my mangled face in the mirror.

During this time, I cannot circumvent my need to write to release my newfound insights and explosion of feelings. Below are a few blog entries I posted online just after my accident, once home from the hospital. I composed most in my head while bound to the bed by life-sustaining devices. As though I had been channeling great philosophers, the insights flooded me and I could barely keep up as I fought—despite my medicated haze—to keep typing.

I wrote the editorial below after an exhausting call with my dear friend Leti in Panamá. I call her God's attorney because she never, not once, neglected to remind me of God's hand in everything. And when misfortune indeed came her way, she handled it with the grace and strength that only a true believer warehouses at heart.

Yet most striking, was the cameo later made by another special someone...

A Tale of Compassion between Mother and Daughter...

Had a very real moment last night. This one I'll cherish forever.

I received a phone call from my best friend in Panamá; it was the first time we had spoken since my biking accident on April 10th. Just hearing her voice cracking on the line, provoked an eruption of emotion—feelings I had buried deep inside and had forbidden to surface.

"Darah, I admire you so much. Look at all you've been through; you are one of the strongest people I know."

"This is all part of God's plan for you. Have faith. He's testing you and strengthening you. You are a leader."

"I just don't believe God is paying attention anymore," I cried.

She pleaded with me to keep fighting through my struggles. And keep believing.

"Soon it will be over and you'll have tranquility and stability again. Be patient," she begged.

It was rounding eleven-o'-clock at night and the house was quiet. But someone was listening, and very intently indeed. Despite her claims not to understand Spanish anymore, she seemed to capture the gist of the entire conversation.

And when my newly ten-year-old daughter emerged from her room, her eyes were wide with tears.

She overheard me wailing about our stressful life situation—one that extends far beyond my recent hospitalization and injury.

"Mommy, I didn't know you felt like that. You're so tired Mommy, and in spite of your pain, you love me so much and are willing to host my birthday sleepover tomorrow night," she stated insightfully.

Instantly, my little girl matured. She had caught a glimpse into an adult world she never knew existed.

"I know you are doing the best you can, Mommy. And I appreciate you now more than ever. It doesn't matter about what you can't give me now. I just need you," she whimpered.

We hugged. She thanked me for fighting so hard to keep our family happy and united—despite my bouts of exhaustion, the unbearable stress and physical pain.

She felt compassion for her mom.

"I admire you so much, Mommy."

Words I needed to hear.

For the first time she saw me as an independent woman, a friend, and much more than just "her mother."

The moment was propitious to confide in her, in a loving way, just how hard many of us parents work to make life enjoyable and less cumbersome for our children.

Overnight, our intimacy deepened and emotional bond strengthened.

A new child awoke in my home this morning—one full of gratitude and understanding.

In the above heart-wrenching conversation with my dear Leti—where my supposedly-sleeping-eavesdropping daughter unwittingly discovered sides to her mother she never knew existed—I expressed my stomach-lurching fear of the future, a future painted black. The desperation reflected in the quivering lilt of my voice, and when she realized she could not uplift my spirits, she began to cry as well. Through her throaty sobs, she pleaded with me to trust in God and the plan He had for me.

"Algo grande vendrá de todo esto. Paciencia,"[55] she said.

At the conclusion of the intimacy shared during this life-impacting conversation, she promised to do all she could to rescue me from the bowels of despair, from my desire to give up. She vowed to help me obtain the funds needed for the costly, reconstructive dental work that soon would play a starring role in the ensuing twenty-four months.

True to her word, the next day Leti called to inform me she'd paired up with another friend, Annette, to coordinate a relief effort and appeal to the hearts of the Jewish Panamanian community.

One thing that sets the Panamanian Jewish community apart from any other I have known is its unwavering commitment to helping others through tzedekah.[56] Many of these families are blessed with good fortune and are more than willing to bestow their generosity upon less-fortunate others. Leti and Annette typed a heartfelt email and sent it out in masses—to appeal to potential benefactors.

The letter reminded everyone of who I was and all my family and I had been through the past five years. It described in

---

55 Something big will come from all of this. Patience.
56 Charitable giving, typically seen as a moral obligation.

harrowing detail, the tragic fall and resulting medical problems. It underscored the fact that my insurance defined all dental and periodontal procedures as "cosmetic" and therefore, would cover nothing. Many, many folks from the community did remember me—remember, it is a very small community and many were our friends. I was the lone gringa[57] who lived down there for eight years, birthed four babies on Panamanian soil, and had left only two and a half years before.

Suffice to say that the unanticipated outpour of love and assistance that flowed my way was overwhelming.

My heart soared. I never felt so appreciative to a people or tethered to a community as I did at that time. Incidentally, there was no way to thank the individuals that contributed toward my recovery. Most everyone preferred to remain anonymous.[58]

My Panamá. My people. We hadn't been forgotten. We still mattered.

So, together with donations received from our local community—after my mother's closest friend, Judi prepared and disseminated an equally powerful memorandum—miraculously, I acquired all the monies necessary to finance the forecasted dental procedures.

The firestorm inside my heart started to cool.

The next blog article came after my sister-in-law, Sandri, in cahoots with my mother, worked on me tirelessly to live the moment and stop waiting for the next act of life to begin. As I am sure you have noticed, I had been living with my head lost in the future, anticipating something that had yet to arrive—if it ever were to arrive at all.

Living Each Day Like It's Our Last...

My "good stuff" arrived from overseas sixteen months ago. I have yet to unpack it. And refuse to use it. Yet.

After all, we are moving soon so why bother? This is what I tell myself and everyone I meet. Such items are tangible representations of a life we no longer lead—a financially stable one—and one lost abruptly a little over two years ago.

---

57 American woman
58 Giving anonymously, with no contact with the receiver, is considered (spiritually) the highest form of giving tzedekah.

Thus, convinced it is all superfluous, and I'll be equally happy with the bare essentials, I pretend it doesn't exist. And I never miss it. Yes, we are just as happy as a family—if not happier—than we have been in years.

And under such rationale, I graciously have been accepting secondhand furniture or household items—despite having my own belongings stashed away in the garage.

Three main excuses I give for living this way are:

- My kids are young and will destroy it anyway.
- I'll wait to have nice things for when they're older.
- I don't need visual reminders of our shared past; it's the here and now that matters.

But the other night my mother, in collusion with my visiting sister-in-law, piqued my interest. They took me through a visual tour of how much lovelier my domestic world would be by hanging paintings and family photos on the walls. They encouraged me to assemble my good, dining room table and unpack some of our nice, unbroken ornaments.

"Get rid of this crap. This table is falling apart. Your dishes are chipped. Why are you recycling disposable forks?"

Inadvertently, I had grown accustomed to the other extreme—a plentiful life full of nothing but the raw necessities.

"Really, you aren't moving tomorrow despite your daily affirmations," my realist mother challenged.

And she was right.

Then it hit me.

I almost died thirteen days ago in a terrible biking accident. However, I got lucky and my jaw took the brunt of a fall, sparing my brain and body from any irreversible trauma.

And home recovering in the warmth embrace of my family, here I am living for tomorrow.

Yet who really knows how many more days any of us have left on this planet?

So with a clear, defined mission, we transformed my humble abode into something a little more elegant—a little prettier.

And guess what?

My heart's content. I awake to a house full of family photos plastered all over the walls. My eyes dart about our home delighting in little treasures, remnants of joyful memories we spent as new parents and newlyweds.

I don't want to live with regrets.

I want to pay attention to the details. Now.

And celebrate life by beautifying my external world once again.

In the following piece, I recount my struggle to face my reflection in the mirror and embrace my undesirable fate. Yet despite my obvious disappointment, my grasping self felt empowered to continue fighting to reclaim the glory days and recapture that piece of my identity now lost. My outlook—one that tinkers on the cusp of idealism—had me absolutely convinced that I can will it all back again.

Hanging onto Vanity...

Remember the days when you rolled out of bed, ran wet fingers through your unkempt hair, brushed your teeth, and were good-to-go?

Today at forty, life is far different and a slight transformation is called for immediately upon awakening.

Here's the drill: I roll out of bed and tiptoe into the bathroom. Time is of the essence. My unruly hair—which somehow over the years, has changed in volume and texture transforming into a frizzy, style-less mop—gets matted down with a generous handful of water. I gingerly twist the mane into the grip of a gigantic hair clip and allow some loose stands to cascade down my cheeks.

I pour a handsome lot of mouthwash into my recently-broken mouth to woo good-morning kisses. A thorough rinsing of the face ensures any nighttime debris washes away.

I wrap a fluffy pink robe around my weary body, anoint myself with an irresistible floral spritzer, glue in my flipper, (teeth) greet my husband, and wake the kids.

Life's adversities have taken their toll, no doubt. I recently admitted it to myself after hearing ad nauseam, "Mommy was this really you?"

"When was this picture taken?"

Yes, the remnants of a monster-sized brain tumor removed five years ago didn't disappear with its extraction. My face still bears a slight paralysis with a left eye that flutters independently from the right. My recent biking catastrophe that thrust me face-first into the street seven weeks ago, despite surgery, further accentuates my asymmetrical grin.

Lest I forget, pushing out five kids and raising this spirited bunch has expedited the aging process.

Undoubtedly, our life experiences reflect the choices we make. Mine has been an adventurous life full of passion, spontaneity and a degree of recklessness. But no regrets.

It's been a journey that has churned out one confident woman. One proud of her scars.

And despite all the imperfections and calamities, wanderlust and adventure still tug at my heartstrings.

I never want to stop tasting all life has to offer.

I still believe in fairies and believe all battle wounds will magically disappear in time.

Frankly, it helps not to linger too long in front of the mirror anymore. This way it's easy to imagine myself as I was before: unbroken. Just like my spirit is today.

You may call me delusional. I don't care.

Because, I'm still living my glory days.

They ain't over yet.

After much introspection achieved during countless hours holed up inside my dark bedroom, it became painfully clear that much of my disenchantment was rooted in a lack of patience and gratitude. No matter how I hard I tried to deny it, deep down, I knew my bounty wouldn't arrive until I owned and lived these two virtues. Daily.

Patience and Gratitude...

Two recurring themes have been defining my life: patience and gratitude. Putting these virtues into practice on a daily basis, is always a constant struggle. Being such a poor student, a tsunami of examples has had to flood into my life so that by age forty, I could begin to get it. I've had to lose almost everything—material and non-material—in order to capture, on a cellular level, its importance.

Gratitude

People always say to pray when things go well, not simply because we lack something. This is the hardest for most people— myself included. It's almost counterintuitive. During times of struggle and desperation, when we have nothing more to lose, we tend to feel grateful for the littlest of things. Our hearts are vulnerable, our eyes are sharp and appreciation flows easily.

Because many of us suffer from short-term memory loss, we forget to be thankful once our prayers are answered. In fact, we press on and demand more.

Like a weak muscle that requires constant training to strengthen, the daily exercise of acknowledging all we do have and are thankful for needs to become an integral part of our daily routine—lest we forget and lose it unexpectedly. Life is unpredictable and change happens abruptly—without warning.

Patience

Likewise, in this modern era of technology overload, we have come to expect immediate gratification. Our collective patience has waned. Nobody understands what it means to wait anymore. The cliché: "Good things come to those who wait," holds no value or importance—most notably, for our children's generation.

I am guilty of this syndrome. Yet life has shown me repeatedly, that when I cleave to something or grow emotionally attached, it slips through my fingers. By keeping nothing more than a loose grip combined with a focused intention on what I want and where I want to go, can I live in the moment and remain open to spontaneous opportunities.

I call it living in a constant state of stand-by. And by remaining semi-detached, my desires flow back into my life effortlessly—without the need to force anything. Deepak Chopra calls this The Law of Detachment.

By counting our blessings, thereby reminding ourselves daily of what we have, we stay in the present and learn to enjoy our kids, our families—our lives. And just when we least expect it, life shifts gears and surprises us with little gifts.

Because only when we first prove to be happy without "it," will "it" eventually come.

Patience and gratitude. Finally, I'm starting to get it.

Don't assume that upon arriving at the above realizations, my behaviors and actions converted into a living manifestation of these philosophies. Mainly, my analyses helped me identify the existential struggles at hand. Thus, I became increasingly aware of the laws of nature I'd been violating consistently. Nonetheless, despite ongoing failed attempts, I fight like hell to convert my revelations into action. Each day, a new battle takes place as I strive to bring into alliance the forces of good and evil that reside within me.

Pearls of Wisdom...

- o Shift focus to the mundane to detach from physical pain.
- o Share emotional strife with a trusted friend.
- o Keep your eye on the future, but your heart and body in the present.
- o Exercise patience and gratitude as a vehicle to uplift spirits.
- o Know and accept yourself.

24. *Same Accident, More Surgeries*
& A Cemetery of Teeth

Six weeks after my surgery, the wires came out. Once my jaw began to heal, I noticed something wasn't quite right. My mouth would not close completely and remained in a creepy, half-open, Neanderthal-like position. It looked as if I were panting. My lips couldn't touch and there was virtually no contact between what pieces were left of the upper and lower back molars.

After several consultations with two independent periodontal specialists, my dentist and the oral surgeon himself, the options were on the table. The chances of this happening are rare, I was told, but sometimes the jaw doesn't heal properly. The result is little to no occlusion between the top and bottom halves of the jaw.

Shit. What now?

Basically, it boiled down to three options:

1.) Live with a gaping open bite and adapt,
2.) Consult with an orthodontist to wear terribly invasive and unflattering appliances for years, that may or may not move the jaw into alignment, or
3.) Go back under the knife for a controlled fracture to re-set the jaw and wire it down for another six weeks.

After much deliberation with my husband and wrestling with my own consciousness, the answer became painfully obvious. I had to go back under the knife.

I didn't want to live with a dysfunctional mouth for the rest of my days, never being able to chew food again. To my dismay, I'd become a mouth breather.

Once I made the decision, Dr. McNichol introduced me to one of my now-favorite people in the world, Dr. Reza. Dr. Reza—a brilliant young surgeon with a heart of gold—was in his last year of residency and was ablaze with passion for the type of reconstructive surgery I needed. He had the knowledge to get the job done.

Dr. Reza spent hours on my case. He meticulously snapped photographs capturing all angles of my mouth. He constructed models of what he planned to achieve after surgery and split hairs to measure every crevice of my mouth. From the look of it all, the time he invested in the preparation and scores of colleagues and department heads that came to observe and weigh in on this special case, I knew this was something big.

"It's going to be a lot more painful than the first one, Darah. A lot more," he said. "We have to make at least four breaks between the upper and lower jaw in order to bring it into alignment."

Bring it, I thought to myself. Just give me good drugs for the pain and help me take care of the kids during the recovery. Then, I'll be fine.

We scheduled the operation for mid-August and I worked aggressively with a splint—thanks to the kindness of an occupational therapist named Lisa who loaned it to me free-of-charge for four months. I had to exercise the jaw to loosen it up, to enable the mouth to open wider than the current twelve millimeters—which isn't even enough to bite into a slice of toast.

I sat immobile several times a day, with this revolutionary contraption with jutting metal rods wedged deep into my mouth, and tried to relax while my jaw did yoga. I had no choice; I desperately needed several root canals and crowns in places the dentist could not physically reach. Instead of letting these teeth continue to rot and induce searing pain, I set out to repair what I could before they wired my jaw into submission for six more weeks.

Gradually, the ligaments stretched enough to allow the dentist to bond and crown the fragmented back molars. This greatly reduced the chances of the teeth further corroding during the anticipated wiring stint. Thanks to the jaw yoga, my toothbrush finally squeezed its way in there. Most importantly, the pain that emanated from the exposed nerves had been eliminated.

I was as ready as I'd ever be...

It's Monday morning, August 29, 2011, and we sneak out of the house before dawn breaks. The kids are still sleeping. I packed my bag the night before and Mom, our next-door neighbor, creeps in through the garage door to lie down until it is time to awaken the children for school. The original plan of getting this over with during summer break fell through.

Once processed through Admissions, a hospital staffer accompanies us to the OR waiting room. I never saw any of this before. Last time here, I was rushed in half-conscious through the emergency entrance, and bypassed all the protocol.

Joaquín and I sit in silence, hands intertwined, as voices from the Today Show waft in the background.

"Darah Zeledón. Please come this way," in pops the head of a robust, Hispanic woman in scrubs. "You sir, must wait here until called and then we'll escort you into pre-op."

I kiss Joaquín and follow the lady out.

When we see each other twenty minutes later, I am lying on a tea trolley donning a dreary, blue-spotted hospital gown. All sorts of electrical devices are stuck into my veins and dangling overhead.

"I love you, Mi Amor. You're gonna do great. See you later," he kisses me on the forehead and squeezes my hand gently.

Joaquín immediately jumps on I-95 and heads south to Miami to continue a series of interviews he begun a month before. A promising new job waits in the wings. There is no way in hell I am going to ask him to hang out and potentially sabotage this first golden opportunity.

Dr. Reza waltzes in minutes later and tosses me an encouraging smile.

"Good morning. You ready, Darah?"

I shake my head yes and watch carefully as he whispers to the surgical nurses. They scribble notes on pages wedged into a thick manila folder while glancing over at me every now and then.

After a short while, the team approaches my gurney and bombards me with questions about my post-surgical reactions to anesthesia, specific painkillers and narcotics. "No Diludaid," I exclaim to everyone within earshot.

"We got it. Okay, time to go," one of them says.

Almost instantly, the anesthesiologist comes from behind and stretches a mask over my nostrils. "Let's get you nice and comfortable before we go anywhere, shall we?"

In rushes a cold stream of nitrous gas.

That's all I remember.

When I emerge from surgery six hours later, my face is the size of a gigantic, misshapen watermelon—much more swollen than it had been after April's operation five months earlier. Score one for me. I made it out alive after another long round in the surgical boxing rink!

At least this is all finally behind me, and I will have my jaw back in alignment.

My head is mummified. Incubated and with a catheter shoved inside me, my legs are weighted down with inflatable, humming boots that keep my circulation flowing. A syringe is taped to the top of my right hand and another one is jammed into my left forearm. Whatever meds they are channeling into my veins keep me sleepy and relaxed.

I give a thumbs-up and Joaquín snaps a photo with his phone.

All good. I'm floating....

Joaquín stays with me that first night and is visibly uncomfortable with the set-up. For starters, the crappy, cot bed wedged between my own and the wall wrecks havoc on his back. I watch him toss and turn all night. Between the light-switch-flipping staffers that continuously parade in and out, and the strange, boisterous visitors that storm in to watch late-night television with my roommate, neither one of us sleeps at all.

The following morning, after Joaquin takes off for Miami, an aide wheels me down to radiology for an MRI and Panorex to ensure that all the bones secured with titanium plates and screws were firmly in place.

When I get back to my room, I rest a little and listen to my roommate argue with her belligerent boyfriend. She had been a victim in a serious car collision and couldn't move her legs. The specialists march in and out to examine her, unable to confirm whether she'll be confined to a wheel chair for a few weeks or the rest of her life. Her boyfriend's insults and scoldings hover in the background and lull me to sleep.

Hours later, the nurse on rotation sticks her head in from behind the curtain. "Time to wake up and take your liquid medication," she toots and snaps me awake. My mouth is wired shut. My ghastly huge and discolored lips stretch beyond recognition, and the entire neck and throat region is engorged, bruised and traumatized. I am unable to suck through a straw. The only way I can imbibe liquid is through a tiny syringe—the same way I administered antibiotics to my cat after her surgery.

Within minutes, a crew of white, lab coats appears at the partition.

"Hey, Darah. How ya feeling?" the imposing Dr. McNichol saunters in with a shadow of resident-loyalists at his heels.

"I've got some news for you, Sweetie."

"This morning's test results reveal that a few of the bones on the left side of the jaw didn't fuse together as we'd anticipated during surgery. Seems they're separating already. So we just need to 'go back in there' day after tomorrow to fasten them together with a small, titanium plate."

I go pale.

You have to be freaking kidding me? Another operation? Why didn't you blanket the whole damn face with titanium? God knows I'm already unrecognizable as myself!

I nod solemnly, defeat and sadness mirrored in my eyes. But I am unable to speak or even mouth a question. The vocal chords are unbearably sore and weakened as well.

I stretch my neck and glare regretfully at those damn shears, once again, affixed to the wall and looming over me like a dark, ominous storm cloud. I can't get myself worked up over this. Instead, I dial my husband's phone number—who by this time, already arrived to Miami on his first official day of work—and hand the phone to the doctor. Let him explain the whole mess to Joaquín. No tengo fuerza.[59]

Joaquín is infuriated and so is Mom. Yet what can we do? We are at the mercy of these specialists and need to trust their judgment—trust that this was what must be done. Strangely, despite my recent history of (feigned) courage, this second surgery—scheduled for two days later—scares the living daylights out of me. Just the idea of them manipulating my battered, tender face fills me up with breath-holding fear.

The chaotic narrative churns inside my weary, drug-induced head. I don't want to be put under the knife again. My body is withering into a heap of dried-out bones. Oh God, please be gentle! I'm so scared!

Two days later at seven in the morning, I lay on the gurney in the holding pen, next up on the roster for surgery. I arrive early. I watch as the surgical nurses, aides, surgeons and physicians file in one by one—latte in hand—routinely reporting for work. I listen attentively while they joke with one another about their blind date faux pas, missed sister's birthday and all the mundane.

A few glance over at me—this helpless lump of a body—after

---

[59] I don't have the strength.

reading my name off the day's agenda. Each minute seems to pass in slow motion as I stare blankly ahead reading and re-reading the same notices, wipe-board scribbles and memorandums hanging on the wall.

I wait by myself. Joaquín had to leave early for work to that new job he started two days ago—a day after the first surgery. This was the first position he had found in almost three years that was truly commensurate with his skills and experience. For that reason, I did not dare ask him to stay. Little did I know at the time, this job would become a personal beacon of hope that would lighten my spirits and illuminate the path through a most difficult recovery. It would propel me to trump over excruciating pain.

But at this very moment, I am all coiled up in a fetal position and feeling terribly alone. My body is frail and I feel exceedingly vulnerable. The profusion of narcotics toy with my senses. I am unable to cry as my puffed-up, blackened face lacks elasticity. It went through hell two days before. Cold and shivering, fear and doubt hijack my brain and I begin to think that maybe, just maybe, this time I'm not going to make it through...

Three hours later...

This second time out I appear more distorted and beaten up than ever before. The left jowl protrusion is triple the size of its right side counterpart. It looks like I have a tennis ball tucked inside there. Additionally, the recovery from these two surgeries proves to be much longer and more painful than after April's tumble off the bike.

Joaquín and Mom take turns spending the night with me and it is a good thing because not even the dying get much attention around here. Most of the shift nurses are so desensitized they hardly respond to a patient's request other than the scheduled administration of medications. Mom and Joaquín serve as my lawyers; they physically track down these burnt-out, cell-phone-yapping nurses to convey my needs.

A week later, the head surgeon discharges me and sends me home.

The kids are in school and I spend my mornings cuddled up in bed, focused on nursing myself back to health. The small amount of progress made toward facial symmetry after the 2006 brain surgery has vanished altogether. Somehow, during this last round of operations, in addition to the recent, predicted Fifth Nerve damage, my Seventh Nerve took a hit and the prior left-side paralysis has become more pronounced than it had been in years.

Shit. I miss my old, familiar face. Miss my smile. But I'm still me, still the same person inside. Right, right? Can you see that?

My kids and husband still look at me with the same eyes so nothing else matters.

Reflective and grateful—especially when I don't linger too long in front of the mirror—I string together a few words that best describe my observations about the collective, emotional growth-spurt experienced by the household during my extended recovery. And how, had I truly known what I was delving into, would've stuck with the Neanderthal mouth.

What We've Learned from Mom's Hospital Stint

It is both comforting and humbling to see that in my absence, things operate fairly well.

In fact, prior to surgery I was so consumed with everyone's smooth transition, I didn't make time to ponder the aftermath of what ten hours of major surgery would look like. It's a good thing I was distracted by the kids because had I known what I do now, I would've opted to jump off a bridge in lieu of bearing this anguish.

Nonetheless, from all of life's "challenges," we can extract hidden blessings and opportunities. As a family, we've learned a thing or two from this latest one.

Kids...

- They're more cognizant of their (flailing) limbs, and learn the necessary self-control to slow down and be with Mom.
- Kids are more sensitive to the suffering of others, (slightly) less egocentric, and no longer see Mom as a workhorse, but as a human being.
- They triumph over their initial shock and fear provoked by my post-surgical, distorted appearance and show compassion and love.
- Kids learn resiliency and adaptability as they ride the routine changes Mom's absence and subsequent fragility begets.

- Kids witness firsthand the importance of helping others as friends, family and neighbors collaborate to keep our lives running smoothly.
- Teamwork: Kids learn to (temporarily) put their sibling differences aside and work together for the benefit of Mom's healing, sanity and general good.
- They're not the only ones who drool.

Mom...

- I experience the benefits of passivity and slow-living as I move more deliberately.
- For the first time, I extend patience and acceptance (also) to myself, and do not demand too much.
- No longer do I equate perpetual "busy-ness" with the importance or success of my day.
- I know what it feels like to be ignored, invisible, and neglected. I also know what it feels like to "fall in love" with whoever takes a moment to feed and care for me.
- I have gained a greater appreciation for how much caring people matter and enhance our lives.
- When looks are distorted and the body goes, the mind is all that remains. Ultimately, our thoughts and words are of most interest to others and will be our legacy once we're gone.
- Small, realistic, and achievable goals are enough; the key is always to move forward and celebrate the smallest of victories.
- I adore and appreciate my husband and mother more than ever before.
- I no longer need caffeine to survive.
- I drool; therefore, I exist. (Kids complain that I leave tiny puddles of spit everywhere. So I tell them to get over it, and remind them how each one drooled upon me mercilessly until age four.)

Undeniably, humor is the secret sauce that keeps me buoyed in rough waters. Because as Erma Bombeck says, *"If you can't make it better, you can laugh at it."*

Pearls of Wisdom...

- o   Be fearless and take calculated risks.
- o   Use music, journaling, painting or other crafts to record reflections.
- o   Be especially kind to the "self" after a setback.
- o   Surrender to trusted others—wholeheartedly.
- o   Use humor to lighten up dark moments.

25. *Stability, Self-Acceptance & Brighter Days*

I was blessed with a team of very patient and talented professionals that have been working hard to help me restore what I lost—my old, bucky mouth. It's funny because finally I had the chance to improve my imperfect smile—one that never had been corrected with braces or appliances of any kind. Offered a new and improved mouth—a start-from-scratch one—the only thing I wanted was to restore what had become a mere relic of my past.

I bet you would, too. Think about it: major deformations aside, if you had to choose the same double-jointed fingers, bony knees or slight overbite again over a flawless, brand-spanking-new one, I bet you would want your own signature design back.

I know you would; it's what makes you unique. It's been six years and I'm still working on reclaiming mine.

The A-ha Moment (September 12, 2011, home again from the hospital only four days.)

"She can't wait to get away from me," I overhear her cry to my husband on the phone. "No, it's not like that Mimi," he assures my mother. "She simply loves to travel and is always looking for the next adventure."

Then it dawned on me. God, does she love me. And wants me around. But why?

I have been such a terrible daughter for years—aloof, unaffectionate, and quietly harboring resentments for things gone wrong. But mostly, for the constant rebuke of her ways—ways in which, despite my denial, I was just like her. Yet she heroically came through for us back in November 2008, mid-recession, when we arrived bankrupt and full of hopelessness. She opened her home and embraced her bewildered, tender-aged grandchildren upon our abrupt migration back to South Florida after eight years of the good life in Central America.

She helped us out as best as she could have, despite the financial burden seven additional people squeezed into her three-bedroom town home represented, and the emotional toll it took—

no doubt—on her marriage.

She spared us from homelessness.

And now strangely, she needs me. What can I possibly offer her other than grief?

The knot in my throat rises and swells, and suddenly transforms into full-blown sobbing. It's all pouring out in this un-stuck moment of enlightenment. And of all times, this awakening comes now that my jaw is wired shut, face still swollen and numb from last week's two surgeries, and whilst in the throes of a migraine.

My sinuses start to bleed from the implosion of emotions.

What's more, Joaquín doesn't seem to notice my chest heave when I ask him for the hot packs. It is 10:30pm and we're sort of watching the US Open. I tell him I am in agony and continue to bawl my eyes out once the big, blue gummy packs blanket my battered face. And he goes on and on about his new job and how, for the first time in years, it is an excellent career opportunity—something professionally-challenging that eventually could bring in good money.

I exhale a sigh of relief. Our luck just took a turn for the better. I know it because I feel it.

After over five years of struggling, family tragedy, bankruptcy, and me, in and out of hospitals. After five long years of letdowns and false hopes taking us down dead end roads, this is how this breakthrough moment unveils? I had rehearsed this scenario a million times in my mind; it was supposed to be accompanied by fireworks, a camera crew, and some larger-than-life announcement written across the mid-day sky. Something epic.

But, no. This is bittersweet. We don't know where it will lead us. Back to Latin America or keep us in the US?

It's been exactly three months since Joaquín landed his job with the Venezuelans. He sealed the deal, signed the dotted line and married these guys the day of my second jaw surgery on August 29, 2011. We didn't know if we'd be moving to Guatemala—there was loose talk about it upon his hiring—but nonetheless, his employment infused me with hope. It gave me something to focus on other than my own inability to swallow or breathe.

In fact, because of Joaquín's new gig and all it represented, I avoided asphyxiation, right there, in the hospital bed and once back home. Because deep down, I knew we finally had come up for air, after holding our breath for several long, despairing years. This singular reality anesthetized me more than any of the potent narcotics that flowed through my veins days before.

And yes, after two back-to-back jaw surgeries, I felt like hell and looked worse. Even so, life was better. Our existence no longer was defined solely by a struggle to survive; conflicts that previously had zapped all our energies and time now almost entirely disappeared from our everyday life. A semblance of routine and stability filled the void where gratuitous chaos had been the homeostasis for many years.

The familiar cries of my loyal companions, anxiety and desperation—voices I muffled and embattled for years—slowly died down. I found solace in writing—truthful, soul-searching, meaning-of-life writing. I preferred this form of communication above all others perhaps due to my sensory impairments and inability to multitask. And desire to appease my budding introvert.

Throughout it all, I grew in character and depth. I learned to handle crisis like a full-fledged grown-up.

And despite this newfound adulthood finally founded in my late thirties, I discovered that even in the aftermath of radical life-changing experiences, residual parts of my former self still lingered. Somehow, I would have to embrace it all and integrate the old, carefree dabbler with the new, war-torn, grown-up version.

With a natural inclination to walk the fine line between good and evil, my yetzer hara[60] is an ever-present force I reckon with constantly. Although more than anything else this proclivity for mischief is born out of curiosity, luckily, I possess an equally strong pull toward righteousness and justice—a worthy contender that keeps my wayward tendencies in check.

Despite the existential tug-of-war that accosts my soul, each day I strive to channel this smorgasbord of emotions, destructive tendencies and impulses in a positive direction. Because if nothing else, I've learned that problems are disguised opportunities for personal growth.

My overriding goal is this: discover what I'm made of so I can strive to be the woman I want to see reflected in my children's eyes. These five children, in addition to my loving husband, keep me on

---

60 Hebrew for "the evil inclination" or more commonly known as man's natural tendency to misuse or abuse things the physical body needs to survive.

task; I cannot and will not let them down. My life-force is driven by a hunger to be accountable. Without them, I'd probably end up in prison for something.

For many of us, the struggles of the heart never end. We must trust in the process—growth and character are born from pain and suffering. There is no way around it—no shortcuts. An easy life will not yield the same results.

When trouble strikes, all we can do is stay the course and wait out the storm. Persevere. We have to find comfort in or in spite of the uncertainty, and accept that many of life's questions are unanswerable.

Most important, we ought to check ourselves constantly to ensure that our moral compass guides us in the direction of integrity. Living a principled and virtuous life day after day is not easy. Succumbing to pressure and temptation—especially when we are down—is human nature. Let's face it: we're all prone to bouts of moral lapse from time to time.

If most of the time, however, we can avoid lustful behaviors and bad decisions that drag us into ethical pitfalls, we'll reap the reward of a good night's sleep, and countless other intangible remunerations.

Above all else, we must not take this life or ourselves too seriously. My unremitting faith in God, trust in the natural cycle of life and incomparable feistiness has kept me together and keeps me moving forward. Most definitely, my ability to laugh at myself between bouts of kvetching[61] also helps.

Time marches on to the next event, to a new setting—to another stage of life. It moves quickly and will not wait for us to catch up. Nor does it discriminate between good times and tough times. Both answer to the same set of universal time-space constraints. So really all we can do is hop on board and go with it.

I made a daily choice. Despite assertions otherwise, my practiced self-deception/idealism wasn't a result of naïveté or stupidity. This suspended disbelief was my preferred defense mechanism. This kid-like ingenuousness paired with actively pining for change was the coping skill that kept me hanging in a state of anticipation, expecting a better tomorrow. My feet dangled above ground level all the time. Intentionally.

---

61 Yiddish for complaining.

Unlike the days of yesteryear, this time around I did not undergo a crisis of faith. Approaching my fourth decade of life, I solidified my belief that it was better to believe than not-believe. The answers to questions of faith—any faith—are unknowable. Period. In truth, at the end of our days, we have done nothing better for ourselves than having chosen to live life entrusting God or some other omnipotent entity to help shoulder life's burdens. At the very least, just to lighten the load. Even if in the end, it's all a crock.

For many years, we lived as observant Jews, abiding by most of the rules of Orthodoxy—insomuch that they defined our lives. With each freshly studied religious doctrine and subsequent integration into our already-rigorous religious routine, my spark of spirituality dimmed. Only once I got honest with myself and others, and stopped the charade—stopped living a lie—did I feel God's presence in every breath, in every moment. And recognize Him everywhere.

My evolution toward a more secular lifestyle did not happen overnight as you've read. It gained traction gradually, over a period of years. I wrestled with my own conscience to overcome and unlearn specific things I had been told—things I wholeheartedly accepted as indisputable truths. Only after confronting my own demons was I able to break free from the reins of dogma.

When things turn sour herein lies the perils of believing karma is delivering a message, or that it is owed to a neighbor's evil eye, or bad spell cast. The guilt I bore from my belief that in some cosmic way I ushered in our family's misfortune almost impeded my ability to cope and work through it at full throttle.

One example of this indoctrination is something I learned during one of my religious classes in Panamá. The moreh[62] spoke often of women's natural spiritual elevation in comparison to that of men. We discussed ways we women can use our divine "gifts" to improve our family's lot. He explained that a woman's degree of religious observance, or adherence to Jewish law, Halakcha, directly and positively correlates with the husband's ability to make money, or parnasa.[63] By this rationale, all men married to devout Jewish women should be financially well-off. Filthy rich even.

I spent many years judging myself harshly, afflicted with

---

62 Hebrew for male teacher.
63 Hebrew for income, sustenance from which to live a plentiful life

remorse, feeling that I alone was responsible for our family's financial woes. For many long years, I was convinced this was the underlying reason the doors to economic independence constantly slammed shut in my husband's face.

If only I weren't such a hypocrite, such a phony, and obeyed the Jewish laws willingly and joyfully, like so many other wives seem to do, I reflected time and again.

My husband had been such a believer; it took me years to muster up the courage to confess my internal struggle to him. When I did, I apologized for sabotaging our family's ability to forge ahead financially.

"Don't think like that, Mi Amor," he replied when I finally unloaded my burden. "It's only manipulation and you aren't responsible for anything."

Thankfully, by the time I came clean, like myself, he was past the punitive cycle as well. Pragmatism had filled the void. It was the only doctrine that made sense now.

Piety has many intangible benefits, no doubt. Naturally, it offers little by way of insulation or protection from bad things happening. I've seen the most spiritually devout people fall apart during tough times, despite a previously-asserted, unshakable faith. Staunchly following Halakcha—Judaism's treasured book of laws— replete with timeless wisdom and mystical explanations makes theoretical sense, but was not practical for us. We needed to be no-nonsense because of the way our lives had been unfurling.

No longer was I apologetic or feeling guilty for my vanishing religiosity. No longer did I try to conceal the two tiny tattoos I'd etched into my skin when young, wild and free.

In fact, I remember how an hour before brain surgery in 2006, an Orthodox Rabbi approached me in the waiting area. He said, "Bargain with God for your life. Vow to remove the tattoos and in exchange God should spare your life and that of your unborn child." Under the gun and feeling vulnerable, I did. Later on, I ran into problems once back home in Panamá and needed a beit din[64] to exonerate me from my promise.

Judaism will always be an integral part of my identity, a defining characteristic of our family life and traditions. Judaism's eternal wisdom fills in many gaps, and resides in the gulf between

---

64 Three Jewish men over the age of thirteen that act as a panel of judges with regards to issues of morality.

cold-hard science and blind faith. I do believe the Torah, or Old Testament, is God's gift to Jews—to the world. It provides a blueprint for righteous and compassionate behavior. It serves as a moral compass, and following such a path is transformative. Within the framework of Jewish ethics,[65] we learn what we must do to be a mensch.[66] It is that beautiful, that simplistic.

However, an orthodox lifestyle steeped in restrictions and relative separation from the outside world and a diet confined to expensive kosher food was not feasible for us—a family struggling to survive.

On a deeply personal level, I shed the duplicitous exoskeleton of piety and was free to explore my deep, unqualified faith. My relationship with my Maker grew more intimate, more authentic and more constant. There was no more pretending and man was it liberating. Released from bondage, I was able to live my truth; namely, that just behavior propelled by a desire for good pretty much summed it all up.

Only when I stripped my spirituality down to its bare bones, did I throw my hands in the air and find patience and gratitude. And God. Yes, I first remember really finding and desperately needing Him while climbing that seventy-foot Strangler Tree in Costa Rica's Osa Peninsula back in 1996. However, our relationship has matured since then. Not only do I now feel connected to Him in moments of desperation, but I trust in His guidance and allow events to unfold serendipitously.

Over the past six years, I had become a chameleon—a true master at adapting to the fluctuations of fate, holding onto nothing more than my own thoughts and flesh-and-blood family. Each day was marked by innovation and re-invention. A realist who never lost hope, each day I embarked on a personal journey to start fresh, as if yesterday's bad luck never existed. Borderline la-la land, I know, but it worked to preserve sanity.

My strength came from a place buried deep within my core, where seeds of rage were first planted when I was diagnosed with that mammoth-sized brain tumor. These seeds sprouted into a fierce defiance that began to stir and eventually transformed into a

---

65 The book Pirkei Avot, meaning Chapters of the Fathers is a compilation of ethical teachings and proverbs. Because of its contents, stemming from the Rabbis of the Mishnaic period, it is also called Ethics of the Fathers.
66 Person that radiates integrity and honor and other admirable character traits.

volcanic force when Adam died. Once erupted, its energy nourished my restless spirit and kept me pressing on indefinitely—despite my crumbling world.

All the suffering, stress and losses have made me into the person I am today. During this metamorphosis, I became a warrior. I led my family through a labyrinth of instability and insecurity.

In 2006, my life began to unfold like a soap opera. I didn't sign up for this. There were only two choices: adapt and plough through, or shrivel up and perish. I chose the former. I had three tiny children at the time, and was pregnant with my fourth. They all looked toward me to be strong. My husband needed me to hold it together. So I dove into a parallel reality and fancied myself a soldier. My mission came into sharp focus: safeguard the well-being of the family—at all costs. By evoking my rich childhood imagination, and assuming the mindset of an embattled combatant, I pushed on through years of darkness.

Although we still have our bouts of chaos that disrupt the status quo, eventually everything does come full circle. I always knew it would, just never knew when. Tom Petty nails it when he sings: *The waiting is the hardest part.*

Look, reading the signposts is not only fun, it adds an element of mystery to life. It makes room for moments of spontaneity, surprises, and innovation. For me, it is the very life force, the drive that rules my sense of optimism about the moment, the future, and life in general. It's what keeps me from getting "stuck in the moment" because these moments called life are impermanent. An understanding of this singular reality spurs me on to await something extraordinary—something fresh—to color my world.

That's how I knew the dim colors of our destiny had brightened the day Joaquín returned from work and told me about the International Congress in Barcelona. I felt the earth move under my feet as the words casually rolled off his tongue. I didn't know how we'd manage a single logistic between the kids and lack of funds. Yet intuitively, I knew we were fated to return to the place where all the magic had begun twelve years before.

Barcelona was calling us back.

I pray that my children will one day understand all we did to safeguard their emotional and physical well-being and how our endless well of love for them inspired us to keep pedaling against hurricane-like gusts. I hope that when they come face to face with adversity, they'll demonstrate a staunch resilience coupled with an unremitting faith that "this storm will too pass." I also wish that in a shorter time than it took their own mother to do so, they will learn to accept and love themselves and live their own individual truths. And when their inner conflicts and insecurities blend away, and they settle comfortably into their own skin, they, too will reap the intrinsic rewards honesty and transparence of purpose bestows upon us—one of them being a heart full of joy.

I know my story is just one of many. Most certainly, many, many other tales are testament to the unbreakable will of the human spirit. Throughout humankind we've witnessed countless people whose challenging circumstances have catapulted them to incalculable levels of courage and greatness.

However, if a story is not told, one's story—no matter how grand or insignificant—an entire life can be forgotten.

I am nothing more than an ordinary woman, a mere speck of dust in the history of the human race. And this is my story.

Epilogue

After that breath of fresh air, our Barcelona rendezvous, once again, the wind was at our back and things began to turn around rather quickly. Joaquín changed jobs immediately upon our return and joined the ranks of a successful European company. We talked again about moving, and having more space for our kids to spread their wings, play and for all of us to enjoy a tad of privacy when needed. After many long hours of combing through neighborhoods, researching schools and navigating our way through shady contracts that eventually fell apart, we found a home—our very first home we could call our own.

The kids finished out the school year and we moved two days later. That following summer was glorious. The kids and I stayed home submerged in the swimming pool, explored our new surroundings, and acclimated to the new set-up. I kept busy looking after them, running the household asylum, unpacking and organizing. Before we knew it, fall came barreling around the corner and it was time for the kids to start their new school. As usual, I pumped them up for the change—new friends, new teachers, a new adventure—and we were all enthusiastic to embrace the unknown.

On school day number three, I signed all five out early and took them to their routine, dental cleaning appointment. I floated on top of the world, so thankful for the change of tides.

When we returned home, after deactivating the alarm, a heavy scent wafted in the air—the house reeked of gasoline. The gardeners recently left, but this intoxicating odor never penetrated the interior of the house like this before. I took the kids around the back of the house to check things out and behold: our new home had been burglarized!

The perpetrators entered through my bedroom sliding-glass door, leaving minuscule shards of glass scattered everywhere—even blanketing the bottom of the swimming pool. Peering inside my new bedroom, my heart hammered inside my chest. Upon further exploration, I came to the sick realization that they pilfered every piece of valuable and sentimental jewelry I owned and had riffled through all our drawers, seizing documents and countless treasures.

My heart tanked. I wanted to close my eyes and run away, yet had all five kids looking to me for guidance and reassurance. I led them to the front lawn where we all plopped onto the ground, huddled together and cried as we awaited the police's arrival. Hands intertwined, we thanked God none of us were home when it happened.

Joaquín showed up a short while after and stepped inside as I conversed with the trio of cops that arrived almost instantly to tell me nothing I didn't already know. That is, except for comforting me with the notion that our homeowners insurance didn't cover the replacement of my jewelry because the remiss insurance agent neglected to offer Joaquín a "floater policy." But that's another story.

So, why would I put this narrative in the epilogue of all places? To illustrate the point that although circumstances improved immeasurably, it wasn't all smooth sailing and happily-ever-after following our personal turning point, Barcelona. Blindsided by this crisis, I had to walk the talk, and put my own *pearls of wisdom* into practice immediately—knocked down once again after feeling so up. After my slotted time mourning the loss of all my sentimental belongings purchased with nothing more than the fruits of our own blood, sweat and tears, I detached and moved on.

Don't get me wrong: this un-jeweled woman would love nothing more than her precious treasures back, but moving forward is the only option. Perhaps something better is on the horizon and I just can't see it yet? I'd like to consider it that way. Regardless, bumps in the road there will be always, but the important lesson is to use the *pearls* as shock absorbers. They enable us to develop resilience, to keep pedaling, even when it burns so badly our aching bodies beg for mercy.

The *pearls* also afford us the chance to be spectators of our own thoughts, feelings and actions and mindful of our power to choose how we react and respond. Onward I march, pressing on into the uncertainty—not knowing what awaits me at the end of each day. I am confident that by staying authentic and courageous, and true to my higher purpose of inspiring others, everything, somehow, will turn out fine.

And be just as it should, a little *crooked*.

Acknowledgments

I am truly blessed. So many people over the years, directly and indirectly, helped me write this book. Many friends first encouraged me to continue documenting my soap-opera-of-a-life when I first started publishing it on blogger.com. They were among the very first who demonstrated interest in my writings at its unpolished inception. Some of these early supporters were: Derek Price, Russell King, Ana Margarita Goode, Sandra Graves, David Silverman, Amy Silverman, Bernita King, Maris Zilant, Tamara Stark, Joaquín Zeledón, Heather Sobierski, Virginita Weeden, Lillian Faigenbaum, Leti Kolangui, Michelle Chandler, Celia Shapiro, Robert Chandler, Dorita Eisenman, Bridget Straub, Stacey Magadov, Sally Abadi, Alejandra Zafrani, Bonnie Eisenson, Leslie Crouch, Rebecca Fichtel, Gabriel Constans, Kayelle Allen, Angelica Pastorelli, Lorne Fisher, Alyssa Cohen-Freeman, Stephanie Newman, Debbie Appleton, Jenny Levin, Kelly Rothschild, and Dana Turtletaub.

A big thank you goes out to my early draft readers as they tirelessly read through one error-laden draft after another only to be slammed with (yet) another revision days, sometimes just hours, later: Bethany Vedder, Judy Turtletaub, Evelyn Lauren, Charlene Pacenti, Nancy Levy, Ana Karla Gherman, Penny Weiner, Judy Wiener, Judi Robaina, Judy Turtletaub, Sheree Sharkan, Dorita Eisenman, Sally Abadi, Tamara Stark, Bernita King, Chrissy Plunket, Warren Gherman, Maris Gherman, and Lynette Benton. Your input, suggestions and spot-on critiques empowered me to keep writing and editing over and over again—till I couldn't even stand to look at the damn thing anymore.

Grateful to all the writers, editors, publishers and other dynamic professionals who provided invaluable advice and assistance over the years: Michael Stark, Alex Glass, Jesse Green, Monique Raphel High, Hope Clark, Nellie Sabin, Dr. Deborah Gilboa, Fran Lewis, Randy Roth, Peter Jaegar, Helen Jonsen, Kelli Daley, Jennifer Cohen, Elisabeth Wilkins, Judy St-Somer, Lori Ortiz, Rochelle Weinstein, Kiki Bochi, Meredith Miller Chandler, Shawana Bridgers, Beth Smith, Patricia Laster, Linda Gaissenheimer, Judith Marks-White Meyers, Michael Befante, Karen Frankel, Lisa Napoli, and Jerry Sepulveda.

Thank you to all the people who interviewed me on their websites, talk-radio and television shows having found my story inspirational and the empowering message behind it valuable: Dana Hilmer, Allan Holender, Lillian Brummet, Toni Quest, Greg Giesen, Jeanne White, Susan Greenman, Michael Dresser, Lillian Cauldwell, Fey Ugokwe, Johnny Tan, Paolo Pugni, Robin Gorman Newman, Lynette Benton, Marsha Cook, Allyson Tomchin, Stephanie Goldberg Glazer, and Teana McDonald.

In awe of all those higher souls who helped me gain insights and spiritual understanding throughout my tumultuous journey: Leah Gila Banayon, Fradel Laine, Gabriel Benayon, Rabbi Aaron Laine, Moreh Cohen, Leti Kolangui (God's attorney and my BFF), Rabbi Mordechai Lichy, and Rabbi Dr. Gideon M. Goldenholtz.

To all generous and compassionate spirits who made donations after my horrific biking accident: there are too many to name, but you know who you are and words prove adequate to express my most heartfelt gratitude. You collectively saved me from a cemetery of broken and missing teeth. May God bless each and every one of you and your loved ones with good health and happiness always.

To my amazing team of doctors and occupational therapists who worked indefatigably and painstakingly to reconstruct my broken face, jaw and mouth: Dr. Reza Movahed (I love you, I really do!), Dr. Shawn McClure (You too, doc!), Mrs. Lisa Grace, Kurt Klein, Dr. Darren Snow, Dr. Dan Mazor, and Dr. Raul Chanis. To the special doctors that helped me through my days in Panamá: Dr. Juan Antonio Carbone, Dr. Carlos Velarde, Dr. Ana Celia Arango Jimenez, Dr. Carlos Briceño, Dr. John Golfinos and his right-hand nurse practitioner, Jessica Shafrick, and Mom's crush, the so very handsome, Dr. Thomas Roland.

To my incredibly talented and brilliant publisher, mentor and success coach, Jodi Nicholson, who, from the moment she saw I'd dropped the f-bomb in my book, never hesitated to tell it to me straight. For your unique ability to dole out the hard-to-swallow candor and polish it off with a generous dollop of enthusiasm and encouragement, I am forever grateful. You help me laser-focus every inch of the way, recognizing from the get-go, my mind's natural tendency to drift, in and out of outer space. You hold me accountable to my tasks, calling me out on all my overzealous "ridiculousnesses" — *Is that even a word?* I will always cherish the serendipitous way we found one another then chatted for hours like childhood pals, sharing philosophies about life and purpose. Clearly, more evidence that living in a state of stand-by, both expecting nothing and anything at all, truly does usher in the most rewarding surprises.

To my intimate group of friends and family who remained at my side whilst in the throes of manic writing binges. You picked up my slack when I neglected to feed the kids—or even acknowledge their existence at all—and negotiated with countless loads of unfinished laundry: Judy St-Somer, Judy Carlish, Trish Sheldon, Maris Gherman, Warren Gherman, and my rock of Gibraltar, role model and moral compass, Joaquín Zeledón.

Thank you all from the bottom of my heart. It's been a long, arduous journey to get here, a dream come true. I do believe in fairies; I do, I do!

Having accomplished this goal, I press on like a warrior, in the realization that the "real work" now begins: taking the worst tragedy of my life, the loss of my brother, and using it to fuel my higher purpose. That being, reaching out to touch others with the objective of helping a few lost souls find their way home.

Thank you, my beloved "Little Man," for a second chance to be a good, big sister—one that never stops paying attention.

With love and gratitude,

Darah Zeledón
Girl with the Crooked Smile

Florida Initiative for Suicide Prevention's Adam Silverman Memorial College SUN Program

- Declaration of Charity -

...*stop suicide*

A percentage of the proceeds from the sale of each copy of this book will go to *the Florida Initiative for Suicide Prevention's (FISP) Adam Silverman Memorial College SUN Program*, named for Darah's younger brother who committed suicide in 2006.

These programs are geared to teach critical problem-solving and life-coping skills to college kids and adolescents.

FISP is a 501(c)(3) nonprofit volunteer organization that started in 1987. To learn more, if you need help or to get involved please visit www.fisponline.org.

To learn more about the SUN programs offered, or start one in your area please visit http://fisponline.org/programs/sun-programs/.

Author's Note: I'd like to personally thank each and every one of you who purchases this book, ultimately contributing to the greater cause of reaching out to loved ones who need reassurance that no matter what circumstances befall them, life's still worth living. Together we can make a difference if, at the very least, we remember to pay attention to those around us, and nurture daily our most treasured relationships.

I was lucky; my kids and loving husband fueled my desire to keep nudging forward. Others aren't as lucky, or feisty as I am, or sadly, don't count on the same support I was blessed with. These folks need a little more coaxing, someone to take them by the hand and show them that they too, can get through and prevail.

As for me, if I can inspire just one person to keep the faith, I've done my job.

About The Author, Darah Zeledón

A self-proclaimed dynamo, Darah's the devoted mom of five and wife of one amazing husband, Joaquín. When she's not mothering or "wife-ing," she shines as many other things... an accomplished author, inspiring speaker, motivational coach and humanitarian.

Darah is known throughout social media as the Warrior Mom. She is fluent in Spanish, holds a B.S. in psychology, M.A. in international relations and is a Certified Life & Success Coach (CLC, CPSC). As a seasoned writer, she joined *The Miami Herald's* www.momsmiami.com as a featured blogger in 2010, and in 2011, began writing for the print publication, The Parent Notebook, as their family editor and founder of the witty and provocative *"This Parenting Gig"* column.

As an inspirational speaker, Darah shares globally her vibrant story of tragedy to triumph, always authentically and with passion.

With her straight-talking message of faith, courage, and perseverance, her tales and teachings empower others. She adeptly weaves her *Pearls of Wisdom* into all her talks and shows that by overcoming hardship, you can emerge stronger, more confident, and more resilient.

Depending on her mood de jour, you'll usually find Darah swinging wildly between the frivolous and the philosophical. Connect with her on Twitter @darahzeledon, on her Facebook page at Girl with the Crooked Smile, or her website http://DarahZeledon.com.

Darah Zeledón
author | speaker | coach

www.girlwiththecrookedsmile.com

Praise For Darah Zeledón

As featured blogger at MomsMiami.com, Darah makes insightful, uplifting observations on the mom life that so many can relate to. She brings in her own experience as a mother of five to share wisdom we can all use to get through the hectic weeks with our children. Darah's humor and voice are great assets to the site.

—*Charlene Pacenti, Editor-in-Chief Miami Herald's Momsmiami.com*

On the surface, Darah's specialty is that vast area known as "mothering." Her blog, WarriorMom.net discusses the joys and chaos of motherhood with humor and energy, as well as with deep wisdom and originality. However, Darah's message is even broader than that and touches all of us who weather life's unpredictable storms—whether or not we are mothers or parents. Her *Pearls of Wisdom* emerged from the trials she overcame in her adult life; she presents them as a gift that we can all use to get through trying and terrifying times in our lives.

—*Lynette Benton, Author, Teacher, Writing Coach*

Darah is a very creative writer, and has written several pieces for our online magazine, Angie's DIARY, since 2010. Her subjects have a wide-range, and our editors and fellow writers rate her work as outstanding. She was recently awarded with a VIP status.

—*Angelica Pastorelli, CEO at Angie's Diary*

Darah is an enthusiastic and gifted writer who offers substance, wit and wisdom in all of her blog posts for EmpoweringParents.com. Darah is able to mix common sense advice with humor and compassion in a way that resonates with readers on a very personal level. I always look forward to her new posts, both as her editor and her fan!

—*Elisabeth Wilkins, Editor*
Empowering Parents at Legacy Publishing Company

Darah is a creative and gifted writer. She consistently expresses her point of view in a way that women respond to. I know if I give Darah an assignment she will come through.

—*Beth Smith, Co-founder Hybrid Her*

Darah is a smart, witty and insightful blogger. We are happy to have her as part of our team.

—*Kelli Daley, Working Mother Media, Manager of Online Services*

Darah writes with joy in an engaging way. She is a terrific addition to workingmother.com and the working mother community.

—*Helen Jonsen, Working Mother Media, Editor-in-Chief*

Darah is a terrific writer who delivers witty, poignant content for my SaneMoms.com site on a regular basis. She's prolific, easy to work with, and shares her personal stories from an honest and down-to-earth viewpoint. She's a great addition to my team of writers, and highly recommended as a contributor for any publication looking for relevant and humorous parenting content.

—*Bethany Rule Vedder, Founder of sanemoms.com*
Owner of Thin Line Designs

Your energy always inspires me!!   — *Margaret Stall, raving fan*

Way to go girl, that's the attitude! Love everything you've written and good to know you are being the "extraordinary you" that I am so fond of.

—*Virginita Weeden, raving fan*

Darah is a genuine, heart-centered dynamo! As an inspirational author, speaker and coach, she authentically shares her core intuition and natural abilities for empowerment, hope and motivation. She consistently delivers valuable insights, direction and guidance combined with "real life" coping skills, humor and a unique "fire" that's sure to bring about positive results with confidence and clarity.

—*Jodi Nicholson, Author, Speaker & Success Coach*
Founder & CEO, A Fabulous Group of Companies, Inc.

Darah Zeledón *aka Warrior Mom* is a true voice for women all around the world. Her honest real life thoughts, anecdotes and feedback encourage us to take stock in how we overcome obstacles in our lives and to help us find comfort in accepting who we are as women, mothers and fabulous beings. Darah is a true inspiration to our generation of just doing what it takes to get the job done.

—*Allyson Tomchin, LCSW*
Psychotherapist and Co-host of 3 Loud Women

Darah, you've got a new fan – me. This book is amazing! I've read every chapter, and believe me, I left you a bunch of stars... wish I could leave more. You have my heartfelt prayers, hopes and best wishes for the success of this remarkable book.

—*Patricia Laster, Ph.D*
Free to be Me